SALES AND KEY ACCOUNT MANAGEMENT

To Sue, with love, and to Bill Woodward,
wherever he may be and whatever he may be selling.

SALES AND KEY ACCOUNT MANAGEMENT

Jim Blythe

THOMSON

Australia • Canada • Mexico • Singapore • Spain • United Kingdom • United States

THOMSON

British Library Cataloguing-in-Publication Data

A catalogue record for this book is available from the British Library

ISBN 1–84480–023–7

Text design by Design Deluxe

Typeset by J&L Composition, Filey, North Yorkshire

Printed in Italy by G. Canale & C.

CONTENTS

PREFACE

This book sets out to explain how **modern sales managers** (and **modern salespeople**) handle marketing at the individual level. It covers the theoretical and conceptual basis of selling, selling techniques and situations, and the motivation and control of the sales force. The book also covers the growing areas of sales management: key-account management, customer relationship management, telesales, and legal aspects of selling.

Selling has often been regarded as the Cinderella of marketing, associated with manipulative techniques and dubious ethics. In fact, though, successful salespeople are aware that such practices are counterproductive. Good salespeople help to find solutions for their customers' problems, and are often creative in doing so: their knowledge of the product range, coupled with the customers' knowledge of his or her needs, produces creative solutions to business problems.

Specific issues covered include:

- the strategic role of selling
- the relationship between selling and marketing
- **B2C** and **B2B** buyer behaviour
- planning and executing effective sales presentations
- aftersales activities
- major-account management
- exhibition and trade-fair management
- selling in a global context
- legal and ethical issues
- motivation, remuneration, monitoring and feedback

In writing the book, I have tried to show that the practice of selling bears no relationship to the 'selling concept' often portrayed in marketing textbooks. Salespeople are marketing professionals who deal with all the issues marketers deal with, and solve problems for individual customers in real time, in front of the customer, without the benefit of recourse to the market-research figures or even the marketing department. Salespeople usually work alone, applying their intelligence and product knowledge to the customer's situation: they are judged on how much they sell, not on how many hours they put in. Not surprisingly, the highest-paid marketing professionals are usually salespeople – and selling is still the most common starting-point for a marketing career.

Author's acknowledgements

I would like to thank everyone who has contributed directly or indirectly to this book. Firstly, my wife Sue, who understands when I am 'on a roll' and leaves me to get on with it, even at four in the morning. Secondly, everyone at

Thomson Learning – Jennifer Pegg, Laura Priest and the production team who have turned my files into a book. Thirdly, my students past and present, who come up with the right questions and make me rethink my position on so many issues, and who sometimes contact me years later to tell me how they are getting on. Fourthly, my brother Henry, who is a key-account manager in computer software: his advice and anecdotes have helped me to forget how much richer than me he is, and concentrate on what a good brother he is. And finally the salespeople and sales managers I have worked with and for – heroes all!

Acknowledgements from Thomson Learning

Thomson Learning would like to thank the following reviewers who have commented on the content and presentation of *Sales and Key Account Management* during the proposal and manuscript processes:

- Phil Bretherton, University of Central Queensland
- Suzanne Cole, University of Aberystwyth
- Per van Freytag, University of Southern Denmark
- Richard Gay, University of Northumbria
- Bob Hartley, University College Northampton
- Cathy Pickup, East Berkshire College

About the author

Jim Blythe BA, M.Phil., M.A.Ed.D., Ph.D., Dip.M., MCIM is Reader in Marketing at the University of Glamorgan. He has been a salesman and sales manager, and eventually became a company director before joining Glamorgan Business School in 1991. Since then, his academic career has been characterized by a prolific writing output: he is the author of eight textbooks and some twenty academic papers. His research interests include exhibitions and trade fairs (for which he is best known), sales management (in particular the uneasy relationship between sales and marketing), and the marketing of innovation.

Jim is a member of the Academy of Marketing and the American Academy of Marketing Science, and is frequent speaker at conferences and training seminars. He has also published works on teaching and learning, and is regular contributor to practitioner journals.

WALK THROUGH TOUR

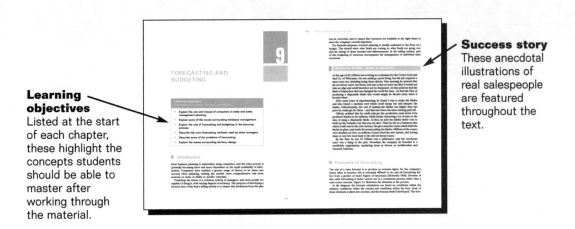

Learning objectives
Listed at the start of each chapter, these highlight the concepts students should be able to master after working through the material.

Success story
These anecdotal illustrations of real salespeople are featured throughout the text.

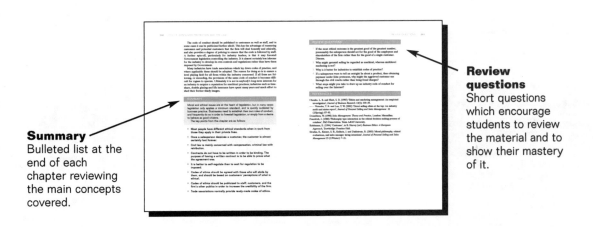

Summary
Bulleted list at the end of each chapter reviewing the main concepts covered.

Review questions
Short questions which encourage students to review the material and to show their mastery of it.

Accompanying website
Visit the *Sales and Key Account Management* accompanying website at www.thomsonlearning.co.uk to find further teaching and learning material including:

For students
- Multiple choice questions for each chapter
- Sample essay questions for each chapter
- Additional cases
- Practical exercises
- Related web links

For lecturers
- Downloadable PowerPoint slides
- Tutorial exercises

SELLING AND ITS STRATEGIC ROLE

1

Learning objectives

After reading this chapter, you should be able to:

- Describe the main categories of salesperson and their key functions.

- Explain the role of personal selling within the overall marketing communications mix.

- Explain why salespeople may not regard themselves primarily as being communicators.

- Describe the characteristics of salespeople.

- Describe the characteristics of sales managers.

- Explain the strategic role of selling.

■ Introduction

Selling probably employs more people than any other branch of marketing. Most marketers have, at some time or another, worked in sales; many stay in selling for their entire working lives. Personal selling is often regarded as the most powerful weapon a marketer has; the salesperson can engage in a dialogue with a prospective customer, developing solutions to the customer's problems based on the firm's product range. The interactive nature of selling makes it the most effective means of bringing in business.

On the other hand, personal selling is also widely regarded as being an expensive option; and certainly, if selling is considered as a communication tool, the number of contacts made and the level of information passed on by salespeople is far below that of mass media such as advertising. In fact, salespeople do not regard themselves as being mere communications devices in the employ of the marketing department. Most salespeople would regard their problem-solving role as being what sets them apart from the other elements of the communications mix, and there is even some debate as to whether personal selling is primarily a communications activity at all.

SUCCESS STORY – JOHN ILHAN

Looking out across the creek at his parents' house and seeing burnt-out cars is one of John Ilhan's early memories of growing up in a tough North Melbourne suburb. He was the son of poor immigrants from Turkey, but he grew up embracing the Australian way of life, the expansive have-a-go approach and the incredible opportunities available.

He dropped out of La Trobe University, despite being the only student from his school to make it to university, and got a job selling cars for Ford. Then the mobile telephone craze arrived – and John jumped on the bandwagon. At first, he sold for Strathfield Car Radio, and quickly became their best salesman – but he left when they owed him $1100 in commissions and hadn't paid him for six months. 'I thought, hang on – all I knew how to do was sell phones,' he said.

At that time, the telephones cost around £3000, and he had no money to buy stock. So he would sell a phone to a customer, go out and buy the phone, deliver it, and pick up the money to pay for it. 'If you liked me and liked what I was offering I would drop it into your home or office,' he says.

Now he owns a chain of mobile phone shops called Crazy John's. 'Building a culture for the company, that's what did it,' he says of his success. 'Getting good people around you, looking after them.' So the lesson of Strathfield has not been lost.

Now, at age 38, John Ilhan looks out at the ocean from his $6 million beach house in fashionable Brighton, Victoria. A far cry from the burnt-out cars of his slum childhood.

Strategy and selling

Strategy is about placing the company in an appropriate position to be able to compete effectively and survive. In some cases this is achieved through product superiority or through price competitiveness, but in many markets (especially in business-to-business environments, where most personal selling takes place) the product is either homogeneous (for example oil products) or must be manufactured to tight specifications. This means that product differentiation is impossible. Equally, competing on price is likely to lead to price wars, unless the firm is

TALKING POINT

IBM is rarely the cheapest in any given market, and does not offer anything that is technologically more advanced than other companies, especially in the PC market; PCs (and indeed other computers) need to be standardized in order to run the same software and be compatible with each other. In fact, IBM made its PC hardware patents freely available to other manufacturers during the 1980s in order to ensure that the IBM/Microsoft operating systems and hardware would become the industry standards rather than the competing Apple Macintosh systems. So why would anyone buy IBM? The reason is that the sales force is trained to seek solutions to customers' business problems, and to solve the problems using IBM equipment and software. The company also has an outstanding reputation for its aftersales service, which is again a function of the sales force, and for its technical support systems, which are a function of the technical sales force.

able to adopt a cost leadership position; in any event, competing on price almost always leads to reduced profit margins.

It is popularly assumed that buyers buy only the physical product. In practice, the buying process is more complex, because buyers also buy a reputation, an aftersales service regime, and even in some cases the likeability of a company. For the buyer, the main contact with the supplying company is the sales representative – it is often said that the sales rep *is* the company, and from the buyer's perspective this is probably the case. Therefore the sales representatives are often the only differentiation between one supplier and another.

The sales force can also be used to target specific strategic customers, as is often the case with key-account management. For example, persuading a major retail chain to accept a particular credit card is likely to mean that smaller retailers will also be compelled to follow suit.

According to research conducted by Hurcomb (1999) there are four success factors in strategic customer selection, all of which are related to the sales force. They are:

1 Deselection of strategic customers is as important as selection. In other words, it is as important to choose which customers should not be sold to as it is to choose those who should be sold to.

2 Selection depends on more than turnover and profitability. Choosing the correct strategic customers should also enhance suppliers' capabilities and improve efficiency and effectiveness.

3 Establishing partnerships is important (although the research indicated that many firms are still caught in the outdated buyer–seller mindset).

4 The most effective corporations approach selection with considerably more diligence than other firms.

The most effective companies in the survey were effective at securing and subsequently growing the business with strategic customers. This is very much a

> **TALKING POINT**
>
> The L'Oreal Kerastase range of products is sold to a carefully selected group of hairdressing salons. Salons must achieve a high standard of training, quality of work and professionalism before they can be selected as Kerastase franchisees. The L'Oreal Professional sales force, who calls on hairdressing salons as part of its normal selling task, has a major role in selecting appropriate salons.
>
> This is, of course, marketing at its most refined. The company deliberately chooses not to supply the brand to a group of potential customers which it feels do not reflect the brand values of Kerastase. Although L'Oreal is quite happy to supply their other professional brands (Luocolor, Constructor, etc.) to these salons, Kerastase remains an exclusive brand.

sales-force-led activity: the sales force not only opens up new business, but by making regular calls and taking an interest in the customer's business it helps to increase the mutual involvement.

Top companies also scored well on locking out the competition. Competitive lockout occurs when there is a substantial barrier preventing competitors from taking over the business. In some cases this will result from a contractual agreement, in others the lockout occurs because the supplying company has built in some factor (technical or service) which the competitors are unable to match. For example, a component manufacturer might supply goods which are protected by patent, ensuring that the customer becomes reliant on those components which are protected.

Targeting specific customers in this way will help in positioning the supplying company; if the aim of the company is to operate in an exclusive, specialist niche the sales force is able to select exactly those customers who will fit the pattern, and ignore those who don't.

Finally, salespeople are able to position the brand and themselves by the way they dress, act and speak about the products they sell. Salespeople selling to boards of directors of major corporations dress very differently from salespeople who sell to farmers, and still differently from salespeople selling stereo systems. Even within product categories differences can be marked – Ford salespeople are likely to differ in approach from Bentley salespeople.

■ Categories of salesperson

Salespeople have been categorized in various ways by different researchers and writers. A commonly-used categorization is Newton's categorization (Newton 1969), shown in Table 1.1. Each type of selling demands a different type of salesperson, and a different approach to the job.

As with most models, Newton's classification is very much a simplified view of the real world. A more complex and comprehensive classification is that developed by McMurry and Arnold (1968), and shown in Table 1.2. This classification offers nine different types of selling situation, with correspondingly nine different types of salesperson. The categories are listed in order of difficulty of making the sale, and (consequently) of creativity on the part of the salesperson.

The classification of salespeople is important because it affects every aspect of managing the sales force. Remuneration packages are different for each type of salesperson, as are training, recruitment, motivation and retention packages. For example, a missionary salesperson never actually takes an order, so a commission-based remuneration package would be difficult or impossible to operate. Likewise, the training programme for a missionary salesperson would differ greatly from that of an order-taker. Retaining creative salespeople is a difficult task, because successful ones are able to find work anywhere and may leave for a better-paying job, while unsuccessful ones cannot earn a living and leave the selling profession altogether. The differences between the different categories of salesperson (in terms of management) will become clearer as the book progresses.

TABLE 1.1 Newton's classification of sales types

Sales type	Description	Success factors
Trade	The salesperson calls on regular customers showing them new products and taking orders for existing product lines.	The emphasis is on building long-term relationships, sales support such as promotional deals and service aspects, and being helpful as well as persuasive.
Missionary selling	Spreading the 'good word' about the company's products to people who do not themselves use or stock the product. This is typical of the pharmaceutical industry, where missionary salespeople seek to persuade doctors to prescribe particular drugs, or in the construction industry, where missionaries approach architects.	The emphasis is on good coverage and presentation to ensure that the influencers know of the products, the benefits and the competitive advantages. Younger salespeople are better at this type of selling, and success relates to the number of calls and the coverage of the territory.
Technical selling	These salespeople are primarily technicians who have some sales training. Their function is to explain the technical aspects of the product to users and others in situations where the product itself is highly technical or where its use presents specific problems. Typical examples exist in the computer industry and in the hairdressing industry.	Success in technical selling stems from having a high level of product knowledge and technical skill. Technical salespeople tend to be well paid, and are paid on salary rather than commission. Young people are often chosen to be trained for technical sales jobs, so supervision needs to be closer than would be the case for older, more experienced people.
New business selling	These salespeople seek out new accounts, or work in an industry where there is very little repeat business. They operate by calling on entirely new customers and selling from scratch.	New business salespeople tend to be older than average, and to have less formal training than other categories of salespeople. They also tend to enjoy the challenge of persuading new prospects to buy, and are also good at handling rejection. The evidence is that such people are hard to find and to retain.

There are many other ways of categorizing salespeople, and frequently an individual salesperson will cross the boundaries between the categories. Since McMurry and Arnold's classification was originally developed, telephone selling has become much more important, and the concept of key-account selling has emerged (see Chapter 5). Given that marketing thinking has changed greatly over the past 30 years, it is perhaps surprising that so little appears to have changed in the area of personal selling; the theories and practices underpinning personal selling have undergone relatively little re-thinking during that time, and much that was relevant 50 or more years ago remains valid even today.

TABLE 1.2 McMurry and Arnold's classification of sales types

Type of salesperson	Description and explanation
Inside order-taker	Function is to serve the customer who is already (at least mainly) committed to the purchase. For example, retail shop assistants.
Delivery salespeople	Salespeople who sell fast-moving lines to retailers from a van. Typical examples are snack products, where the salesperson calls regularly on retailers and restocks their shelves, perhaps showing them new lines in the process.
Outside order-taker	Again, this salesperson calls on retailers and takes orders which are delivered later. Sometimes these salespeople will also check the retailer's stock levels or offer other services such as merchandising; order-taking is primarily a service function.
Missionary salesperson	These salespeople do not take orders directly; the description is the same as that for Newton's classification.
Technical salespeople	Engineers or technicians who have been given sales training, and who sell to other engineers and technicians.
Creative salespeople – tangibles	This category covers direct selling of home improvements such as double glazing or kitchens, vacuum cleaners, and many industrial products.
Creative salespeople – intangibles	Typically this category is concerned with financial services such as insurance and pensions, or (in the business-to-business context) advertising, consultancy services or professional services such as law or accountancy.
Political or indirect salesperson	In some ways similar to the missionary salesperson, these people deal with large-scale contracts for raw materials such as bulk oil, steel products for motor manufacturers, or other major contracts.
Multiple salespeople	These salespeople develop long-term relationships with organizations over a number of years, perhaps selling major items such as aircraft or computer systems.

■ Personal selling and the communication mix

Personal selling as it is practised should not be confused with the selling concept. The selling concept is often cited as a stage in the development of marketing, and assumes the following:

- Customers will not ordinarily buy enough of the product without a persuasive sales talk.
- Customers can be fooled into buying more of a product than they really need if the salesperson is clever enough.
- The customer won't mind being fooled, and will still be glad to see the salesperson again.
- Customers' objections to the product or the company are artificial obstacles to be overcome rather than genuine problems to be solved.

This contrasts with the marketing concept, which attempts to anticipate customers' needs and solve their problems profitably.

The selling concept can still be found in many companies, but it is a corporate philosophy rather than a set of tactics; most professional salespeople would reject the selling concept as being not only incorrect but personally offensive, since they do not wish to be associated with the fast-talking, glib liars so often portrayed in fiction.

Marketers usually think of personal selling as part of the promotional mix, along with sales promotion, advertising and publicity. Personal selling is different from the other elements in that it always offers a two-way communication with the prospective customer, whereas each of the other elements is usually a one-way communication. This is partly what makes personal selling such a powerful instrument; the salesperson can clarify points, answer queries, and concentrate on those issues which seem to be of greatest interest to the prospect. More importantly, the salesperson is able to conduct instant market research with the prospect and determine which issues are of most relevance, often in an interactive way which allows the salesperson to highlight issues which the prospect was not aware of.

As with other forms of marketing communication, selling works best as part of an integrated campaign. Salespeople find it a great deal easier to call on prospects who have already heard something about the company through advertising, publicity or exhibition activities, and many salespeople regard it as the main duty of the marketing department to deliver warm leads (or even hot ones). Equally, marketers regard it as part of the salesperson's responsibility to sing the same song by communicating the company's core message, in conjunction with the other communications methods.

Salespeople and marketers often have divergent views about the relationship between selling and marketing, and this is occasionally a source of conflict between them (Dewsnap and Jobber 1998). Conflict between salespeople and others within the firm has potentially far-reaching effects; some authors have shown that such conflicts have a direct effect on the buyer's commitment (Tellefsen and Eyuboglu 2002).

A marketer's view

Peter Drucker has been quoted as saying that 'the aim of marketing is to make selling superfluous' (Drucker 1973). Drucker went on to say that there will always be some need for personal selling, but that marketers should aim to produce products that are so ideally-suited to the customer that the product sells itself. This view of personal selling has coloured marketing thinking for over 30 years – it is often coupled with Levitt's statement that 'Selling focuses on the needs of the seller; marketing on the needs of the buyer' (Levitt 1960). The result of this somewhat negative view of selling is that marketers have tended to adopt a suspicious view; at worst, salespeople are perceived as being associated with the selling concept (which has little to do with the practice of selling) and at best they are viewed as a necessary evil, filling in the gaps in the communications mix by tailoring the communication to fit the prospect's prejudices and preconceptions.

On the positive side, salespeople are believed to be able to find, inform and persuade customers in a way that has yet to be bettered by any other communications medium. Personal selling has been described as 'The interpersonal arm of the promotion mix' (Kotler *et al.* 2001), as 'An interpersonal communication tool which involves face-to-face activities undertaken by individuals often representing an organization, in order to inform, persuade or remind an individual or group to take appropriate action, as required by the sponsor's representative' (Fill 1995), and as 'The process of identifying potential customers, informing them of a company's offer mix, and finding a match between the benefits offered and customers' needs through personal communication' (Adcock *et al.* 2001).

These descriptions of personal selling emphasize heavily the provision of information, and the element of persuasion. Personal selling is one of several possible options available to the marketer for communicating the company's messages to the customers; its major advantage over other communications is that the message can be tailored to fit the prospect's need for information. This is very much a marketer-oriented view; marketers appear to be working to the model shown in Figure 1.1.

In this model, the marketing people make decisions about product, about distribution, and about price and then feed these decisions into decisions about promotion. They then use the promotional mix to develop an integrated communications programme, including personal selling, which is then delivered to the customers. Feedback from the customers is collected via marketing research and through feedback from the sales force.

Marketers and writers about marketing seem to be unanimous in their belief that personal selling is the most powerful promotional shot in the locker; equally, they seem to be unanimous in believing that it is the most expensive.

Because of the supposed high cost of personal selling, and the knowledge that there are many other ways of communicating effectively with customers, marketers will sometimes look for ways of eliminating the sales force – after all, if a cheaper way can be found to get the message across, it would be irresponsible not to seek it out.

To summarize the marketers'-eye view, the sales-force functions and their potential replacements are shown in Table 1.3.

Overall it would appear that Drucker's view that selling will ultimately become superfluous, and Levitt's view that selling is about the needs of the seller, have encouraged marketers to view selling as the enemy.

In fairness, Levitt's statement may have been misconstrued. It would certainly be true to say that the selling *concept* focuses on the needs of the seller. It should also be pointed out that Drucker's statement about the obsolescence of selling could equally be applied to advertising, publicity, or sales promotion; the Drucker

FIGURE 1.1   Marketer's view of the role of personal selling

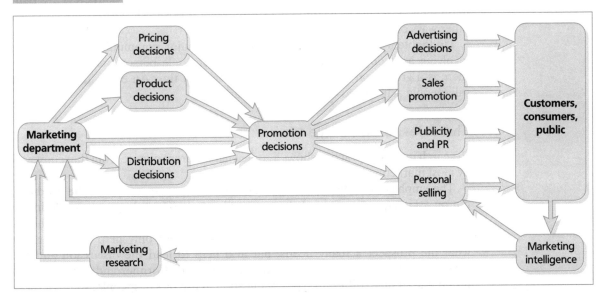

TABLE 1.3 Replacements for sales-force functions

Sales-force function	Marketer's replacement method
Prospecting	Bought-in database; database combination
Evaluating prospects	Database scrutiny, credit referencing technology, response to direct mail
Preparing customer	Combining databases to find most effective approach to the individual
Approaching the customer	Initial mailing, Internet advertisement, direct-response advertising
Making the presentation	Tailored direct-mail, Internet or e-mail negotiation
Overcoming objections	Interactive computer-based (Internet-based) information system
Closing	Internet-based close, credit transfer, e-mail order forms
Following-up	Direct mail

ideal appears to concentrate on perfect product development, which is either some way in the future, or buried in the past along with platonic idealism and the product concept.

At first sight the marketer's model of the role of personal selling appears to allow for the replacement of selling with other (often IT-based) techniques. Since personal selling is regarded as an expensive option, this viewpoint is wholly understandable. A mailing which contacts 5000 good prospects for a cost of £15 000 is a great deal cheaper than a sales rep who would contact around half that number of prospects in a year at a minimum cost of £50 000; even allowing for the sales rep's much better success rate, the cost advantage is obvious. If the marketers are right in thinking of selling as a communication tool, it is obviously cost effective to seek other ways of communicating.

Undoubtedly personal selling does have a major communications element, involving as it does a two-way dialogue between salesperson and prospect, but there is a great deal more to personal selling than this. An examination of what salespeople actually do will make this clearer.

The salesperson's-eye view

Research into sales practice shows a somewhat different picture from that conveyed by most marketing texts.

The emphasis in selling practice is not on telling prospects about the products, but on asking questions about the prospect's needs. The salesperson's role in the sales presentation is not about delivering a persuasive sales talk, but rather is about using appropriate questions. The questions not only help in finding out what the prospect actually needs, but also help to lead the discussion and the subsequent negotiations in a particular direction. DeCormier and Jobber (1993) found a total of 13 different types of question in use by salespeople; some of these were for information-gathering purposes, and others served to control and direct the discussion. Rackham (1991) categorized questions in four dimensions: situation, problem, implication and need-payoff. In each case the emphasis is on asking the prospect about his or her situation, with a view to finding a solution from among the salesperson's portfolio of products. The three key elements in this are firstly that the needs of the buyer are paramount, secondly that the salesperson is asking questions not making statements, and thirdly that communicating the marketing department's message is not relevant to this core process.

Sales trainers and writers have emphasized the problem-solving aspects of selling for many years now, and salespeople are usually told that the most successful presentations are those in which the customer does most of the talking (Lund 1979). Problem solving is at the core of the activity, rather than communication; if the customer is allowed to talk, he or she will (in effect) tell the salesperson how to sell the product.

In the case of services, the marketer and the salesperson will also be concerned with the people, process and physical evidence (Booms and Bitner 1981). Salespeople have a role to play here as well; for example, it is common practice for salespeople to leave something with the customer once the sale is closed (a copy of the order, a brochure about the product, etc.). The salesperson is the main individual in the people element, at least in most service industries, and also often has considerable input into the process.

In fact, a comparison of the salesperson's activities and the marketer's activities shows considerable common ground, as Table 1.4 shows.

The main difference between selling and marketing is that selling is concerned with individuals and individual relationships, whereas marketing is concerned with market segments. Although direct marketing and database marketing seek to target very small segments, even a segment of one, by using information technology, salespeople already do this, face-to-face and in real time, without the benefit of the marketing department's range of resources.

The salesperson's model of the relationship between marketing and sales will look more like that shown in Figure 1.2. From the sales-force viewpoint, it is the sales force which does the real work of finding out the customer's needs and fulfilling them, with the marketing department providing the back-up services of advertising, public relations and sales promotion. Marketers provide information, gained by market research, to the sales force, and also to the production department, but the sales force exists to identify and solve customer's problems. They do this using the range of products supplied by the production department.

In the salesperson's model, the marketing department occupies a subservient role. Since the sales force is in the front line, dealing directly with the customers, it is clear that every other department in the firm depends on them to bring in the business. They are, in fact, the only department which brings in money; everything else generates costs. Sales training programmes sometimes emphasize this; salespeople are told that the average salesperson supports five other jobs, they are told that 'Nothing happens until somebody sells something,' and they are encouraged to think of themselves as the most important people in the firm.

TABLE 1.4 Comparison of marketers' and salespeople's activities

Marketer's activities	Salesperson's activities
Research into the needs of consumers	Needs analysis based on situation and problem questions
Gap analysis	Analysis of needs to identify problems
New product development, designed to meet the consumers' needs	Selection from among the existing range of products to to find closest fit for prospect's needs
Pricing: selecting a price which meets the needs and and expectations of both the customer and the firm	Price negotiation: negotiating a price which meets the needs and expectations of both the customer and the firm
Promotion: developing an appropriate promotion strategy which will equate to the consumers' psychological and behavioural characteristics	Promotion: explaining the features and benefits of the product in terms of the customer's needs, psychology, and behavioural characteristics
Distribution decisions: ensuring that the product is in a convenient place for the consumer to buy it	Distribution negotiations: ensuring that the product reaches the customer in the right quantities and at the right time

Many salespeople regard their relationship with their customers as being more important than their relationship with the firm that pays their salaries – further evidence that salespeople regard themselves as being the most important people in the firm. Research shows that salespeople are often defensive of their good relationships with customers even when this conflicts with instructions from the marketing department (Anderson and Robertson 1995). This may be due to the belief that it is easier for salespeople to find a new company to work for than it is to find new customers.

While there may be some justification for the salesperson's model, the model ignores the interrelated nature of the firm's activities. Salespeople would have nothing to sell were it not for the efforts of the production department, would have no pay-packet and no invoicing without the finance department, would have no deliveries without the shipping department, and so forth. Salespeople may have been given a false view of their own importance, but trainers may feel justified in doing this in order to counteract the often negative image and low status that selling has in the eyes of other departments.

In this model, the sales force collects information about the market from the marketing department's research, and information about the individual customer directly from the customer. Information about the product range, prices and discount structures, delivery lead times and methods, sales promotion and the use of advertising and PR materials (contained in the salesperson's silent seller – see Chapter 3) are all used in negotiation with the customer. This is done with the aim of obtaining an acceptable solution for both parties, regarding both information exchange and product and price exchange.

For many salespeople, the marketing department also has the role of softening-up prospective customers by providing publicity and advertising; the salesperson feels more confident about making a call knowing that the prospect has already heard of the company, and has had the opportunity to form some favourable impressions. In this model the marketing department performs a support function, providing a set of products for the customer to choose from, a price structure for

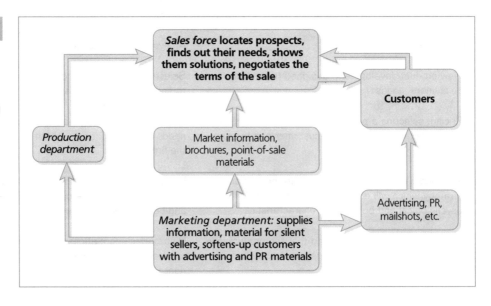

the salesperson and the customer to negotiate around, a distribution system which can be tailored to suit the customer, and promotional back-up in the form of advertising and publicity. Sales promotions might be useful as ways of closing sales (they are sometimes called deal-makers) but the basic problem solving and decision making is done by the salespeople when they are with the customer. In fact, it is this problem-solving and decision-making function that distinguishes the sales force from other promotional tools. The sales force do not think of themselves as being primarily communicators; they think of themselves as being primarily decision makers.

If the salespeople are correct in this view, then it would be impossible to replace them with a database (at least, given the current state of the art). Computers can hold and manipulate information very effectively, but they are unable to solve problems creatively or negotiate effectively, or indeed establish a long-term relationship on a human level. For these functions a human being is necessary.

A problem that arises from this perspective is that salespeople tend to identify very much with the customers. They will, and indeed should, be prepared to represent the customers' views back to the company, and even fight the customer's corner for them within the firm, because this leads to a more customer-oriented attitude within the company. On the other hand, the firm is entitled to expect a certain amount of loyalty from its employees, so the sales force's over-identification with the customers is likely to lead to conflict between salespeople and their colleagues back at head office.

A customer's eye view

The popular image of salespeople is that they are pushy, manipulative, fast-talking and unscrupulous. Although there are undoubtedly salespeople who over-persuade and try to pressurize customers into buying, this approach is usually unproductive. This is for the following reasons:

1 Most selling situations involve the possibility of repeat business at a future date. This means that the salesperson will be calling again, and would not want to be met with a firmly closed door.
2 Most selling takes place in a business-to-business environment, where buyers are generally professionals who are trained to resist a pushy approach. Even in a situation where the salesperson is dealing directly with consumers, it would be true to say that most people would show considerable resistance to a bullying or manipulative approach.
3 Bullying customers into signing for goods only leads to cancellations once the salesperson is gone.
4 This type of high-pressure approach is too emotionally demanding on the salesperson to be sustainable for a long period.

For these reasons salespeople find it is easier and more beneficial to begin by finding out the customer's needs, and then apply a solution to those needs based on the firm's product range. Although marketing writers commonly refer to 'the product', it is very rarely the case that a salesperson will only have one product to offer; in many cases, salespeople even have the capacity to vary products or tailor

FIGURE 1.3

Areas of
knowledge and
the sales dialogue

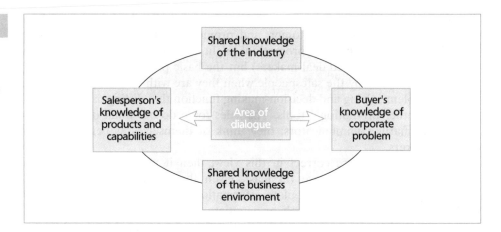

them to fit the customer's needs. For example, computer software houses selling to major customers are able to write customer-specific software for the client; even double-glazing firms tailor-make the windows to fit each house exactly. Salespeople will have considerable knowledge about the products in their own company's range, and probably of those of the industry in general. The customer can therefore pick the salesperson's brains for useful information to help in the problem-solving process. The customer's knowledge of his or her unique situation combines with the salesperson's knowledge of products and industry to generate a creative solution. This is shown in Figure 1.3.

For the customer, the salesperson is a source of information, a source of help in problem solving, and is an advocate back to the supplying company. Good salespeople are also adept at helping their customers through the decision-making process; often this is the hardest part of making a sale.

■ Characteristics of salespeople and sales managers

There is a commonly held view that salespeople are born rather than made; many people have the underlying assumption that selling is a natural talent. There is no evidence to support this view. Although it is possible to identify personal characteristics that are helpful in selling, the effects of motivation and demotivation more than overshadow the effect of these characteristics. In other words someone who has a talent for selling but no motivation will not sell, whereas someone with little talent but a great deal of motivation will. As a general rule, salespeople will need to be smart, well spoken, empathetic, able to work alone without supervision, and determined. Having said that, most sales managers are able to cite examples of salespeople who have been sloppy, lazy or inarticulate and yet have still managed to sell well.

Salespeople's characteristics

A survey of sales managers came up with the list of characteristics shown in Table 1.5 that the managers looked for when recruiting salespeople (Jobber and Millar 1984). Naturally, these findings do not necessarily equate to the characteristics of successful salespeople – the list could equally be a reflection of the sales managers'

TABLE 1.5 Desirable qualities of salespeople

Qualities	Percentage of sales managers mentioning quality
Communication skills	38%
Personality	32%
Determination	28%
Intelligence	27%
Motivation/self-motivation	27%
Product knowledge	26%
Educational background	19%
Confidence	18%
Appearance	18%
Resilience and tenacity	17%
Business sense	17%
Integrity	15%
Ambition	13%
Acceptability/likeability	13%
Empathy	9%
Initiative	9%
Self-discipline'	9%
Experience	8%
Adaptability	6%
Persuasiveness	6%

prejudices. Having said that, it is interesting to note that persuasiveness comes at the bottom of the list of desired characteristics – and communication skills is at the top.

Motivation and self-motivation also rated fairly highly, with 27 per cent of sales managers mentioning it as an important characteristic. Self-motivation comes largely from the feeling of being in the right job; having work that one finds intrinsically interesting, satisfying and valuable is a major encouragement to work well (see Chapter 8 for more on motivation).

Research into salespeople's motivations for going into selling resulted in Table 1.6 (Galbraith *et al.* 1991). Interestingly, this shows that working methods and independence are more important than earnings as the motivating force behind looking for a job in selling. This is in sharp contrast to the popular view of salespeople as commission-hungry go-getters. Equally, independence is valued more than twice as highly as earnings once the recruit is in the job.

Based on these findings, it would appear that the type of person who would most enjoy a sales job is someone who is independently minded, enjoys personal freedom, likes to provide a service, and enjoys dealing with people.

Sales manager's characteristics

Sales managers are not in the company to do the selling themselves; sales managers are there to create the right conditions under which the sales force can operate effectively. Therefore, although sales managers are almost always competent salespeople, they are not necessarily the best salespeople in the team. Sales managers' responsibilities are as shown in Table 1.7.

Sales managers must function as the coach, not the player. Many newly promoted sales managers fail to make this distinction, and continue to sell to their favourite customers and contacts. In part this stems from a desire to keep in touch with selling techniques, to maintain skills, and to maintain credibility with the rest of the sales force; in part it stems from the desire to hold on to the human contact

TABLE 1.6 Features of most interest and value to salespeople

Features of most interest	Features of most value
Working methods (60%)	Independence (40%)
Independence (13%)	Earnings (18%)
Earnings (12%)	Providing a service (14%)
Company status (5%)	Freedom (11%)
Good training (4%)	Dealing with people (8%)
Promotion chances (2%)	Job satisfaction (6%)
Exclusive territory (2%)	Promotion prospects (1%)

and relationships that have been built up over a number of years. This is under-standable, since (for most salespeople) the customers are a great deal more impor-tant than the company; after all, they spend most of their time with the customers and relatively little time at the company offices.

Sales managers need most or all of the following characteristics in order to do their jobs effectively:

- motivation and enthusiasm
- human relations skills
- higher-than-average energy
- ambition
- a liking for dealing with people.
- persuasiveness and charisma
- flexibility
- sensitivity
- intellectual ability

The critical differences between selling jobs and sales management jobs are shown in Table 1.8.

Part of the function of the sales force is to represent the customers' views back to the company; this sometimes leads them into conflict with their employers, but is a necessary part of what they do, and provides the company with the necessary drive to meet customers' needs more effectively. Just as the salespeople are at the interface between the company and its customers, so the sales managers are at the interface between the sales force and the rest of the firm, and this means that sales managers may need to represent the views of the sales force to the management. This can put the sales manager in a difficult position, but again is a necessary force for change.

TABLE 1.7 Sales manager's role

Role	Explanation
Recruitment	Selecting the right people to join the sales force.
Training	Helping people to develop the right skills for the job.
Motivation	Optimizing the sales force's desire to get the job done.
Planning	Setting the objectives for the sales force, and monitoring the tactical approaches used.
Organization	Ensuring that the correct procedures are adopted, and that resources are available for salespeople to do their jobs.
Monitor	Set up systems and procedures for checking the results of the sales-force activities.
Control	Feeding back the results of the monitoring to enable the sales force to stay on course at the tactical level.

TABLE 1.8 Differences between sales and sales management

Activity	Sales representative	Sales manager
Primary responsibility	Develops accounts	Develops people
Working relationships	Works alone	Works through others
Role	Player	Coach
Part of management?	No	Yes: has the task of selling the company plans to the sales force
Detailed responsibility	Makes calls, sells, provides aftersales service	Recruits, selects, trains, motivates, compensates, sees key accounts, corresponds and works with other corporate departments

Sales managers therefore need some contradictory characteristics. They need to be able to work closely with their colleagues in management, yet stand up for the sales force when necessary. They need to be able to work through others when managing the field sales force, yet work on their own when handling office responsibilities. They need to be empathetic when dealing with the salespeople's problems, yet hard-nosed when dealing with other managers.

SUMMARY

Selling is not merely a matter of being fast-talking and persuasive. The modern salesperson must add value to the marketing exchange; this is done by using the salesperson's superior product knowledge in helping the customer to solve a problem. Without this ability to solve problems for customers the salesperson becomes an expensive form of communication – and one which firms could readily manage without.

This chapter has introduced some of the basic concepts underlying selling and sales management. The relationship between selling and marketing has not always been an easy one; salespeople tend to regard themselves as being the more important of the two, with marketing performing a support function, whereas marketers tend to regard salespeople as a tactical arm for their strategic plans. The personal characteristics and motivations of salespeople and sales managers are somewhat at odds with the popular view taken of each; far from being money-hungry fast-talkers, salespeople are more concerned with independence and providing a service; sales managers do not value persuasiveness in salespeople nearly as much as they value communication skills, intelligence and personality.

The key points from this chapter are as follows:

- Selling is probably the most powerful tool the marketer has available.
- The practice of selling has nothing to do with the selling concept.
- Salespeople and marketers sometimes suffer from a difference of opinion about each others' roles.
- Personal selling is about asking questions, not about telling customers about products.
- Selling is about identifying needs and providing solutions.
- There is no such thing as a born salesperson.
- Money is not the main reason for salespeople entering the profession, nor is it the main source of their satisfaction with the job.
- Sales managers do not have to be the best salespeople on the team.
- Salespeople fulfil many functions in many categories which frequently overlap.

REVIEW QUESTIONS

1 If the main role of salespeople is to solve customers' problems, why do most marketers include it in the communication mix?
2 How can salespeople ensure that they are offering the right product to the client?
3 Why might a top-rated salesperson make a poor sales manager?
4 Why is selling practice different from the selling concept?
5 What factors might account for the view that selling is the most powerful tool of marketing?

REFERENCES

Adcock, D., Halborg, A. and Ross, C. (2001) *Marketing: Principles and Practice*, 4th edn, Harlow: Pearson Education.

Anderson, E. and Robertson, T. S. (1995) 'Inducing multi-line salespeople to adopt house brands', *Journal of Marketing* 59 (2/Apr.): 16–31.

Booms, B. H. and Bitner, M. J.(1981) 'Marketing strategies and organisation structures for service firms', in J. Donnelly and W.R. George (eds), *Marketing of Services*, American Marketing Association.

DeCormier, R. and Jobber, D. (1993) 'The counsellor selling method: Concepts, constructs, and effectiveness', *Journal of Personal Selling and Sales Management*, 13(4): 39–60.

Dewsnap, B. and Jobber, D. (1998) 'The sales and marketing interface: Is it working?', *Proceedings of the Academy of Marketing Conference*, Sheffield.

Drucker, P. F. (1973) *'Management: Tasks, Responsibilities, Practices'*, New York: Harper & Row.

Fill, C. (1995) *Marketing Communications: Frameworks, Theories and Applications*, Harlow: Prentice Hall.

Galbraith, A., Kiely, J. and Watkins, T. (1991) 'Sales force management – issues for the 90s', *Proceedings of the Marketing Education Group Conference*, Cardiff Business School, July: 425–45.

Hurcomb, J. (1999) 'Developing strategic customers and key accounts: The critical success factors', *Journal of Selling and Major Account Management* 1 (3/February): 49–59.

Jobber, D. and Millar, S. (1984) 'The use of psychological tests in the selection of Salesmen: A UK survey', *Journal of Sales Management* 1: 1.

Kotler, P., Armstrong, G., Saunders, J. and Wong, V. (2001) *Principles of Marketing*, Harlow: Financial Times Prentice Hall.

Levitt, T. (1960) 'Marketing myopia', *Harvard Business Review* July–Aug.: 45–56.

Lund, P. R. (1979) *'Compelling Selling'*, London: Macmillan.

McMurry, R.N. and Arnold, J.S. (1968) *How to Build a Dynamic Sales Organisation*, New York: McGraw-Hill.

Newton, D.A. (1969) 'Get the most out of your salesforce', *Harvard Business Review*, Sept.–Oct.: 16–29.

Rackham, N. (1991) *The Management of Major Sales*, Aldershot: Gower.

Tellefsen, T. and Eyuboglu, N. (2002) 'The impact of a salesperson's in-house conflicts and influence attempts on buyer commitment', *Journal of Personal Selling and Sales Management*, 22 (3/Summer): 157–72.

MITSUBISHI–TOKYO PHARMACEUTICALS

The Japanese pharmaceutical industry is highly competitive, as is the case with many industries in this heavily populated, highly industrialized, wealthy country. Additionally, Japanese companies are well aware that they must compete effectively on the global stage as well – so the pressure is on to form alliances and even mergers with other like-minded companies in order to develop the strength to compete against the global majors.

The pharmaceutical industry is also a complex one. Firstly, pharmaceuticals divide into OTC (over-the-counter) products which can be sold without prescription. These are headache tablets, cold remedies, cough medicines and the like which are available from chemists' shops and supermarkets. Secondly, there are the so-called ethical medicines, which can only be issued on a doctor's prescription. From a selling viewpoint, OTC medicines can be sold in much the same way as any other consumer goods, but ethical medicines are sold by missionary salespeople. This is because doctors prescribe the medicines but do not buy them, and the pharmacists who buy them have no influence on consumers' purchase of them. A further complication is that the missionary salespeople involved need to have a good understanding of the highly technical and complex nature of the products. New drugs appear regularly, and the sales representatives need to be able to talk knowledgably about them to medical professionals.

In October 2000, Mitsubishi Chemicals and the pharmaceutical division of Tokyo Tanabe Seiyaku Co. Ltd. merged to form Mitsubishi–Tokyo Pharmaceuticals, Inc. The new company became the leading Japanese pharmaceutical company, with 2300 employees and an annual turnover of over 100 thousand million yen (approximately £540 million). The new company's growth strategy for the 21st century hinged on research and development, internationalization, and a strong sales force. The company found itself with 530 medical sales representatives, with various degrees of training, and with widely differing knowledge of the products, since each company had its own product range. There was therefore a need to develop the domestic sales force rapidly, and in particular to provide them with high-quality, detailed information about the products and the market.

In typical Japanese style, the company decided to seek a solution using state-of-the-art software. Tokyo Tanabe's previous system, Zaurus, had been good at increasing the effectiveness of the medical representatives, but was unable to handle the large amounts of data which were now streaming in from the larger sales force. The system also would not allow the sales force to share information about physicians. Mitsubishi–Tokyo also wanted to use pen-touch computers to access product information. Finally, Katsumi Kurita, the company's sales manager, opted for a system from Dendrite, a software house which specializes in systems for pharmaceutical sales forces. Dendrite developed a system which Mitsubishi–Tokyo decided to call MUSE (an acronym for medical, useful, sensible, expert).

Kurita said, 'We have strong competition in the pharmaceutical industry. A pharmaceutical company must manage knowledgeable, productive information about hospitals and physicians to gain a competitive advantage. The more we develop new products, the more important it is to micromanage and expand efficient medical representative activity. That's how Dendrite's solution is helping us to grow our business in the future.'

The MUSE system has proved much more successful than the old Zaurus system, so much so that the company is planning to extend its use so that the sales force can exchange information more easily with office-based marketing personnel. 'We have to enhance not only the quantity of medical representatives but also the quality,' Kurita says. 'And in the future, when we develop new medicines, we need to provide them with greater strategic information.' Since the company plans to expand its sales force to over 700 representatives, the ambitious sales goals being set will require the most effective and efficient management systems available.

Case-study questions

1 Mitsubishi–Tokyo appears to be a sales-led company. How can this be reconciled with a missionary sales force, which is characterized by the fact that it never actually sells anything?

2 How can the new system help in solving customer problems?

3 Since the company is investing in these information systems, why not simply make the system available to the doctors and hospitals so that they can access it directly, instead of via the sales force?

4 How would you expect the marketing and selling functions to be integrated at Mitsubishi–Tokyo?

5 What conflicts might occur due to having both a missionary sales force and an order-taking sales force?

2

BUYER BEHAVIOUR

Learning objectives

After reading this chapter, you should be able to:

- Describe the main influences on consumer behaviour.

- Describe the consumer decision-making process as it applies in selling situations.

- Explain the main influences on organizational buyer behaviour.

- Describe the differences in approach between selling to consumers and selling to organizational buyers.

- Explain how organizational buyers evaluate suppliers.

■ Introduction

Buyers fall into two main categories: consumers, who are buying for their own or their families' use, and organizational buyers, who are buying on behalf of their organizations. There is a common assumption that consumers are often swayed by emotion, as opposed to organizational buyers who are assumed to operate on a formal, unemotional basis. This is not entirely true: organizational buyers do not leave their human emotions at the door when they arrive at work, nor do all consumers operate on an irrational basis. Within both groups there is, of course, wide variation in decision-making style.

A company or an organization cannot buy anything; a company is a legal fiction, an artificial person which can only act through its officers and employees. Therefore all buying is done by people, just as all selling is done by people. The buyer–seller interface is therefore always on a human level, and nothing can change this in any fundamental way. Organizational buyers are likely to be swayed by emotional considerations, by career ambitions, or by other influences not directly connected with the immediate purchasing role.

SUCCESS STORY – JIM PATTISON

The Jim Pattison Group is one of the biggest corporate success stories in Canada. In less than 40 years the company grew from nothing to a conglomerate which employs 26 000 people, has sales of $5.5 thousand million, has assets of $3.5 thousand million, and has a small stake in almost every aspect of Canadian life. What's more, it is all owned by one man.

When Jim Pattison was only eight years old he began selling garden seeds. He paid his way through university by selling cars to his fellow students, then after graduation he bought a General Motors car dealership, promising his wife that he would be a millionaire by the time he was forty. He far exceeded this aim – within eight years he had 2500 employees in six corporations, with a total turnover of $100 million.

What he learned as a salesman shaped his career. Understanding his customers, ensuring that people get what they want from the deal, respecting his staff, and understanding what motivates people are the basis of his incredible success. He has never forgotten that customers' needs are the driving force of a company, and that the staff are its backbone.

By 1986 his company, the Jim Pattison Group, was the largest company in Canada owned by a single person. His group of companies ranges from food services through manufacturing to transportation and leasing. Jim continues to serve as chief executive, chairman and sole owner of the group, which is now Canada's third largest privately held company. He has been made one of eight inaugural laureates of the Canadian Professional Sales Association Sales Hall of Fame, a singular achievement for a humble salesman from British Columbia.

Consumer behaviour

The consumer decision-making process follows the stages shown in Figure 2.1. *Problem recognition* happens when the consumer realizes that there is a need for some item. Sometimes this comes about through *assortment depletion* (where the item has been used up or worn out) or *assortment extension* (which is where the consumer feels the need to add some new item or items to his or her existing assortment of possessions). At this point the consumer has decided to seek a solution to the problem, perhaps by buying a category of product; the decision about buying a specific brand may come much later. Seeking a solution may also involve

TALKING POINT

Double glazing was first introduced into the UK during the late 1960s. At that time people did not know what it was, and therefore were not aware of a need for it. In the ensuing ten years, salespeople called from door-to-door explaining the benefits, often using high-pressure and even unethical techniques to gain entrance to homes and make sales. In fact, double-glazing salespeople became a byword for high-pressure selling. However, most people were clearly happy with the product – no-one would have gone looking for it, since they did not know it existed, but having installed it most were very satisfied and glad of finding a solution to a problem they did not know they had.

By the late 1980s most homes in Britain had some double glazing, and the market had matured. Everybody now knows the advantages of low maintenance costs, good insulating properties and draughtproofing. Now people approach the double-glazing companies and ask for quotes; salespeople have a much lower profile in the process. Yet this was an industry created by salespeople!

considerable information searching; the answer may not be obvious. Problems can sometimes be pointed out by salespeople. Often a potential buyer may not be aware that a problem exists until someone arrives with a potential solution.

The felt needs can be categorized as either *utilitarian* (concerned with the functional attributes of the product) or *hedonic* (concerned with the pleasurable or aesthetic aspects of the product) (Holbrook and Hirschmann 1982). The current view is that there is a balance between the two types of need in most decisions (Engel *et al.* 1995). In fact, most products contain aspects of both utilitarianism and of hedonism; few products are entirely impractical, and equally few products are entirely devoid of any pleasurable features. In practice, salespeople often emphasize the hedonic aspects of owning the product since these are often the main differentiating features of the products – the basic utilitarian functions would be held in common with most competitors.

 FIGURE 2.1   The consumer decision-making process

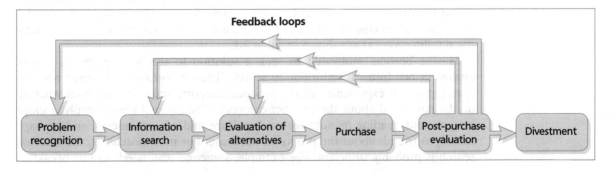

Drive is the internal stimulus that comes about because there is a gap between the *actual state* the individual is in and the *desired state*, or the position the individual would like to be in. For example, becoming hungry leads to a drive to find food; the hungrier the individual becomes, the greater the drive becomes, but once the hunger has been satisfied the individual can move on to satisfying other needs. For salespeople, the actual state of the individual cannot usually be influenced, so most marketing and selling activity is directed at influencing the desired state (e.g. 'Don't you deserve a better car?'). Thus drives are generated by encouraging a revision of the desired state. The higher the drive level (i.e. the greater the gap between actual and desired states) the more open the individual is to considering new ways of satisfying the need; in simple terms, a starving man will try almost any kind of food.

Most people enjoy allowing gaps to develop between the desired and actual states; building up an appetite before going for a meal makes the experience more pleasurable, for example. Each individual has an *optimal stimulation level* (OSL) which is the point at which the drive is enjoyable and challenging, without being unduly uncomfortable or unpleasant. OSL is subjective; research shows that those with high OSLs like novelty and risk-taking, whereas those with low OSLs prefer the tried and tested. Those with high OSLs also tend to be younger (Raju 1980). There is really nothing a salesperson can do to influence someone's OSL, although of course attempts might be made to encourage instant gratification rather than waiting.

Drives generate *motivation*, which underpins the reasons why people take action. The level of motivation will depend on the desirability of the end goal, and the ease of achieving it. The more desirable the goal, the greater the motivation; the easier it is to achieve the end goal, the greater the motivation. Motivations are subjective, so it is difficult to infer motivation from behaviour. Few actions take place as a result of a single motivation, and sometimes a motivation may not even be apparent to the individual experiencing it; in other words, some motivations operate below the conscious level. For example, an organizational buyer may choose to buy from a particular company because he believes they have a good product and will be reliable. In fact he may have been swayed in this viewpoint by the fact that the salesperson was reliable. The characteristics of the salesperson may have been transferred to the brand, which is of course irrational. Equally the buyer may have been motivated by a barely remembered advertisement or casual conversation, and may be entirely unaware of this.

McClelland's (1988) theory of need achievement argues that there are three main categories of needs: affiliation (which is the need to belong to a social group), power (the need to have control over the environment, other people and events) and achievement (the need to achieve personal goals). Examples of these in a personal selling context are shown in Table 2.1.

Having become motivated to seek a solution to the need problem, buyers engage in two forms of information search. The *internal search* involves remembering previous experiences of the product category, and thinking about what he or she has heard about the product category. The *external search* involves shopping around, reading manufacturers' literature and advertisements, and perhaps talking to friends about the proposed purchase. For most purchases, the internal search is probably sufficient. For example, someone who needs to buy breakfast cereal will easily remember what his or her favourite brand tastes like, and will often also remember where it is on the supermarket shelf. When buying a new hi-fi system, on the other hand, a fairly extensive information search might be carried out, involving reading manufacturers' brochures and looking around the hi-fi shops. The purpose of this exercise is to reduce risk; buying the wrong brand of cereal involves very little risk, since the financial commitment is low, but buying the wrong hi-fi could prove to be an expensive mistake. For this reason many retailers offer a no-quibble return policy, since this helps to reduce the perceived level of risk and makes purchase more likely.

The external search is the point at which the salesperson will usually become involved. In most cases, this will only apply to major purchases such as cars or expensive electronic equipment such as computers or hi-fis. From a selling point of view, it is important to distinguish between a customer who is on an information search and one who is actually ready to buy – this is particularly important in areas such as exhibitions, where many people are engaged in information searches rather than purchasing expeditions.

Having found out about several competing brands the buyer will *evaluate* the alternatives, based on the information collected or remembered. The first stage in the process is to select a *consideration set*, which is the group of products which would most closely meet the need. Often buyers use *cut-offs* to establish a consideration set; these are the minimum and maximum acceptable values for the product characteristics. For example, buyers typically have a clear idea of the acceptable price range for the product, and may specify a minimum as well as a maximum price; most people prefer not to buy the cheapest, on the grounds that it is likely to be of poor quality. *Signals* are important when making choices; a particular price-tag, a brand name, even the retailer will have some effect on the buyer's perception of the product. Price is frequently used as an indicator of quality, for example.

TABLE 2.1 Theory of need achievement

Need	Example
Affiliation	A customer might be sold an expensive car on the basis that it conveys an impression of wealth and success. This might enable the purchaser to feel part of a particular social group.
Power	Some buyers like to demonstrate that they have the power in the relationship, but in any event everyone likes to feel in control of situations. Good salespeople allow customers to feel in control by letting the customer do most of the talking; the salesperson guides the conversation by asking questions rather than making statements.
Achievement	Some customers like to feel that they have driven a hard bargain. When negotiating with this type of customer, salespeople can lose the negotiation, thus allowing the customer to enjoy a feeling of achievement by winning.

Legendary salesman Frank Bettger had a straightforward technique for dealing with the subject of competitors. If a prospective customer raised the name of another insurance company, Bettger would say, 'They are a fine company. I'm sure they would provide you with an excellent insurance policy. But I am in a position to do something for you that no-one else can do.' This, of course, would arouse the prospect's interest. In response to the inevitable enquiry, Bettger would say, 'I can give you immediate cover. I have already made an appointment with our company doctor to examine you, and if you are as good on the inside as you look on the outside, you can be insured immediately.' At the time, insurance companies routinely required medical examinations for large policies, so Bettger had a real edge on the competition. The prospect would know that it would be impossible to arrange a medical quickly, and obviously the cover needed to be put in place as quickly as possible – in case of accidents!

Astute salespeople will ensure that the consideration set includes several of the firm's products; some salespeople provide information about competitors' products so as to reduce the search time for the buyer. This means that the buyer can move on to the actual purchase decision more quickly. Failure to provide information about competitors' products creates a risk of the consumer going to a competitor's salespeople, who may be better able to help the consumer through the decision-making process. Equally, salespeople can use their knowledge of the industry and of the available products to help set up cut-offs (perhaps by saying 'You probably won't find anything of the quality you need for less than £3000').

Occasionally the use of cut-offs eliminates all the possibilities from the consideration set, in which case the buyer will have to revise the rules. This can result in the creation of a hierarchy of rules (Bettman 1979). For salespeople and marketers, the challenge is often to ensure that their firm's product becomes a member of the consideration set.

The decision-making process appears lengthy and complex as stated here, yet most of us make several purchasing decisions in a day without going through a lengthy decision-making process. This is because most of us use *heuristics*, or decision-making rules, for most purchases. These are simple 'if . . . then . . .' rules which reduce risk by using previous experience as a guide. For example, an international traveller in a strange city might have a heuristic of only eating in restaurants which are full of locals, on the grounds that the inhabitants of the city would know which are the best restaurants. Heuristics divide into three categories: *search heuristics,* which are concerned with rules for finding out information, *evaluation heuristics*, which are about judging product offerings, and *choice heuristics*, which are about evaluation of alternatives. In major purchases, salespeople can sometimes help in setting up these heuristics by suggesting possible rules, in the same way as cut-offs can be suggested. For example, a salesperson may suggest that the buyer should not consider any product lacking in certain features.

The decision-making process may contain a number of *interrupts*; points at which the search is temporarily suspended. Interrupts come in four categories, as shown in Table 2.2.

An approach–approach conflict occurs when a second product is presented which would probably do the job just as well. This means that the customer has to make a comparison, and the search pattern is temporarily suspended; it is easy for a salesperson to place the consumer in this position when presenting alternatives, but it is equally easy to break the conflict by pointing out the crucial differences between the alternatives. An approach–avoidance conflict might arise when the consumer finds out the product is much more expensive than expected; this risk can be avoided by ensuring that the customer is aware of the price range of the products in advance. Some salespeople even go so far as to suggest a higher price than the one which the product actually costs, in order to prepare the customer for the real price. For example, a customer who expects to pay £300 for a top-of-the-range hi-fi system might be told that £3000 is more realistic. The real price of £1500 then comes as a pleasant surprise.

An avoidance–avoidance conflict might arise when the two alternatives are equally distasteful (an example might be the reluctance to spend money on new shoes while at the same time not wanting to be embarrassed by wearing old ones). In some cases salespeople will try to cause an interrupt, by suggesting something new or by distracting the customer. In most cases, consumers will resume the interrupted problem-solving process once the stimulus has been absorbed and accepted or rejected, so these tactics are seldom really effective.

TABLE 2.2 Categories of interrupt

Category	Explanation and examples
Environmental stimuli	Environmental stimuli arise from events in the surrounding environment; for example in-store promotions. Sometimes these interrupts are caused by salespeople or in-store demonstrators.
Affective states	Affective states are conditions of the individual, for example physiological needs such as the sudden need to go to the toilet or to have a coffee. Salespeople have little influence over these states, but should be aware that a buyer's impatience or irritability may be caused by hunger or thirst rather than any problem with the product.
Unexpected information	Unexpected information often causes the buyer to revise the terms of the information search. For example, a computer salesperson might have to tell a customer that the model he is looking for is obsolete and unavailable; this means that the customer will need to examine the new version of the machine, or look at other makes.
Conflicts	Conflicts occur when the consumer realizes that the original decision-making plan cannot be followed, or an alternative plan appears which is not consistent with the original plan. In these circumstances the customer may need to consult with colleagues or otherwise regroup.

Purchase of the product is often instigated by the salesperson; this is the part of the sale called the close. *Closing the sale* means getting the customer to make a decision; sometimes the decision is positive but more often it is negative. The main function of the closing techniques used by salespeople is to ensure that a decision of some sort is made; if the decision is deferred, it is more likely to be a negative one when it is finally made.

Post-purchase evaluation refers to the way the buyer decides whether the product purchase has been a success or not. This process usually involves a comparison between what the buyer was expecting to get, and what was actually purchased, although sometimes new information obtained after the purchase will also colour the individual's thinking (Oliver 1980). Before the purchase, the information search will have enabled the buyer to form expectations of the product's capabilities in term of *equitable performance* (what can be reasonably expected given the cost and effort of obtaining the product), *ideal performance* (what the buyer hopes the product will do) and *expected performance* (which is what the product probably will do).

Sometimes post-purchase evaluation leads to *post-purchase dissonance*, when the product has not lived up to expectations, and sometimes to *post-purchase consonance* when the product is as expected or better. In either event, the consumer will store the information in his or her memory, to inform the internal search for next time.

Because post-purchase dissonance is unpleasant, people try to reduce it as much as possible. There are four general approaches to doing this:

1 Ignore the dissonant information and concentrate on the positive aspects of the product.
2 Distort the dissonant information (perhaps by telling oneself that the product was, after all, the cheap version).
3 Play down the importance of the issue.
4 Change one's behaviour.

From a sales viewpoint, it is generally better to ensure that the consumer has accurate information about the product beforehand so as to avoid post-purchase dissonance, but if it occurs then salespeople need to reduce it in some way. Research has shown that only one-third of consumers will complain or seek redress; the remainder will boycott the goods in future, or simply complain to others, either of which is a non-optimal outcome from the viewpoint of the marketer (Day *et al.* 1981). Consumers express dissatisfaction in one of three ways: *voice responses* in which the customer comes back and complains, *private responses* in which the customer complains to friends, and *third-party responses*, which may include complaints to consumer organizations, trade associations or TV consumer programmes, or even legal action (Singh 1988). Research by the Coca Cola Company showed that people whose complaints are not dealt with to their satisfaction tell an average of nine other people about their dissatisfaction; those whose complaints are dealt with satisfactorily only tell four to five others about this. This indicates that poor complaint handling is likely to be damaging in the long run; Coca Cola further reported that 10 per cent of those whose complaints were handled well subsequently went on to increase their purchases of company products, showing that dissatisfied customers can be turned round (Coca Cola Company 1981).

The most effective way of reducing post-purchase dissonance is to provide a product that meets the customer's expectations. This is partly a function for the manufacturer, but is also a problem for the salesperson to address since it should be possible to ensure that the consumer's needs are fully understood before a recommendation about a product is made. In other words, the manufacturing department are in charge of developing the right product, but the salesperson is in charge of developing the right expectations.

As a fall-back position, though, every effort should be made to encourage the consumer to complain if things do not come up to expectations. Salespeople should, wherever practical, follow up on sales to ensure that everything is as it should be. For example, a home-improvement salesperson should call back to visit the customer after the work has been done, in case any problems have come to light. Many salespeople are afraid to do this, in case there is a problem which must be dealt with, but it is better to call back to the customer and try to solve the problem than to leave matters until the customer makes a complaint. Also, of course, in the vast majority of cases the customer is perfectly happy with the product and may even offer a recommendation to friends or a repeat purchase.

A failure to solve problems raised by post-purchase dissonance will, ultimately, lead to irreparable damage to the firm's reputation. The evidence from the Coca Cola survey is that consumers whose complaints are resolved satisfactorily can become more loyal than those consumers who did not have a complaint in the first place. In the last analysis, it is always cheaper to keep an existing customer than it is to attract a new one, and therefore it behoves suppliers to give customers every chance to express problems with the service or product provision.

Finally, the *divestment* stage refers to the way the customer disposes of the product after use. This could be as simple as throwing an empty food container into the bin, or it could be as complex as the trade-in of a second-hand car. This stage is of increasing importance to marketers, both in terms of green marketing (dealing with environmental issues) and in terms of the possibility of making sales of new products (for example on trade-in deals). Trade-in was originally invented by General Motors in the 1930s as a way of encouraging motorists to buy new cars, and to facilitate the operation of the second-hand car market; negotiating trade-in deals has since become a standard part of the car salesperson's job.

Most consumer decisions are made without intervention by salespeople, but those which involve complex decision making or which involve a heavy commitment of time or resources often involve salespeople. The range of purchases in this category goes from shoes to houses; in each case the consumer is in need of guidance and help with the decision-making process.

Influences on the buying decision

The main influences on the buying decision are of three types. *Personal factors* are features of the consumer that affect the decision process, *psychological factors* are elements of the consumer's mental processes, and *social factors* are those influences from friends and family that influence decision making. Personal factors are shown in Table 2.3.

Involvement can also be a major factor in consumer decision making. People often form emotional attachments to products, and most people would be familiar with the feeling of having fallen in love with a product – even when the product itself is hopelessly impractical. Involvement can also operate at a cognitive level, however; the outcome of the purchase may have important practical consequences for the consumer. For example, a rock climber may feel highly involved in the purchase of a climbing rope, since the consequences of an error could be fatal. Whether this is a manifestation of a logical thought process regarding the risk to life and limb, or whether it is an emotional process regarding a feeling of confidence about the product, would be hard to determine.

Psychological factors in the decision-making process are shown in Table 2.4.

Customers' attitudes to products and companies can be complex. They vary according to *valence* (whether the attitude is positive, negative, or neutral), according to *extremity* (the strength of the attitude), *resistance* (the degree to which the attitude can be changed by outside influences), *persistence* (the degree to which the attitude erodes over time), and *confidence* (the level at which the consumer believes the attitude is correct).

The traditional view of attitude is that affect towards an object is mediated by cognition; Zajonc and Markus (1985) challenged this view and asserted that affect can arise without prior cognition. In other words, it is possible to develop a gut feeling about something without conscious evaluation. In the selling context, much of this gut feeling comes from the attitude towards the salesperson; liking the salesperson tends to spill over into a liking for the product.

From the salesperson's viewpoint, attitudes are important since they often precede behaviour. Clearly a positive attitude towards a salesperson is more likely to lead to purchase of the firm's products than a negative attitude; for the consumer, the salesperson *is* the firm. There is, however, some evidence to show that people often behave first, then form attitudes afterwards (Fishbein 1972), which is why car salespeople usually allow the customer to test-drive vehicles. Trial is considerably more powerful than advertising in forming attitudes (Smith and Swinyard 1983).

TABLE 2.3 Personal factors in the buying decision

Personal factor	Explanation
Demographic factors	Individual characteristics such as age, gender, ethnic origin, income, family life-cycle and occupation. Sometimes a young sales representative might not be accorded much credibility by an older buyer, or vice versa. Equally, some salespeople and buyers have difficulty relating effectively with people from different ethnic backgrounds.
Situational factors	Changes in the customer's circumstances. For example, a downturn in a firm's business might lead it to cut back on purchases.
Level of involvement	Involvement concerns the degree of importance the customer attaches to the product and purchasing decision. Involvement is sometimes about the emotional attachment the customer has for the product, sometimes about the consequences of buying the wrong product. For example, a buyer may feel obligated to continue to buy a product from a firm which has proved helpful in the past, on the basis of returning a favour. Equally, an aircraft manufacturer would pay great attention to the control systems being bought in, because the consequences of failure could be catastrophic in a way that, say, the quality of the tray tables would not.

Social factors influence consumers through *normative compliance* (the pressure exerted on the individual to conform with the behaviour and attitudes of their social group), *value-expressive influence* (the need for psychological association with a particular group, usually by buying products or acting in ways that show that one accepts the values of the group) and *informational influence* (the need to seek information from a group about the product category being considered). Of the three, normative compliance is probably the most powerful, and works because the individual finds that acting in one way leads to the approval of friends or family, whereas acting in a different way leads to the disapproval of friends and family. This process favours a particular type of behaviour as a result. Salespeople are able to use normative compliance by implying that the product is *de rigueur* for the customer's social group or industry.

Peer-group pressure is an example of normative compliance. The individual's peer group (a group of equals) will expect a particular type of behaviour,

TABLE 2.4 Psychological factors in the purchase decision

Psychological factor	Explanation
Perception	People build up a view of the world by a process of selection or *analysis*; this means that each person has an incomplete picture of the world. The brain fills in the gaps by a process of *synthesis* using hearsay, previous experience, imagination, etc. Salespeople are able to fill some of the gaps during the sales presentation, but will come up against the problem of breaking through the selection process; often customers will reject on principle what the salesperson is saying.
Motives	The internal force that encourages the consumer towards a particular course of action. Motivation has both intensity and direction. Salespeople can sometimes affect the direction of the motivation, or the nature of it, or its strength.
Ability and knowledge	Ability affects some buying decisions; a professional musician is likely to spend more on instruments than a beginner would, and the same is true of computer systems, aircraft and other complex products. Likewise, an individual who knows a great deal about a brand or product class already will be harder to persuade; it is much better to try to add to the customer's knowledge wherever possible since this is likely to increase the opportunities to trade up.
Attitude	Attitude has three components: *cognition*, which is to do with the buyer's conscious thought processes; *affect*, which is about the buyer's emotional attachment to the product, and *conation*, which is about planned courses of behaviour (see Figure 2.2). In order to change attitudes, salespeople need to begin by destabilizing one component of the attitude. Usually this will be cognition, because it is easier to inject some new information than it is to change an emotion or a behaviour.
Personality	Personality is the traits and behaviours that make each person unique. Personalities change very slowly, if at all, and can be regarded as constant for the purposes of selling. Typically marketers aim for specific personality types, such as the gregarious, the competitive, the outgoing or the sporty, but salespeople need to adapt their own behaviour to fit in with the personality of the buyer. This is not always easy.

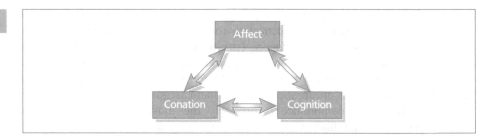

FIGURE 2.2

Balanced attitude

TALKING POINT

Parceline, the UK parcel delivery company, runs Mercedes trucks. The decision to buy Mercedes rather than the much cheaper Ford Transits used by competitors Securicor was based on several factors. Firstly, the Mercedes trucks had longer service intervals, which meant that they were off the road less frequently for routine servicing. Secondly, the Mercedes trucks had a better reputation for reliability. But the clincher for the decision was that Mercedes has a more upmarket image, which would rub off on Parceline.

including, probably, some purchase behaviour. For example, most cigarette smokers take up smoking in their early teens or younger; the pressure to be part of the group is stronger than government health warnings.

Organizational buyer behaviour

Organizational buyers differ from consumers in that they are (at least theoretically) more formalized in their buying behaviour. The major areas where organizational buying differs from consumer buying are as follows:

- bigger order values in terms of both cost and quantity
- organizational buying may be reciprocal; the firms may buy each other's products as part of a negotiated deal
- fewer buyers, because there are fewer firms than there are individuals
- more people become involved in the decision-making process
- fewer sales in terms of the number of deals
- more complex techniques exist for buying and for negotiating.

Organizational buyers are buying in order to meet the organization's needs, but it is important for salespeople to remember that the buyers also have personal needs. These might be a need for prestige, for career security, for friendship and social needs. Some buyers have a need for the satisfaction of driving a hard bargain, or the process may be affected by the buyer's personality, attitudes and beliefs (Powers 1991). The astute marketer, and particularly the astute salesperson, will not ignore the personal needs of the buyers.

Regarding the organization's needs, however, the chief considerations of most buyers appear to revolve around quality, delivery, service and price (Green *et al.* 1968). This often means that buyers will be working to a set of specifications about the products. Organizational buying behaviour revolves around the purchase methods given in Table 2.5.

New-task buying involves making a purchase for the first time. In this case the buyer will need to adopt extensive problem-solving behaviour, which usually means spending considerable time talking to salespeople. The salesperson may be in a position to establish a relationship which might last for many years, but new-task situations usually involve considerable negotiation, since there is little, if any, previous experience to draw on, at least on the part of the buyer.

Straight re-buy tasks are routine; the buyer is simply placing an order for the same products in the same quantities as last time. This requires very little thought or negotiation on the part of either buyer or seller. Often buyers and sellers conduct these deals over the telephone rather than spending time and money on a face-to-face meeting.

Modified re-buy involves some change in the purchase order, for example a larger order value or a different delivery schedule. Sometimes the re-buy can be modified by the salesperson, for example by suggesting that the buyer orders a slightly larger value of goods than usual, or by altering the delivery schedule in some way. Again, the negotiation level involved might be relatively high – the buyer will only place a larger order if there is some benefit in doing so.

Another complication from the salesperson's viewpoint is that the demand for organizational products will often be dictated by factors outside the buying organization's control. For example, *derived demand* occurs because the buyers are using the products either for resale, or to use in making other products. The

TABLE 2.5 Organizational buyers' methods

Method	Explanation
Description	The organization lays down exactly what is required, and the buyer is given the brief of finding the best supplier. He or she will then ask manufacturers to quote prices, and will make a judgement based on price and reliability of delivery.
Inspection	Inspection is carried out for variable goods, such as second-hand plant and equipment. Car dealers will usually inspect the cars before buying, for example.
Sampling	This is commonly used for agricultural products. A buyer might sample, say, wool from an Australian sheep-station and fix a price for it on the basis of its quality. Often these decisions will be made by reference to a very small sample, perhaps only a few strands of wool.
Negotiation	Typically used for one-off or greenfield purchase situations. This involves the greatest input in terms of both the buyer's skills and the salesperson's time.

demand is therefore dictated by the demand for the end product, and the salesperson has no control over that. Frequently the demand for a component will be *inelastic*; for example, the price of wheel nuts will not affect the demand for them much, since they form only a tiny proportion of the price of a car and also the car cannot be made without them. This means that negotiating a lower price for the nuts is unlikely to lead to increased orders, unless the firm is one of several suppliers of nuts. *Joint demand* occurs because the demand for one type of product dictates the demand for another. For instance, if the demand for petrol rises, so will the demand for car tyres in the following months – as people drive more, they wear out the tyres faster. This can be useful to salespeople in predicting demand, provided some way is available of knowing what the demand for petrol is.

Fluctuating demand is more common in organizational markets because a small reduction in consumer demand for a product will lead to de-stocking, which causes a big reduction in production. A rise in consumer demand is likely to lead to re-stocking, which causes a bigger than expected rise in demand for components. In this way the fluctuations in demand for organizational products are more extreme than for consumer products.

Decision-making units

Organizational buying decisions are rarely made in isolation. Usually several people are involved in the process at different stages, as shown in Table 2.6 (Webster and Wind 1972).

These categories are not, of course, mutually exclusive. A user might also be an influencer, or a gatekeeper might also be an initiator. The categories were originally developed to explain purchasing behaviour within families – which may be an example of the closeness of organizational marketing and consumer marketing.

In general, members of the decision-making unit (DMU) tend to be more risk averse than consumers. This is because DMU members have more to lose in the event of a wrong decision; for a consumer, the main risk is financial, and even that is a limited risk since most retailers will refund or exchange products which have been purchased in error. For organizational buyers the risk includes loss of face at work, perhaps loss of promotion, and in extreme cases even dismissal. The professional persona of the organizational buyer is compromised by serious mistakes in purchasing, whereas consumers have little to lose.

As a result of the greater risk involved, organizational buyers use a variety of risk-reduction strategies (Hawes and Barnhouse 1987). In order of importance, these are:

1 Visit the supplier's operation to observe its viability.
2 Question other customers of the supplier about their experience of doing business with the supplier.
3 Multisource the order to ensure a backup source of supply.
4 Obtain penalty clause provisions from the supplier.
5 Talk to colleagues about the vendor.
6 When choosing a supplier, give preference to companies the firm has dealt with before.

7 Confirm that members of senior management are in favour of dealing with the supplier.

8 Limit the search for, and ultimate choice of, suppliers to well-known firms.

9 Obtain the opinion of a majority of co-workers that the chosen supplier is satisfactory.

Organizational buyers have many of the same influences on their decision making as do consumers. The desire to play a role, or to drive a hard bargain, or a desire to be liked and respected would be as powerful in an organizational buyer as in a consumer. These influences might cause a buyer to place an order with a salesperson who is perceived as friendly and helpful, and deny it to one who is perceived as pushy. Buyers are also influenced by a set of environmental influences, as shown in Table 2.7 (Loudon and Della Bitta 1993).

Organizational factors derive from the corporate culture as well as from strategic decisions made by senior managers. The procedures, structure, work patterns, reward systems, status, authority and communications systems will all affect the

TABLE 2.6 The decision-making unit	
Member	**Explanation and examples**
Initiators	These are the individuals who first recognize the problem. An initiator is often a salesperson from a supplying organization; recognizing problems and initiating the purchase process is an important role for salespeople.
Gatekeepers	Secretaries and receptionists control the flow of information to the decision makers. Often they see their role as being primarily to prevent interruptions to the decision maker's work pattern and will act as a barrier to salespeople.
Influencers	These are individuals who have the ear of the decision makers. Influencers are difficult to identify; they could be people within the firm whom the decision maker trusts, or they could be friends or advisers outside the firm.
Users	These will actually use the product. For example, if the organization is contemplating the purchase of a new computer system, the IT department will be involved in the decision.
Deciders	These are the ones who make the real decision. They are not necessarily buyers, but they do hold the real power in the buying decision. Usually they are the more senior people in the decision-making unit, and are hard to get to because they are surrounded by gatekeepers.
Buyers	These are the individuals who are given the task of getting quotes from suppliers, negotiating (often within a very specific brief) and handling the paperwork.

TABLE 2.7 Environmental influences on organizational buyers

Influence	Explanation
Physical influences	The location of the firm relative to its suppliers may be important. Many firms, especially those operating in a global environment, like to source supplies locally whenever possible. Sometimes this is because the buyers prefer to deal with someone from their own cultural background, even when rational decisions about cost and delivery would indicate that a foreign supplier would be better.
Technological influences	The level of technological sophistication among local suppliers will determine what the buyer can obtain. For example, a company in Zambia would not be able to find local suppliers of robotic machine tools, and would have to buy from Japan or Europe. Also, technology needs to be compatible; technical standards within the European Union are not yet fully agreed, so it is sometimes easier for companies to buy from former colonies of their home country, where standards are the same, rather than from a much nearer supplier within the EU.
Economic influences	Macroeconomic issues such as the national taxation regime or the level of demand within the country will affect what a buyer can obtain because they affect the demand for the buying company's products. On a more subtle level, economic issues affect buyers' confidence levels. A widespread belief that the country is about to go into an economic decline will almost certainly make buyers reluctant to commit to major investments in stock, equipment and machinery. At the microeconomic level, a firm experiencing a rapid boom in business will have more confidence and a greater ability to pay for goods, as well as a greater demand for inputs.
Political influences	Governments frequently pass laws affecting the ways in which businesses operate. In the international arena, trade sanctions, preferred-nation status and selective aid to industries affect the ability of firms to do business. The political stability of countries also affects business confidence.
Legal influences	Laws often lay down technical standards which affect purchasing behaviour. Firms may be compelled to incorporate safety features or environmentally protective features, for example. Laws are also passed which regulate the behaviour of buyers and sellers.
Ethical influences	In general, buyers are expected to act at all times for the benefit of the organization, rather than for personal gain. Bribery or excessive business gifts are not usually considered ethical, although in some countries and cultures bribery is expected, which leaves the salesperson with a difficult ethical problem. In general, buyers tend to be reluctant to do business with a salesperson whom they believe to be acting unethically – after all, if a salesperson is prepared to cheat, he or she cannot be trusted not to cheat the buyer.
Cultural influences	Culture establishes the values, norms and beliefs of a society. When dealing internationally, cultural influences are paramount; in the UK, for example, it would be customary to offer a salesperson a cup of tea or coffee, whereas in China it might be customary to offer food. Dim sum originated as a way for Chinese businessmen to offer their visitor a symbolic meal, as a way of establishing a rapport. Corporate culture ('the way we do things round here') also affects the way buyers behave because it encompasses the organization's ethics, attitudes towards suppliers and customers, and beliefs about the company's direction.

buying function. Figure 2.3 shows the main categories of organizational influences on the buyers' behaviour.

Task influences are those which are dictated by the nature of the buying problem. The buying task for a retailer differs from that of a manufacturer, because the retailer will be selling the products on virtually unchanged, whereas the manufacturer needs to consider how the product will fit into a specific process. Even within a supermarket the tasks may vary; for example, negotiating with a manufacturer to produce own-brand products, negotiating with an electronics manufacturer to supply new tills, or negotiating with a building firm to provide maintenance services are all activities which a supermarket might engage in. The structure of the organization falls into two categories, the formal and the informal. The formal structure is represented on the organization chart, and shows the level of seniority of the buyer and his or her levels of autonomy and responsibility. The informal structure is the network of social obligations, friendship, internal liaisons and political jockeying which, in most cases, actually determines staff behaviour on a day-to-day basis. The informal structure dictates issues such as rivalry or co-operation between buyers, buyers' attitudes towards the boss, buyers' political ambitions regarding other departments, and so forth. From the viewpoint of a salesperson, the complexities of the informal structure are probably impenetrable, but such issues often form a key element in the success or failure of a sale, especially in a key-account management situation. The informal structure also dictates who will be the influencers in a purchase decision.

In the global situation, the informal network also has the added dimension of cultural differences. The oriental factor of not wishing to lose face might be crucial in doing business, as might the typically Greek attitude of not wishing to challenge authority openly.

The technology of the organization may act to control or even circumvent much of the buyer's role. Computer-controlled stock purchasing often removes the buyer from the equation simply because the parameters for purchase do not allow for any negotiation. Models for inventory control and price forecasting are also widely used, again obviating the need for input from the buyer or at least reducing the scope for manoeuvre. In circumstances such as these the salesperson will need to work through other members of the decision-making unit in order to change the system; this is an important part of key-account management.

Finally, the people involved in the organization will, in part, determine its culture. They will, at the very least, determine how the rules are interpreted. In many cases the organization's founder will have set his or her personality firmly on the

FIGURE 2.3

Organizational influences on buyer behaviour

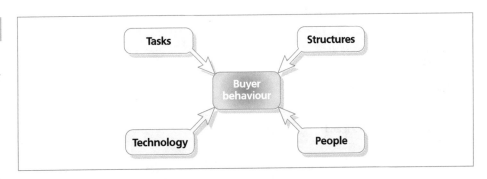

corporate culture; Tom Watson of IBM, Richard Branson of Virgin and Anita Roddick of Body Shop are examples of charismatic corporate founders whose organizations reflect their personalities.

The buygrid framework

Organizational buying can be seen as a series of problems, the solution to each of which leads to a further problem about which a decision must be made (Cardozo 1983). From the viewpoint of the salesperson, it is possible to diagnose problems by examining the sequence of decisions – provided, of course, the decision sequence can be discovered. Often a salesperson can simply ask the buyer what is the sequence of decision making.

The result of this type of analysis is the buygrid framework, shown in Figure 2.4. The most complex buying situations occur in the upper left portion of the framework and involve the greatest number of people and buying influences. This is because new tasks require the steepest learning curves and the greatest amount of effort in seeking information. Also, because they represent the riskiest purchase situations, more people will be involved in the decision, which means more debate and negotiation than would be the case for straight re-buys.

FIGURE 2.4   The buygrid framework   *Source: Robinson et al. (1967)*

	Buying situations		
	New task	Modified re-buy	Straight re-buy
Anticipation or recognition of a problem (need) and a general solution			
Determination of characteristics and quantity of needed item			
Description of characteristics and quantity of needed item			
Search for and qualification of potential sources			
Acquisition and analysis of proposals			
Evaluation of proposals and selection of supplier(s)			
Selection of an order routine			
Performance feedback and evaluation			

TALKING POINT

When IBM set up a key-account operation to service their account with Lloyds Bank (one of the UK's largest banks), they set up a special office in Canary Wharf, near to Lloyds headquarters. The various specialists from IBM worked from this office, and eventually more than 100 individuals from IBM were based permanently at Canary Wharf.

It is rumoured that one office comedian at IBM even had a sign made reading 'Lloyds Bank Canary Wharf Branch' and put it on the office door. This identification with the customer was actually deadly serious – such a large account deserved extra effort from the company, and the effort was made.

The buygrid framework has been criticized because it oversimplifies the situation. As in consumer decision making, the process is nowhere near as logical and mechanical as implied in the framework. The sequence may not be as clear cut, and events may not happen in the order implied by the framework. For example, a salesperson might approach a firm with a solution for a problem which the firm did not know it had, thus cutting out several stages in the decision process. Secondly, suppliers make great efforts to differentiate themselves from competitors as effectively as they can so that the buyer may not have any other potential suppliers for the product. Thirdly, the model assumes a rationality which may simply not be there.

Because of this occasional lack of rationality, salespeople need to be aware of the buying motives of each member of the decision-making unit. This is because each member of the DMU will apply different criteria for including or excluding suppliers (Kelly and Coaker 1976). For example, a finance director might be concerned with low prices, whereas the production engineer might be concerned with reliable deliveries. In the case of key-account management, the differences between buyers is often overcome by the use of a team approach to making sales. Although the salesperson (here called the key-account manager) is responsible for initial contact and for orchestrating the process, other specialists are brought in as necessary to deal with financial aspects, engineering aspects, delivery aspects, and so forth. In this way each member of the DMU is talking to a fellow specialist, with whom there will be a common technical language and professional understanding of the specialism.

Evaluating suppliers

Buyers need to evaluate suppliers for capability in the first instance, then for performance after the sale has been concluded. This is a process of ensuring that the supplier can keep the promises that the salesperson made. Assessing suppliers for capability is a combination of assessing financial stability, technical expertise, reliability, quality assurance processes and production capacity.

Table 2.8 shows some of the ways in which buyers can assess potential suppliers. All of these methods rely on judgement on the part of the buyer, who may not in fact have the necessary skills to judge accurately what are the supplier's capabilities.

Evaluating performance is somewhat easier since it relies on actual experience rather than guesswork and estimates. Some basic evaluation methods are outlined in Table 2.9. All of these methods involve considerable subjectivity. In each case, the output of the exercise will be expressed numerically, which has the unfortunate effect of giving the outcome a spurious credibility. The evaluation exercise itself should be reviewed periodically to ensure that it is still realistic, and that the assumptions on which it is based still hold true.

TABLE 2.8 Assessing suppliers

Attribute	Assessment method
Technical capability	Buyers sometimes visit the suppliers' premises to examine production equipment, inspect quality control procedures, and meet the engineering staff.
Managerial capability	Buyers will discuss systems for controlling processes, will meet the managerial staff, and may even become involved in planning and scheduling supplies.
Financial stability	Buyers may check that the accounts filed at Companies House (or the equivalent company registration offices in the supplier's home country) are up to date and show that the firm is solvent. They may also run a credit check, and examine annual reports if these are available.
Capacity to deliver	Buyers might ascertain the status of the supplier's other customers – would any of these take priority if capacity could not meet demand? They may check the production capacity of the supplier, as well as warehouse buffer stocks and reputation in the industry.

TABLE 2.9 Evaluation approaches

Approach	Explanation
Categorical plan	Each department in the buying firm is asked to provide a regular rating of suppliers against a list of salient performance factors. This method is subjective in some ways, depending on the performance factors selected, but is easy to administer and comprehensive.
Weighted-point plan	Performance factors are graded according to their importance to the organization. For example, delivery reliability might not be as important as product reliability. The supplier's total rating can be calculated and fed back to the supplier if necessary, in order to enable the supplier to improve the offering.
Cost-ratio plan	This involves the buyer in calculating the various factors in terms of what each one costs the corporation. For example, poor delivery reliability might cost the company in terms of lost production or wasted time spent progress chasing. Good supplier performance reduces costs, poor supplier performance increases costs.

Policies and procedures

Salespeople need to take account of the policies and procedures of the potential buying firm. Organizational buyers almost invariably operate within strict budgets, and have upper limits on the size of deal they are able to agree to. This means that salespeople are sometimes unable to make a sale simply because the buyer is not authorized to sign off an agreement for the full price of the order. The salesperson may need to present again to a more senior buyer, or even a group of company directors, if the order is too large for the buyer to agree to.

The payment policies of companies are also likely to be relevant. Many large firms insist on lengthy credit periods – three months is not unusual – whereas the salesperson's own company may have a credit limit of only 30 days. This is a clear area for conflict to develop between the buying company and the selling company, with the salesperson caught in the middle. On the other hand, it also offers rich opportunities for salespeople to negotiate, provided the buyer is authorized to vary the credit terms.

Co-ordinating paperwork, or computer-based systems, may also provide a useful negotiating tool for salespeople when negotiating larger deals or long-term relationships. Setting up compatible systems allows the business to be transacted more easily, and tends to lock in the buying firm, since changing supplier will also mean changing the paperwork systems.

Tactical role of the salesperson

Organizational salespeople gain a distinct advantage if they are able to get to the deciders in some way rather than wait for the buyers to make the first contact by issuing a tender. Tenders are usually very specific, so that the tendering companies will all be quoting on the same basis; this means that the buyer will be making the decision on the basis of price. The only way to get the order in those circumstances is to be the cheapest, and this inevitably results in reduced profits. Approaching the decision maker beforehand means that the salesperson has a chance to persuade him or her of the importance of product features which the competition cannot provide; this will ensure that the tender contains specifications that are difficult or impossible for the competition to meet.

This means that the role of the salesperson is crucial in organizational markets. Salespeople are able to identify potential customers and approach them with a solution for their specific problem; even in cases where the buyer is going to invite tenders from other firms, the salesperson can often ensure that the tender is drawn up in a way that excludes the competition.

In the final analysis, organizations do not make purchases. Individuals make purchases on behalf of organizations, which means that salespeople are always dealing with human beings who have their own needs, failings, attitudes and blind spots. Purchasing decisions are not always made entirely rationally; often the personal relationship between the representatives of the buying and selling companies has the biggest role in the purchase, because organizations do not sell things either. Business is not only about profits and balance sheets; it is about people and their relationships; establishing an atmosphere of mutual trust and respect is a necessary precursor to any business transaction.

SUMMARY

Buying decisions are not made purely on the basis of a rational recognition of a need; still less are decisions made for purely utilitarian purposes. Human beings, whether buying for themselves or on behalf of the firms who employ them, have complex emotional and social needs as well as practical, everyday needs. This is reflected in buying decisions, both in the outcomes and in the process.

Here are the key points from this chapter.

- Consumers buy because they recognize either assortment depletion or assortment extension needs.

- Complaints should be actively encouraged, because they give the opportunity to resolve post-purchase dissonance and, often, create loyal customers.

- Normative compliance is probably the most powerful factor in attitude formation and decision making.

- Industrial buying is complex because of the number of people involved.

- Gatekeepers, users, influencers, deciders and buyers are all involved in organizational decision making. None of them should be ignored if the deal is to go through.

- The route to success in organizational marketing is to make sure the tender has something in it that the competition cannot match.

REVIEW QUESTIONS

1 How might a salesperson increase a customer's motivation to buy?
2 What are the main differences between organizational buyers and consumers?
3 What is the difference between assortment depletion and assortment extension?
4 How can a salesperson use heuristics to reduce post-purchase dissonance?
5 How can a salesperson use interrupts to influence buyer behaviour?

REFERENCES

Bettman, J. R. (1979) *An Information Processing Theory of Consumer Choice*, Reading, MA: Addison Wesley; chapter 7.

Cardozo, R. N. (1983) 'Modelling organisational buying as a sequence of decisions', *Industrial Marketing Management* 12 (Feb.): 75.

Coca Cola Company (1981) *Measuring the Grapevine: Consumer Response and Word-of-Mouth*.

Day, R. L., Brabicke, K., Schaetzle, T. and Staubach, F. (1981) 'The hidden agenda of consumer complaining', *Journal of Retailing* Fall: 86–106.

Engel, J. F., Blackwell, R. D. and Miniard, P. W. (1995) *Consumer Behaviour*, 8th edn, Fort Worth, TX: Dryden Press.

Fishbein, M. (1972) 'The search for attitudinal-behavioural consistency', in J. E. Cohen (ed.) *Behavioural Science Foundations of Consumer Behaviour*, New York: Free Press.

Green, P., Robinson, P. and Wind, Y. (1968) 'The determinants of vendor selection: The evaluation function approach', *Journal of Purchasing* (Aug.).

Hawes, J. M and Barnhouse, S. H. (1987) 'How purchasing agents handle personal risk', *Industrial Marketing Management* 16 (November): 287–93.

Holbrook, M. P. and Hirschmann, E. C. (1982) 'The experiential aspects of consumption: Consumer fantasies, feelings and fun', *Journal of Consumer Research* 9 (Sep.): 132–40.

Kelly, P. and Coaker, J. W. (1976) 'Can we generalise about choice criteria for industrial purchasing decisions?', in K. L. Bernhardt (ed.) *Marketing 1776–1976 and Beyond*, Chicago, IL: American Marketing Association: 330–333.

Loudon, D. L. and Della Bitta, A. J. (1993) *Consumer Behaviour*, 4th edn., London: McGraw Hill.

McClelland, K. (1988) *Human Motivation*, Cambridge: Cambridge University Press.

Oliver, R. L. (1980) 'A cognitive model of the antecedents and consequences of satisfaction decisions', *Journal of Marketing Research* 17 (Nov.): 460–9.

Powers, T. L.(1991) *Modern Business Marketing: A Strategic Planning Approach to Business and Industrial Markets*, St Paul, MN: West.

Raju, P. S. (1980) 'Optimum stimulation level: Its relationship to personality, demographics, and exploratory behaviour', *Journal of Consumer Research* 7 (December): 272–82.

Robinson, P. J., Farris, C. W. and Wind, Y. (1967) *Industrial Buying and Creative Marketing*, Marketing Science Institute Series, Boston: Allyn and Bacon Inc.

Singh, J. (1988) 'Consumer complaint intentions and behaviour: Definitions and taxonomical issues', *Journal of Marketing* 52 (Jan.): 93–107.

Smith, R. E. and Swinyard, W. R. (1983): 'Attitude-behaviour consistency: The impact of product trial versus advertising', *Journal of Marketing Research* 20 (Aug.).

Webster F. E. and Wind, Y. (1972) *Organisational Buying Behaviour*, Englewood Cliffs, NJ: Prentice Hall.

Zajonc, R. B. and Markus, H. (1985) 'Must all affect be mediated by cognition?', *Journal of Consumer Research* 12 (Dec.): 363–4.

ACHILLES

Achilles Information Ltd is the British subsidiary of a Norwegian consultancy. Founded in Norway in 1990, Achilles came to Britain in 1993, offering purchasing intelligence to utility companies, oil and gas companies, and the transport industry among others. Although it is a relatively small organization (200 employees) Achilles has made a considerable impact on the purchasing activities of many UK organizations.

Initially, Achilles was a service provider to purchasers, offering advice through its pre-qualification database, which contains details of hundreds of potential suppliers. The database, known as UVDB (utilities vendor database) sources current and potential suppliers of products, services and expertise. Over 50 utilities companies are signed up to the database. More recently, Achilles has extended its services to include supply chain and contract management, extending its range of activities to pick up even more of the burden from organizations.

Achilles now runs what it calls the Verify Scheme. This is a standardized health, safety, environmental and quality assurance scheme which sets up standardized evaluation and pre-qualification criteria to which suppliers must adhere. The scheme is operated by a steering group made up of representatives from the utility companies, and a service-provider group. The Verify Scheme seeks to set up a standardized, industry-wide system for evaluating suppliers, including a system for benchmarking suppliers so that comparison is easy for the potential customers. Service providers have the option of joining the scheme as Patron Members, giving them the right to participate in the discussions, and also giving them access to the online systems.

Achilles also provides a specialist software system, THEMIS, which explains European Union legislation and enables clients to comply with both UK and EU legislation on purchasing. This includes regular updates to take account of decisions made in court, and guidance through the bureaucracy of the EU as regards purchasing.

The privatization of the UK rail network was certainly a boost for Achilles. Where previously the rail system had been run exclusively by British Rail as a national monopoly, privatization meant that the network was split into 27 separate companies, each of whom had specific procurement problems. Achilles set up a system called Link-Up, which enabled rail companies to share information about potential and actual vendors. The system operates a standard capability assessment for potential suppliers to the rail industry, and the information is updated on a daily basis so that assessments of vendors are always current. The effect of this on the rail companies has been radical; they now have all the cost savings of being part of a large network, while retaining their independence.

The company offers many new, Internet-based services including on-line reverse auctions, where suppliers and buyers put in bids, speeding up the negotiation process. Achilles also offers procurement consultancy, training and marketing provision to suppliers.

Vendors, too, are not displeased with the outcome. Achilles provides a standard set of criteria to aspire to, and a standard set of rules to conform to. Once a supplier has met the Achilles requirements, the rest is easy – companies in need of the product will be in touch. Overall, Achilles seeks to smooth the path of selling and purchasing – a task which it achieves well.

Case-study questions

1 How do the activities of a firm such as Achilles affect a salesperson's approach in selling to utility companies?

2 How might buyers be influenced to use a company that is not on Achilles' list?

3 What are the drawbacks from a buyer's viewpoint of using Achilles?

4 Some suppliers who are on Achilles' list may feel that their sales force is no longer necessary. Why might they think this, and why might they be wrong?

5 What is the role of the Internet in Achilles' success?

PREPARING TO SELL

■ Introduction

As with most other activities, successful selling depends on preparation. Most salespeople need to prepare in a mental sense as well as in a practical sense; selling is not just about ensuring a supply of order forms and a suitable stock of sales literature. It is also about having the right mental attitude. Preparation also includes prospecting – finding appropriate people to sell to – and planning the sales presentation.

Sales companies are recognizing that enthusiasm, intelligence, charisma, and the focus to be able to work in a deadline-driven environment are important qualities for salespeople. At the same time, ambitious graduates recognize that a sales career is a good way of fast-tracking up the corporate ladder.

Mark Young is typical of this. He graduated six years ago, and immediately started his career in media sales. 'I would argue that media sales is one of the most challenging, interesting and rewarding careers,' he says now. 'Not only can you earn good money, but you are helping to grow a business. And how many jobs will give you the opportunity to deal with senior decision makers on a daily basis? Or will involve you in speaking to the managing director of a multi-million-pound turnover company?'

James Nurton, editor of *Euromoney*, refutes the image of the salesperson as fast-talking dodgy dealer. 'Our sales force has to be knowledgeable, articulate and very confident. We look for those who can explain our products clearly, persuasively and concisely, who can grasp new concepts quickly, and who can build up strong relationships.' James should know the value of youth and energy – he is still only 26.

'If you're looking for a career that is going to give you responsibility and many challenges then a future in sales is worth pursuing,' says Mark Young. 'On the other hand, if you're the sort of person who prefers a routine 9 to 5 pen-pushing job, then forget it!'

The selling cycle

Figure 3.1 shows the activities which comprise the selling cycle. It describes the process of making a sale, from the point at which the salesperson is looking for a possible customer right through to the aftermath of the sale, in which the salesperson follows up with the client to ensure that everything went well. The process is regarded as a cycle because the salesperson will often use the follow-up call to prospect for more business, either looking for repeat orders from the same customer, or for ideas on other prospects to call on. Normally, salespeople will have several of the cycles running at once, and be spending part of their time on prospecting, part on follow-ups, part on presentations and so forth.

The sales cycle may be long (weeks or months) or short (hours or days) depending on the product, the industry and the nature of the customers. For some industries (for example, home improvements), a short sales cycle is the norm, and the received wisdom is that letting customers think too long about the proposition will only result in their having more time to think of reasons not to buy. In other industries (for example, capital equipment for manufacturing), rushing the sales cycle through would result in lower sales values and fewer sales. Equally, the sales cycle might involve only one visit or might require many visits over a period of months, perhaps talking to several different decision makers.

In some industries and for some products there may be several salespeople involved in generating the business. A salesperson for IBM, for example, may call on the services of technical salespeople, missionaries, systems designers, and even business specialists who can understand the industry the customer is in.

A further explanation of each of the stages of the cycle is shown in Table 3.1. The selling cycle describes the process of making a single sale to a single customer. It does not describe the day-to-day routine of a salesperson, nor does it apply to the far more common situation in which salespeople have a set of relationships with a large number of customers, each relationship being different from the others in that it is at a particular stage and has its own characteristics.

Prospecting is the process of looking for qualified potential buyers. A qualified buyer is one who has a need for the product, has the authority to buy, is willing to listen to a sales presentation, and has the means to pay for the product or the ability to acquire the means to pay. A prospect is not necessarily going to buy the product; the purpose of the sales presentation is to convert someone with the need for the product and the means to pay for it into someone who also wants the product (see Chapter 4 for a discussion of needs and wants). Prospecting is extremely important; in one study of salespeople's effectiveness, it was concluded that good prospecting often differentiates effective salespeople from ineffective ones (Szymanski and Churchill 1990).

Prospecting involves collecting information about markets, individual firms, and even individuals within firms. The information can be collected via newspapers, trade journals and directories, formal market research (which would usually be carried out by a marketing department) or from personal knowledge. Establishing networks within the industry can be extremely helpful for salespeople; networking often results in a salesperson hearing about a potential source of business.

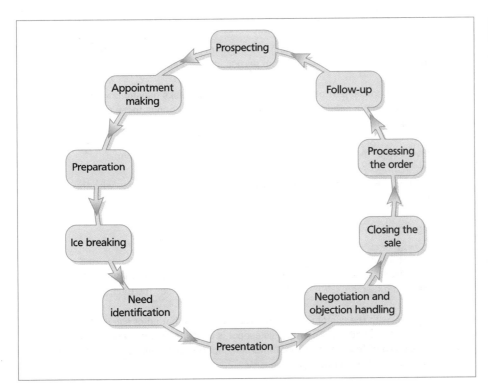

FIGURE 3.1

The sales cycle

At this stage it is very hard to tell whether a prospect (prospective customer) is likely to buy or not; the salesperson is really only seeking out people who might be prepared to agree to an appointment. Often salespeople will telephone possible prospects and ask the receptionist or telephonist to advise on who should be approached for an appointment. Sometimes prospects identify themselves by responding to mailshots or by sending in coupons; sometimes prospects can be identified at exhibitions and trade fairs. Prospecting involves three stages, as shown in Figure 3.2.

FIGURE 3.2

Stages in prospecting

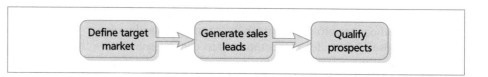

TABLE 3.1 The sales cycle	
Activity	**Explanation**
Prospecting	Sourcing information which enables the salesperson to identify potential buyers.
Appointment making	Selecting the right person to deal with within the target firm and arranging a mutually convenient time to meet.
Preparation	Researching the target company, checking the route for getting there, planning the diary, etc.
Ice breaking	Establishing a human contact by asking some general, information-gathering questions of the prospect. This puts both parties at their ease.
Need identification	This is the most crucial part of the sale. The salesperson asks questions which identify the prospect's needs for the product category and brings those needs to the forefront of the prospect's mind.
Presentation	The explanation of the salesperson's proposed solution for the problem.
Negotiation and objection handling	Dealing with problems raised by the presentation, and discussing these with the prospect.
Closing the sale	Obtaining a decision from the prospect.
Processing the order	Ensuring that the customer's order is dealt with effectively by the supplier, and in accordance with the terms agreed with the customer. This is a good time for the salesperson to run some self-evaluation, to learn from the sales meeting.
Follow-up	Checking back with the customer after delivery to ensure that he or she is completely happy with the product and the firm. This aspect is often neglected by salespeople, perhaps because of fears that the customer may not be totally happy, but it is a good opportunity to prospect for more business.

TALKING POINT

Frank Bettger once advised salespeople that they should never read a newspaper without having a pencil and paper handy. As an insurance salesman, Bettger found the newspapers to be an excellent source of sales leads – the births columns told him who might need extra life insurance for a new family, the business pages told him whose businesses were growing and whose were doing badly, even the sports pages told him who were the up-and-coming athletes who might need insurance.

The same principle can be applied to any industry. Reading the trade press will always provide ideas – but have that pencil and paper handy!

Defining the target market is often carried out by the sales manager or the marketing department, but within a local area the salesperson may need to make a more refined definition of the target market. This will involve developing local knowledge; sometimes this can be obtained by networking with local business people (Michaelson 1998). Local area is not necessarily defined geographically, of course; it could just as easily be a specific industry, or a specific customer group.

The next stage in the process is to develop a sales lead, defined as a potential buyer who is willing to hear a sales presentation. The final step is to qualify the prospect, which involves finding out whether the potential purchaser has a need for the product and the means to pay. Although attempts are often made to qualify prospects before the salesperson's visit, qualification is still best undertaken during the selling meeting. Other methods such as telephone calls asking whether the buyer is solvent, or more general research methods, might be offensive to the prospect, expensive, and unreliable.

Sometimes existing or former customers can be considered as potential prospects for new products. Existing customers are more likely to be receptive to new products than are complete strangers, and former customers will sometimes have changed in their needs or their buying habits in such a way as to become prospects again. Existing customers might also be prepared to recommend friends or business acquaintances who might be interested in the product; these recommendations are called referrals. This method of prospecting is widely used in the insurance industry.

Former customers can be an excellent source of business, even in cases where they were dissatisfied with the company or its products in the past. Correcting whatever went wrong with the previous transactions is often a relatively straightforward matter compared with selling to a prospect who has no knowledge at all of the company or its products. In the business-to-business world in which most salespeople operate, individual buyers move on and are replaced, so a new buyer becomes a prospect even when the previous dealings between the firms were not ideal.

■ Converting leads to prospects

Lead generation is essentially a process of making appointments to present products. A lead is simply the name and address of someone who is prepared to listen to a presentation. A qualified lead also has the means to pay for the product, but a prospect is someone who also has a need for the product (see Figure 3.3). The simplest way to generate leads is to ask buyers directly if they would like an appointment to hear the presentation.

At one time, appointment making was carried out by cold calling on the doorstep. Salespeople would arrive unannounced at the prospect's home or place of business, and try to make an appointment. This approach was common well into the 1990s, and is still encountered occasionally. The main advantage of doorstep cold calling is that the prospect is able to see the salesperson and gain an initial impression of the person as an individual; also, it is harder to refuse an appointment to someone who is physically present. Nowadays, cold calling is often carried out by telephone. The advantages of using the telephone are that it is quicker and cheaper, and also salespeople often find it less psychologically demanding; many people find that the constant rejection of doorstep cold calling is hard to handle. In some firms, the appointment-making function is not carried out by field salespeople at all but by telesales staff who do nothing but make telephone calls asking for appointments.

The main drawback with cold calling by telephone is that many people find it irritating and do not respond positively to it. Increasingly, firms are seeking other ways to find new customers, and inbound telemarketing, which originates with the customer, is on the increase (there is more on telephone selling later in this chapter). Another source of sales leads is the Internet. Websites almost always have a contact number for potential customers to call, at which point they will be put in touch with a salesperson. Note that the website is not a substitute for a salesperson. It offers an opportunity to give potential customers some information about the firm and its products, and to allow some self-qualification of prospects by establishing a need for the product and also, sometimes, giving prospective customers some idea of whether they can afford the product. Websites can even allow customers to gain information on ways of paying for the products. Ultimately, though, unless the product is a simple one such as an airline ticket the customer will need to speak to someone in order to outline the exact problem and obtain

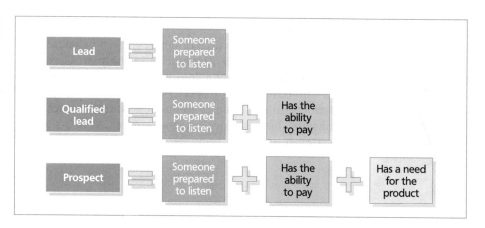

individually tailored advice. The person from whom the advice is sought is, whatever the job title, a salesperson.

Because cold calling is often seen as intrusive, it is under attack from several quarters. Some firms seek to avoid it altogether by putting resources into direct mail or direct-response advertising; others aim to reduce its obtrusiveness by warming the prospects, perhaps by approaching them at exhibitions or other trade functions, or by inviting them to presentations at hotels. Cold calling is unlikely to disappear altogether, since it has proven effectiveness in generating new business, and is often the only way to bring the firm and its products to the attention of a buyer who does not yet realize that he, she or the firm has a problem.

Qualifying the lead (finding out whether the individual or firm has the ability to pay) can be a difficult process. In some cases, research at Companies House (or the local company registration office in a foreign country) can determine whether or not the company is solvent, but this does not tell the salesperson whether the buyer still has funds left in the budget. Even a direct question on this issue may not generate an honest answer, quite apart from the fact that there is no good way of asking without seeming intrusive.

The problem is even greater when dealing with consumers. Clues as to an individual's finances might come from observing how he or she is dressed, observing the standard of the individual's home, and so forth. These measures are hardly reliable, however – the individual may be heavily in debt to fund an unrealistically lavish lifestyle, for example, or conversely may be living frugally but have substantial savings as a result. Confirming the ability to pay is therefore likely to happen during the presentation, when the prospect begins to become interested in the product and starts asking about the price.

Establishing a need for the product will occur early in the presentation (see Chapter 4).

▮ Preparing for the presentation

Preparation for selling involves the following processes:

- Gathering together the necessary information about the prospect.
- Ensuring that all the information needed for the prospect is to hand; for example, leaflets and brochures, price lists and discount tables.
- Checking that supplies of samples, demonstration models and equipment are adequate and working properly.
- Confirming that equipment for producing quotations (computers, tape measures, price lists, discount tables, etc.) is in working order and present.
- Checking the silent seller (see later in this chapter) is complete and up to date.
- Preparing both physically and mentally for the meeting: appearing well groomed, looking after one's health, and developing a positive mental attitude towards the sales presentation.

Gathering information about the prospect allows the salesperson to understand possible problems even before discussing these with the potential buyer. Knowing about the prospect's company also shows commitment, an important element of establishing credibility with the prospect. In most cases, basic research is easily carried out. Visiting the prospect's company website will provide useful background information, but a visit to a news website (e.g. www.thisismoney.com) will provide recent news stories about the firm and its competitors. A good salesperson will already have an in-depth knowledge of the industry in any case.

The information the prospect needs will include information about competitors' products. Again, a good salesperson will be well aware of what the competition is offering, and many salespeople even carry samples of competitors' products in order to make comparisons. Such comparisons should be fair – the credibility of the salesperson can easily be damaged if he or she spends the presentation knocking competing products. On the other hand, the prospect is likely to want to make comparisons, and this is more easily accomplished if the salesperson has the information to hand.

Prior to calling on the prospect, the salesperson should establish the objective of the meeting. In some cases this will not be 'to get the order' since there will frequently be much preliminary work to go through before the sale is made, especially in a major-account context (see Chapter 5). Objectives need to be quantifiable and specific, otherwise they cannot be measured and there is no way of knowing whether the objective was reached. For example, a sales meeting which has the aim of 'establishing a rapport with the client' may be worthy, but cannot be measured and is not sufficiently specific. A sales meeting with the objective of 'arranging for their production manager to see a demonstration of our machine tool' has an identifiable outcome – either the appointment was made or it was not.

Any long-term goal will be based around winning the order, but in a situation requiring multiple calls the following sequence of objectives might apply (Falvey 1989):

1 Telemarketing qualifies a lead.
2 An appointment is sold to the prospect.
3 The salesperson holds a meeting with the purchasing manager and one or two potential users of the product to learn their needs.
4 A proposal is developed.
5 Another meeting is called to present and evaluate the proposal.
6 A contract is negotiated to set out the terms and conditions of the sale.
7 The final order is signed.

Further calls may be made as part of the firm's aftersales service, and as a way of generating referrals. This sequence is by no means prescriptive; different circumstances may well lead to different sequences, and stages may be left out altogether. The majority of sales, especially to consumers, are still initiated and concluded in one meeting.

Physical and mental preparation

Salespeople need to be both physically and mentally prepared. Physical preparation means maintaining good health, being of smart appearance and looking the part. In order to establish a rapport with a customer, salespeople will usually dress and act in the same manner as the prospects. This does not always mean that the salesperson will be wearing a smart business suit. For example, some agricultural salespeople would wear tweeds rather than business suits in order to conform more closely to the dress style of their customers. Prospects are more inclined to buy from salespeople whom they perceive to be like themselves, but it is important to note that aspirations play a role here; the prospect has a self-image which is likely to be at odds with their actual appearance. For example, the farmer might actually be wearing mud-spattered overalls and wellington boots when the salesperson calls, but he might like to think of himself as looking like the smart 'gentleman farmer' that the salesperson's tweed suit projects.

Mental preparation involves two distinct areas: firstly, having a very clear idea of what is to be achieved from the meeting, and what to expect from the prospect, and secondly developing a positive mental attitude. The latter means that the salesperson should believe in the product and the firm, and more particularly in himself or herself. This leads to a more confident demeanour, which will convey a positive attitude to the prospect. A salesperson who goes into the meeting believing that a sale will result is more likely to succeed than one who goes in with seeds of self-doubt apparent.

Enthusiasm for the product and a genuine interest in the prospect's needs trigger conformity on the part of the buyer. For the same reason that it is difficult not to smile at someone who smiles at you, it is difficult not to become enthusiastic when confronted with an enthusiastic salesperson. Equally, a salesperson who appears lethargic or doubtful about the product will encourage similar doubts and indifference in the prospect.

Coping with stress is a major issue for salespeople, since the job itself involves frequent rejection by customers and also a degree of conflict between the customer's needs and the needs of the company (Sager and Wilson 1995). Research

TABLE 3.2 Coping strategies

Salesperson type	Explanation
Professional	These people use problem-focused coping strategies. These people possess high levels of drive, and are optimistic; they represented 41 per cent of the sample.
Productive worrier	10 per cent of the sample. These people also use some problem-focused strategies, but are the most likely to use emotion-focused strategies; in other words try to control their feelings and manage the stress rather than seek to remove the source of the stress. This group commonly think that they have little control over their own time.
Bystander	This group are low users of problem-focused or emotion-focused strategies, but perceive themselves as having control over their time. On the other hand, they do not use many time-management techniques. Overall, this group is laid back, confident and laissez-faire – they let the environment run the job for them. They also have the lowest achievement levels, however.
Plodders	This group use few time-management techniques, have a low propensity to use problem-focused strategies and a high propensity to use emotion-focused strategies. This group has a hopeless or apathetic attitude to the job. Optimism is low in this group.

by Nonis and Sager (2003) showed that salespeople have four basic coping strategies, as shown in Table 3.2.

The study found that 48 per cent of salespeople were either plodders or bystanders. This has implications for sales managers, since these groups are less productive and more likely to leave the job than the other two groups. This clearly has implications for selection, training and motivation.

Tools of selling

A silent seller is a file of documents used by a salesperson in the course of the presentation. It includes such items as press cuttings about the company, photographs of the product in use, testimonial letters from satisfied customers, tables of technical details, and so forth. Most salespeople add to their silent sellers themselves, collecting articles and press cuttings, but producing it is one of the functions that a good marketing department can carry out for salespeople.

The silent seller can be used in a number of ways. It can be referred to during the presentation, it can be given to the prospect to read while the salesperson calculates a quote or takes measurements, or individual items in it can be shown to the prospect. An extension of the silent seller is the use of computers by some financial-services salespeople; the computer generates tailored examples based on the client's actual circumstances. For example, a life insurance salesperson is likely to use a laptop to work out a quotation for a prospect. The computer is able to integrate the various factors involved in the calculation much quicker than the salesperson could do it by hand, and a neatly printed personalized quotation can be obtained.

Mobile telephones have become indispensable for field salespeople. They enable the salesperson to confirm appointments, check details with head office, confirm arrival times, and keep customers informed without needing to waste time looking for a public telephone. In the UK it is illegal to use a handheld cellular telephone while actually driving, but even so it is a great deal quicker to pull over for a moment to make a call than it is to look for a public telephone booth. An extension of the mobile telephone is the office in a briefcase which combines mobile telephone, computer, fax and Internet access so that salespeople can fax documents (for example contracts), send and collect e-mails, and make telephone calls from the same piece of equipment.

The salesperson's car is an essential tool of the job. The vehicle itself must reflect the status of the salesperson and the company; it should not be too expensive since customers may feel that the company's prices will be high. On the other hand, the car should not be too downmarket, as this projects an impression of poor quality which reflects on the products. Since salespeople spend a great deal of time in their cars, the car should be comfortable and with sufficient power to be easy to drive. The salesperson will certainly need enough room in the vehicle to carry samples and selling tools such as computers and demonstration equipment, and of course the car needs to be secure against break-ins to protect the valuable contents.

An issue which can easily be forgotten is the service intervals and reliability of the vehicles. The less often the vehicle needs to be off the road for routine servicing or for breakdowns, the less selling time will be lost. The cost of putting a salesperson on the road is variously estimated to be between £40 000 and £60 000 per annum; this is approximately £200 per day. Even without accounting for the lost sales engendered if a salesperson is not mobile, five days lost through breakdowns equates to £1000 in wasted expenditure. Calculated this way, the extra cost of providing a reliable vehicle pales into insignificance.

Telephone selling

Telephone selling (telesales) has been a major growth area in selling for the past 20 years or so. The reasons for the explosive growth in the use of telephones for selling are as follows:

- The increasing ownership of telephones by householders.
- The lower cost of making calls.
- The greater acceptance of telephone selling by businesses and consumers.
- The costs saved in terms of travelling time and expense.
- The much greater productivity in terms of number of calls per hour.

Teleselling can be either inbound or outbound: inbound calls originate with the customer, outbound calls with the selling organization. Inbound calls can be generated by advertising or by mailshots, or even by helplines; outbound calls rely on having good, up-to-date lists of prospects. These lists can be bought in, or can be generated from internal records, directories, exhibition-stand enquiries and so forth. Much outbound teleselling is directed at existing customers in any case.

In recent years, there has been a growing trend towards locating call centres in developing countries, for example in India. The chief advantage of this is cost; a telesales operator in the UK might be paid £7 or £8 an hour, whereas in India a telesales person might be paid £10 a week. The extra cost of keeping a satellite link open is tiny by comparison. The main drawback of this for telesales is the lack of control and lack of face-to-face contact between telesalespeople and the field sales force.

Figure 3.4 shows how teleselling fits into the overall taxonomy of selling jobs (Moncrief *et al.* 1989). Using a taxonomy developed by Moncrief (1986), teleselling's support role is outlined for each category.

In a supporting role, telesales can be used to take orders, confirm appointments, handle re-orders and variations to existing orders, and maintain contact with customers between sales visits. This supporting role creates a problem in terms of organizational design, particularly as regards setting boundaries between what is the responsibility of the field salesperson, and what is the responsibility of the telesales person (Moncrief 1989). Turf wars can easily result where field salespeople feel that the telesales people have overstepped the mark. One way of reducing this problem would be to establish a close link between the individual telesales people and specific field salespeople, with a clear understanding that the field salespeople are the ones in charge.

When teleselling is used in a primary role, it can provide extremely cost-effective servicing of accounts. Teleselling will work best as a primary method in circumstances where the selling process is routinized, cash value of orders is low, there is a widely-dispersed customer base, and the products themselves are not especially complex. If profit margins per order are small, using teleselling rather than a field sales force is indicated.

Some firms have adopted a combination role for field sales and telesales in which the telesales people have responsibility for small or remotely situated accounts, leaving the field sales force to concentrate on the larger, more accessible accounts.

Some accounts cannot be serviced by telesales. Major or key accounts, new accounts, and any accounts where the buyers would expect face-to-face service are examples of customers who would not respond well to telesales, and may even be offended. The selling process complexity, contact requirements and importance of the purchase require face-to-face contact in such circumstances.

An extension of teleselling is telemarketing, which includes customer care and marketing research as well as selling. Telemarketing has been defined as any meas-

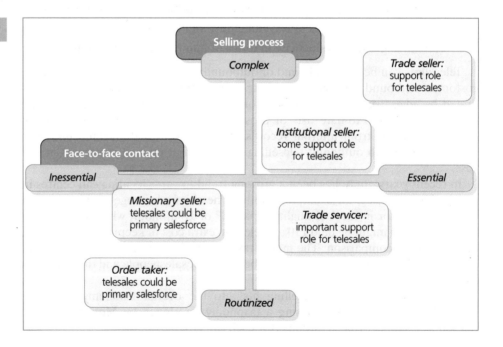

FIGURE 3.4

Telesales and selling roles

urable activity that creates and exploits a direct relationship between supplier and customer through the interactive use of the telephone (Jobber and Lancaster 1999).

Telemarketing needs to be carefully planned and controlled if it is to succeed cost effectively. The potential for causing mistrust and outright hostility is considerable if the exercise goes wrong, and skill and diplomacy may need to be brought into play to correct any mistakes. Table 3.3 offers a checklist for managing telemarketing.

Telephone selling will not replace personal calls; most customers prefer to deal face to face with salespeople rather than impersonally, over the telephone. The reason for this is that selling is a personal interaction rather than a purely economic one. People need to see each others' faces in order to read emotions and moods, and to put the meeting on a human level.

TABLE 3.3 Managing telemarketing

Activity	Management
Define objectives	Possible objectives are to generate leads, to improve aftersales service, to take orders or to qualify prospects. Objectives need to be set in order to evaluate achievements.
Planning	Ensuring that each potential customer is contacted, and that no potential customer is approached too often, requires careful planning and de-duplication of calling lists (removing duplicate names). Handing each telesales person the telephone directory and expecting them to deal with these issues themselves is wholly inadequate.
Employing appropriate contact staff	Selling by telephone demands particular skills, notably patience and resilience. Good communication skills and a clear voice are essential; often, women seem less threatening over the telephone, so the profession is female dominated.
Establish good relations with other staff	Field sales staff in particular need to be involved at an early stage, in order to avoid duplication of effort. Staff in other departments should also be made aware of what the telemarketing department is doing. This will minimize friction and encourage a supportive and co-operative atmosphere.
Ensure that the customers understand the nature of the telemarketing effort	Customers need to appreciate the benefits of the system; the system should, of course, be designed with the intention of benefiting the customer as well as the firm.
Measurement, feedback and control	Measurement of response rates, speed of dealing with customer complaints or orders, sales or appointments made, and measures of customer satisfaction with the service are all areas that can be measured. Information gathered should be fed back to the staff involved so that they are able to correct and improve their own performance against the measures set.
Managing the lists	Ensuring that defunct businesses or deceased customers are removed, that customers do not appear more than once (perhaps under a slightly different name – this is the bugbear of list management) and ensuring that other details are correct and up to date.

▮ Journey planning

In most cases, salespeople will spend more time travelling than they do selling. There is clearly scope for improving productivity by planning the journeys in the most efficient way possible; this is not always as straightforward as it might appear. The issues are as follows:

- Overall journey time should be minimized.
- Travel time during the best selling period of the day should be minimized.
- Relative importance of different customers should be recognized.
- Possible traffic problems need to be anticipated, for example rush hour through a major town, bottlenecks near airports, etc.
- Availability of motorways or trunk roads within the territory.
- To some extent, fuel efficiency and mileage efficiency should be considered, but not where these conflict with saving sales-force time.

Table 3.4 shows some of the methods used for route planning. In all three methods, the road system will dictate the route planning to some extent. For example,

TABLE 3.4 Route planning methods

Method and description	Advantages	Disadvantages
Circle system: The salesperson divides the territory into a rough circle centred on his or her base. Each segment of the circle is covered on a separate day of the week (or of the month) so that, over the period, every segment is covered.	The salesperson ensures that each customer is visited on a regular basis, and that the journeys are kept short.	This method relies on having a fairly evenly distributed group of customers, all of similar value. It also assumes that a regular weekly or monthly call will be appropriate for those customers.
Hopscotch system: The salesperson travels out to the furthest point of the territory and works back, travelling either side of the journey line as appropriate.	This method means that the salesperson can complete the longest part of the journey before the start of the business day, returning to base at a reasonably early hour in the evening.	The method relies on the salesperson being able to control the appointment times. If a customer wants a visit before noon, or has some other specific requirement, the hopscotch method will not accommodate this as well as the circle system would.
Petal system: Similar to the hopscotch system, except that this time the route is a circle rather than a straight line. The salesperson travels out to the territory before the start of the business day, and returns after the close of the business day.	This method works best where the territory is a large one. The salesperson can be based at an hotel in the area and cover the territory within a fixed time period.	Again, this relies to an extent on being able to control the appointments. Also, the road network does not necessarily lend itself to a circular route.

in the UK the M4 corridor (the area either side of the M4 motorway) contains a large number of high-tech industries. Along this hundred-mile stretch of road, the obvious routing approach to use is the hopscotch method. Conversely, in the Highlands of Scotland a petal route might be more appropriate. Inevitably, callbacks and appointing problems will mean that the most efficient route is unlikely to be achieved in any case.

Computer-based models are available for determining territory size (see Chapter 9) and these can also be used for route planning. Salespeople who have been provided with laptop computers are able to use these for the purpose, and, to some extent, can amend the route according to changing circumstances.

The problem with territory design and journey planning is that the sales process is not routinized in most cases. Attempts to develop models to manage the process have not been universally successful, because the decision rules necessary to the process cannot be operationalized or standardized effectively. For example, an early attempt by Thompson and McNeal (1967) tried to integrate such factors as the probability of achieving success on each visit, ranking each customer according to their net expected value, and availability of selling time.

Unfortunately the model relied on several assumptions:

1 Salespeople will sell only one product and price is constant for all customers.
2 Sales are made on an ad hoc basis, i.e. there is no continuing customer–salesperson relationship.
3 The expected cost of the call is the same for all customers.
4 The expected time spent in a call is the same for all customers.
5 Customers may be classified on the basis of their relative propensity to buy as exhibited during the most recent sales call.

In fact, all these assumptions are unrealistic. Few salespeople have only one product to sell, and almost all are able to negotiate prices. Secondly, the majority of salespeople establish some kind of ongoing relationship with their customers, even if it is only that the calls are regular and they become friendly with the buyer. Thirdly, the cost of the call will depend on location of the customer and the time spent in the call, each of which is likely to be variable. Fourthly, time spent in a call will depend on what is to be discussed, and is not entirely under the control of the salesperson.

Finally, it is extremely difficult to judge in advance what the customer's propensity to buy will be. A customer may appear reluctant to buy, simply as a negotiating ploy to extract more favourable terms from the salesperson; equally, an apparently eager customer might well have found another supplier between calls. In short, journey planning is not simple, and is unlikely to be susceptible to mechanistic planning processes.

■ Setting targets and activity management

Although targets are usually set by sales managers, or agreed between the salesperson and the manager, many salespeople fine tune the targets in order to ensure the correct activity level. To do this effectively, the salesperson will need to know how many calls it takes to make a sale, what the average order value is, and how many cold calls it takes to make an appointment. In some industries the ratios may be based on different factors; a soft-drinks salesperson is likely to make a sale of some kind on every call, but may be able to affect overall sales by using specific merchandising techniques.

For example, a salesperson may be given a target which is expressed in monetary terms, either in terms of gross sales (turnover) or in terms of profit. This can be broken down in terms of daily activities provided the salesperson knows his or her ratios. Figure 3.5 shows how this works for a home-improvement salesperson.

For this salesperson, the average appointing rate is 6.7 cold calls for each appointment made. This means that the salesperson will have to contact, on average, 6.7 people to get one appointment. The closing rate on the appointments is one in every three, so two out of three sales calls will not result in a sale. Again, this is an average – the four appointments made on Wednesday resulted in two sales, whereas the two appointments from Thursday resulted in no sales. Finally, the average order value is £6418.

If this salesperson were to be targeted to sell £100 000 worth of business per month, the activity level needed to achieve this could be calculated by working backwards using the known average ratios. £100 000 would be equivalent to approximately 16 average orders. To sell 16 average orders, the salesperson will need to make 48 appointments, which will mean making 321 cold calls.

This approach to planning was advocated by Frank Bettger (1949) as a means of self-motivation. It enables the salesperson to maintain activity levels even when sales are not forthcoming, and it also helps to ensure a planned and self-disciplined approach towards hitting a target which may seem too large to be attainable. It is generally accepted that steady, carefully-paced activity is better, in the long run, than short bursts of intense, high-energy selling.

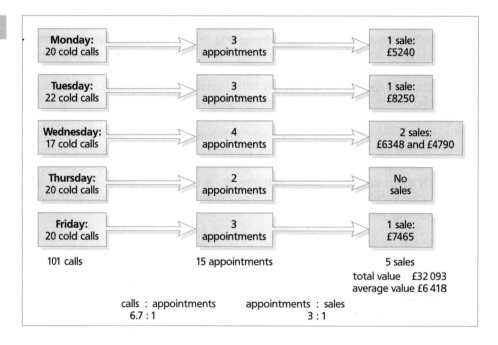

FIGURE 3.5

Sales planning for a home-improvement salesperson

The approach is possible in most industries, although it does not work in key-account management (see Chapter 5). For most salespeople it provides a framework within which to plan the daily or weekly activity. Some take it further, and break down the commission payments earned on each sale in terms of number of appointments made or number of cold calls; this can be a useful self-motivator, since it allows the salesperson to value cold calls, even on the basis of the unsuccessful ones. In the case above, assuming a 5 per cent commission rate on sales, the salesperson is earning an average £3.17 for each cold call, whether it is successful or not. This can be a comforting thought when the morning's calling has been less than successful.

SUMMARY

As in any field of activity, thorough preparation will improve success rates. For salespeople this is even more true than it is for other professions; salespeople rely heavily on appearing relaxed and confident, and good preparation helps to ensure that this is the case.

Key points from this chapter are as follows:

- Sales cycles run concurrently; most salespeople will be dealing with all the stages at once, but with different customers.

- Qualified prospects have a need, have the authority to buy, a willingness to hear a presentation, and the means to pay for the products.

- Cold calling is still effective, but is being replaced by other warm-calling techniques.

- Clear objectives should be established for any sales meeting.

- Physical preparation is important; looking the part means being halfway to acting the part.

- Journey planning, sometimes called routing, is about ensuring efficient use of a salesperson's time.

- Individual targeting helps with self-motivation.

REVIEW QUESTIONS

1 If sales can be easily made by telephone at a tenth of the cost of personal calls, why not do away with the field sales force altogether?

2 How might you motivate a salesperson who had made, say, 25 sales presentations without making a sale?

3 What objectives might you establish for the first meeting with a firm which is planning to buy a complete new computer system?

4 How would you decide which journey-planning system would be the most effective for a heavily industrialized area such as the English Midlands region or the Ruhr Valley?

5 Why should the designer of a telemarketing system ensure that the benefits to the customer are made known?

REFERENCES

Bettger, F. (1949) *How I Raised Myself from Failure to Success in Selling*, Englewood Cliffs, NJ: Prentice-Hall.

Falvey, J. (1989) 'Without a goal for every call, a salesperson is just a well-paid tourist', *Sales and Marketing Management* 141 (June): 92.

Jobber, D. and Lancaster, G. (1999) *Selling and Sales Management,* London: Pitman.

Michaelson, G. (1988) 'It's a small world if you've got a big network', *Sales and Marketing Management* 140 (Aug.): 74.

Moncrief, W.C. (1986) 'Selling activity and sales position taxonomies for industrial sales forces', *Journal of Marketing Research* 23(2): 261–70.

—— Shipp, S. H., Lamb, C. W. and Cravens, D. W. (1989) 'Examining the roles of telemarketing in selling strategy', *Journal of Personal Selling and Sales Management* 9(3): 1–20.

Nonis, S. A. and Sager, J. K. (2003) 'Coping strategy profiles used by salespeople: Their relationship with personal characteristics and work outcomes', *Journal of Personal Selling and Sales Management* 23 (2/Spring): 139–50.

Sager, J. K. and Wilson, P. H. (1995) 'Clarification of the meaning of job stress in the context of sales force research', *Journal of Personal Selling and Sales Management* 15 (3/Summer): 51–64.

Szymanski, D. M. and Churchill, G. A. Jr. (1990) 'Client evaluation cues: A comparison of successful and unsuccessful salespeople', *Journal of Marketing Research*, 27 (May): 163–74.

Thompson, W. W. and McNeal, J. U. (1967) 'Sales planning and control issues absorbing Markov chains', *Journal of Marketing Research*, IV (Feb.): 62–6.

INDIA CALL CENTRE

India Call Centre is a joint venture between VCare Technologies Ltd and Shyam Garments Ltd. It is the vision of Vishal Gupta, Raj Kumar Gupta and Ronald D. Bell; the company provides every possible variety of telesales and telemarketing, all from a base in New Delhi.

Raj Kumar Gupta is the CEO of Shyam Garments, one of India's largest clothing manufacturers. His experience in operations management, coupled with Bell's knowledge of the telecommunications industry, enabled the three men to set up India Call Centre under the control of Vishal Gupta. The company seeks to exploit the low-wage environment of India, coupled with the increased availability of cheap international telecommunications, to provide a low-cost call centre which serves the English-speaking world.

Because of the time differences between India and the rest of the English-speaking world (North America, the UK, Australia, New Zealand and Ireland) the call centre has to operate 24 hours a day. Employees are meticulously trained – they have speech training so that they speak with the accents of the countries they are contacting, they have cultural awareness training so that they understand the customs, traditions and even the sense of humour of the countries they are dealing with, and they have rigorous training in the legal limitations on telesales in each of the target countries. This means, in total, that a buyer in, say, Wisconsin will not be aware that they are not speaking to a fellow-American. A customer in Cork might imagine that the telesales operator is a Dubliner rather than a Delhi-ite, and Britishers will hear a UK regional accent rather than a Northern Indian one. Staff assume Western names so as to maintain the illusion.

For clients of the call centre, this adds up to an impeccable service. The staff are, to all intents and purposes, nationals of the countries they are calling, but of course they earn around one-twentieth of the salaries, which means a substantial saving on the overall cost even when the cost of maintaining a permanent satellite link is discounted. This is not without its costs to the staff, of course. Call centre work is demanding at the best of times – irate customers, negative responses, the knowledge that one's supervisors might be listening secretly in order to monitor the calls, and so forth are common to all call centres. But for the Indian call centre staff, there is the added knowledge that they must maintain a masquerade, even denying their own nationality.

On top of this, the staff are given a rigorous sales training which includes up-selling (moving customers to a more expensive product) and cross-selling (moving them to another product or an additional product in the range). Needless to say, the telesales operators are already educated to a high standard – all are college graduates, with a high standard of written and spoken English, and often with business qualifications as well. By Indian standards the jobs are well paid and conditions are good, but this does not prevent some staff from feeling over-pressured. Some staff burn out early and leave, but others stay on because of the prospects for advancement – the bottom line is that US call centres experience an 80 per cent per annum staff turnover, whereas Indian call centres experience less than 15 per cent staff turnover.

Other problems are apparent in shifting operations to India. The infrastructure is somewhat shaky, so that companies need to ensure emergency back-up electricity supplies, and in some cases need to transport employees to and from work. In some parts of India the political situation is unstable, and of course employees in Western countries fear for their jobs, unable to compete with low-wage economies like India.

However, in the relatively prosperous city of New Delhi, India Call is able to thrive. Growth for call centres is running at 70 per cent per annum, with no sign of slowing down, and the Guptas intend to make every effort to grab their share. Offering a slick, efficient and well-managed service to their Western clients is the first rule of this game. Pramod Bhasin, chief executive of GE International Services, said recently, 'Corporations come to India for the cost savings, but stay for the quality.'

Case-study questions

1 What other drawbacks might manifest themselves for a company using an Indian call centre?

2 Why might staff turnover at Indian call centres be less than that at US ones?

3 Why would a firm choose to locate its call centre in India rather than in its own country, apart from the cost savings?

4 What might be the key competences that India Call Centre Ltd needs to have in order to sell its services to the West?

5 Pramod Bhasin refers to quality of service. What factors might have contributed to this quality?

4

THE SALES PRESENTATION

Learning objectives

After reading this chapter, you should be able to:

- Explain how to open a sales presentation.
- Describe ways of keeping control of the presentation.
- Explain how decisions are arrived at.
- Explain how different closing techniques help the interview to reach a conclusion.
- Describe some basic ways of structuring the sales presentation.
- Describe the basics of negotiation.
- Explain how negotiation tactics work.

■ Introduction

Salespeople are often portrayed as slick communicators, using a set of standard techniques to persuade prospects to buy. In fact, there is a great deal of variation between presentations; it is impossible to use a standard, formulaic approach because each customer is different, and has a different set of problems to address. Equally, each salesperson is different, and will play to a different set of personal strengths and weaknesses.

A sales presentation is, at its most basic, a conversation between individuals. Companies do not buy goods from other companies; people buy goods from other people, sometimes on behalf of the organization. All selling is therefore an interaction between human beings.

This chapter examines the sales presentation as it applies in small-account selling. The approaches described apply only to situations where there is a one-off sale such as a photocopier or a home improvement, and when the individual sale is not a crucial one for the company. In situations where the sale is of major significance, or when the customer represents a substantial part of the firm's turnover, the approach taken is totally different. Major-account selling is covered in Chapter 5.

SUCCESS STORY – PATRICIA GARDNER

Patricia Gardner is a native of New York, and a graduate in sociology from Alfred University. She began her sales career at Xerox Corporation, and was a sales manager within six years. She became expert in closing sales with major multinationals such as TransAmerica and Honeywell, and acquired a reputation for cultural sensitivity and the ability to cross borders with little difficulty. She has lived in such disparate places as Uganda, Mexico, Karachi and Toronto.

This stood her in good stead when London-based company Smartlogik wanted to penetrate the North American market in 2000. Pat built the US sales team from the ground up, running a 15-member international team; during this period she herself closed a multi-million-pound deal with the Thomson Corporation.

Success has brought financial rewards. Patricia's hobby is flying light aircraft, and she enjoys a lot of travel – when she has the time. A millionaire several times over, she sees herself as an innovative leader who sets direction, provides clarity, and transforms strategy into results in a challenging environment. In a Wharton Seminar presentation in 2003 she told the audience, 'My customers taught me everything I ever needed to know. To sell to them, what new products to offer them, and they gave me the exact words to say to get new clients. They taught me that there are thousands of clients out there in the middle tier, and not to be discouraged if Fortune 100 clients wouldn't see me. They taught me to stick to the vertical market that works for me and not to try to be all things to all people. And they taught me that your number one strategy for success is to design a company, and your products, with the customer in mind.'

■ The sales visit

Figure 4.1 shows the sequence of events which leads to an eventual sale.

Opening the sale

Particularly when first meeting a new customer, the salesperson needs to establish a personal rapport. This is established by a showing a genuine interest in the customer and his or her problems; the traditional view of the salesperson as being a backslapping individual with a fund of good jokes is a long way from the truth.

Typically salespeople begin with an ice breaker. This is an opening remark or series of comments which tend to put the relationship on a human level; they are the common politenesses which anybody might use when meeting someone new. Comments about the weather or the state of the traffic help to put both parties at ease before getting down to business, but it is usual to proceed fairly quickly to the business at hand. Often the aim of the exercise is to create a perceived similarity between the salesperson and the prospect; if the prospect feels that they have something in common, this will increase the level of trust in what the salesperson has to say (Dion *et al.* 1995). Salespeople seek to establish relationships with their prospects, because this is a more certain way of making sales (McKenna 1991). It is also a way of making the working day more pleasant.

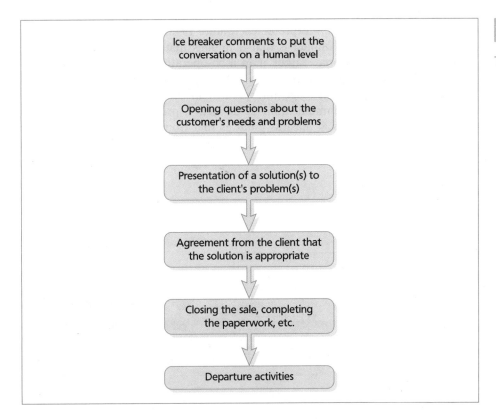

FIGURE 4.1

The sales visit

Sometimes the response to ice breaking comments provide the salesperson with useful information about the company or its problems, even though this is not the primary reason for ice breakers. For example, a comment about the difficulty of parking locally might enable a computer salesperson to extol the merits of working from home.

Non-verbal cues are important in this context. Buyers pick up on expressions, mannerisms, body language and so forth and are influenced by these. Eye gaze, posture, speech hesitation, gestures and clothing were all found to have significant effects on buyers' perceptions of the salesperson and the product (Leigh and Summers 2002).

■ The presentation

The presentation itself is not, in fact, a presentation at all. The word 'presentation' implies a one-way flow of information, a talk or a lecture in which the customer is passive. In fact, communication is not that simple.

Communications theory has been dominated by the Schramm model of communications (see Figure 4.2), a model which is familiar to most students of communication.

In this model, the sender of a message first needs to code the message in order to send it. The code will need to be something the receiver can understand, for example it must be in a language the receiver knows. There must be a medium for the message to travel through (for example television or radio), and the recipient must be able to decode the message. Interference and noise will affect the way the message is transmitted and interpreted (Schramm 1948, 1971).

The problem with this model is that it implies that communication is something that is done to people, rather than a co-operative process. A more modern view of communication is that it is a co-construction of meaning in which the person receiving the message interprets it in the light of previous experience. In this model, communication is an active process on both sides: the input from the receiver is at least as great as that from the transmitter, and the message is likely to be interpreted in many different ways by each different receiver.

FIGURE 4.2

Conduit model of communications

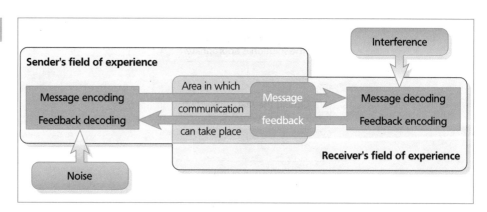

The model implies that communication creates a pool of meaning between the parties. Each person puts something into the pool, each person takes something out, and the pool changes slightly each time (see Figure 4.3)

To stretch the analogy further, when either party puts something into the pool the new input mixes with everything that is already in the pool. What the other party draws from the pool therefore includes some of what already existed. Provided the new material is not wildly at odds with what is already in the pool, the shared meaning will remain close; if the new material is very different from that which already exists between the parties, the person who put the material in may have to add a lot more before the meaning becomes clear.

This model of communications is particularly relevant to personal selling. The personal selling function is, by its nature, a dialogue in which the seller may control the process, but the bulk of the communication comes from the buyer. Salespeople who lose sight of this end up doing most of the talking and lose the sale.

The model also explains another phenomenon in communication, which is that some communications are actively sought out by customers, whereas others are not (Blythe 2003). Unsought communications are those which the seller sends out in the optimistic hope that a buyer will respond: display advertising, TV advertising, billboards and so forth. This includes initial canvassing for appointments by salespeople. Sought communications are those which a buyer specifically looks for: classified advertising, exhibitions, brochures and sales presentations. It is important to distinguish between the two, since the approach needs to be very different; an unsought communication needs to be persuasive and attention grabbing, whereas a sought communication should be informative and factual, because the buyer is already persuaded to a large extent.

Considered in terms of the decision-making process (see Chapter 2), buyers who are at the need-identification stage may be approached using unsought communication. A display advertisement, suitably placed, may make companies realize that they have a problem which had not previously been identified.

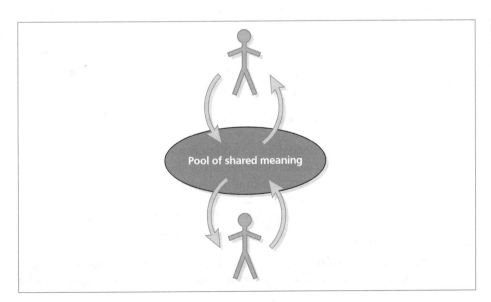

FIGURE 4.3

Pool of meaning

In the wake of the 11th September attacks on New York, British Airways ran a highly successful campaign on UK television aimed at encouraging business travellers back onto BA North Atlantic services. The advertisements contrasted one company pitching for business by sending a beautifully produced glossy brochure to its New York customer, with another company whose sales executive arrives in person. The executive making the personal visit is quickly on first-name terms with the customer, and is greeted as a friend; the brochure is left on the table. The executives who sent the brochure, meanwhile, are congratulating themselves because, in the course of a telephone call, the New York customer said that he liked the spreadsheets.

This advertisement was unusual in several respects. Firstly, it appeared on television, which is rare for B2B advertising. Secondly, it was aimed at a general problem for any business, which is the failure to attach enough importance to personal contacts. Thirdly, the product itself is generic – aeroplane rides across the Atlantic are provided by a very large number of airlines, any of whom might benefit from BA's advertising, since all it did was flag up the problem. Later BA advertising became much more brand-specific, delineating the advantages of using BA rather than its rivals.

Buyers who are at the information search stage may use display advertising because they will be sensitized to look out for it, but will rapidly move towards seeking out communications such as sales presentations in order to obtain hard facts on which to base decisions. At this point an emotive sales pitch is likely to be of a lot less interest than a factual presentation.

In the first instance, salespeople should be prepared to listen to what their customers have to say; selling is not about talking well, it is about listening to people's problems and finding solutions.

Secondly, salespeople need to be ultra-polite, and very aware of the customer's sensibilities. The overall impression should be that the salesperson is a friend in the business – and in fact most salespeople will agree that it is easier to find another company to work for than it is to find new customers. Good salespeople look after their customers, and the best way to encourage people to buy a product is to ensure that it meets their needs as fully as possible, as in any other area of marketing.

Finally, telling lies to customers is counterproductive, since the lie will inevitably come to light once the customer takes delivery of the product. This leads to cancellation of contracts, return of the goods, and even lawsuits – which the customer will almost certainly win. Unfortunately, the same is not true when the situation is reversed; it is a paradox of selling practice that the customer is free to tell any number of lies but the salesperson must tell the truth, despite a popular belief to the contrary.

Although some customers regard salespeople with suspicion, the evidence is that salespeople actually seek to develop and maintain good relationships with their customers even when this conflicts with instructions from their marketing departments (Anderson and Robertson 1995).

For the customer, the salesperson is a source of information, a source of help in problem solving, and is an advocate back to the supplying company. Good salespeople are also adept at helping their customers through the decision-making process; often this is the hardest part of making a sale.

Canned presentations

In the past, companies have tried to standardize the sales presentation, and in some cases this has advantages. Salespeople were sent out with a carefully worded script to work from, and a set of ready-made answers for the most common objections and problems raised by customers. The advantages of this approach are:

1 The salesperson can be trained fairly quickly.
2 The company can be reasonably confident that the sales force is giving all its customers the same basic message.
3 The sales presentation can be written so that it closely mirrors the company's other marketing communications.

Such an approach often comes across as a hard sell, since the customer is not being treated as an individual, but rather as a unit in a mass market. Although a hard-sell approach might work for some products and some companies (Chu *et al.* 1995), this generally only applies to low-risk, low-cost products. In most other cases (which means most cases in which a salesperson is involved) the sale will only be successful if the customer's needs are being met, and, more importantly, the customer perceives that these needs are being met. By using the salesperson as a mere mouthpiece for the marketing department, the company is losing the main strength of personal selling, which is the ability to help customers to solve problems (see Chapter 1).

For these reasons salespeople find it is easier and more beneficial to begin by finding out the customer's needs, and then apply a solution to those needs based on the firm's product range. Although marketers commonly speak of 'the product', it is very rarely the case that a salesperson will only have one product to offer; in many cases, salespeople even have the capacity to vary products or tailor them to fit the customer's needs. For example, a machine-tool salesperson would have considerable latitude in redesigning the products to fit a particular task. In the consumer selling situation, a kitchen salesperson would usually design the kitchen for the customer, working together with the customer to find an optimum solution.

Asking questions

The obvious way to find out the customer's needs is by asking questions. The traditional approach, which was developed by E. K. Strong in the 1920s, is to divide questions into two types; open questions and closed questions. An open question has a number of different possible answers, whereas a closed question can only be answered 'yes' or 'no' (Strong 1925). Here are some examples of open questions:

'How do you calculate the maintenance costs on your equipment?'

'What difficulties have you encountered in doing your own maintenance?'

'How do you prefer to receive shipments?'

And some examples of closed questions:

'Would you like me to show you how you can save on maintenance?'

'Shall I put you down for the 24-hour call-out service?'

'Should we deliver to the main warehouse?'

Open questions are actually opening questions; they are the main tool the salesperson has for finding out about the customer's needs. Closed questions tend to be closing questions, used towards the end of the sales presentation to bring the customer to the decision point. Questions have a further important function in that they enable the salesperson to keep control of the direction in which the presentation is going. Questions are powerful in directing people's thoughts; anybody with small children knows that the constant stream of questions is both distracting and wearing because the child keeps triggering the adult's mind to think of a response. Questions demand attention in a way that statements do not. For example, here is a dialogue between a salesperson and a prospect:

SALESPERSON: The equipment needs a concrete base to attach to so that it doesn't move around when it's operating.

PROSPECT: I don't like the sound of that. We have wooden floors in the factory.

SALESPERSON: Would you like me to show you a model that vibrates less?

PROSPECT: I think that would be a good idea.

SALESPERSON: Of course, being a smaller machine, it would have a smaller output. Would that be acceptable?

PROSPECT: Possibly, yes. Look, is this going to take long? I have another appointment.

SALESPERSON: We can be finished in about 15 minutes, but would you prefer it if I came back another day?

PROSPECT: No, 15 minutes is fine.

In the first instance, the prospect has raised an objection about the machine; the salesperson uses two questions to bring the presentation back on track. In the second case the prospect tries to cut the presentation short, but the salesperson asks an appropriate question which prevents the presentation ending. Of course, the prospect might ask the salesperson to come back another time, but that doesn't mean that the presentation has ended, merely that it has been postponed. It is generally preferable not to do this, though; apart from the extra work involved, the prospect may not be available, or a competitor might have got in first and closed the sale. Controlling the presentation by asking questions also tends to avoid confrontation.

The presentation itself is, in part, the transfer of knowledge from the salesperson to the prospect. Salespeople will, of course, have considerable knowledge about the products in the range, and probably of the industry in general.

One method of structuring the presentation to the customer's needs is to adopt the NASA structure, shown in Table 4.1.

If at any stage the salesperson is unable to get an acceptance, he or she should go back to needs and review what the prospect's problem is. The NASA system places the emphasis on finding solutions to the prospect's need problem; researchers have demonstrated that this is the most effective way to achieve success in selling (Lund 1979).

During the solution part of the presentation, the salesperson is explaining about the particular product which seems to fit the prospect's needs. Because the presentation revolves around the specific customer, it is essential to refer back to those needs at each stage. People do not buy physical products, they buy what the product will do for them. The classic example is the hot water bottle; people do not buy a rubber bag with a stopper in it, they buy a warm bed.

This means that a simple description of the product's features is entirely inadequate; the features must be converted to benefits if a sale is to result. Features are about what the product is; benefits are about what it will do for the customer.

Handling objections

Objections are queries or negative statements raised by the prospect in the course of the presentation. The prospect may, for example, say that a particular feature of the product is not wanted, or is an expensive frill. In most industries the same objections tend to crop up over and over again; common ones are, 'We can't afford it,' and 'I need to consult someone else about this'.

Although objections are often seen as being barriers to making the sale, good salespeople recognize them as requests for further information. Provided the

TABLE 4.1 The NASA model	
N	*Needs*: The salesperson asks the prospect about his or her needs; what problems does the prospect have?
A	*Acceptance*: Having ascertained the needs, the salesperson confirms with the prospect that these are in fact the needs, and obtain the prospect's acceptance of the problem.
S	*Solution*: The salesperson shows the prospect how the solution will meet his or her problem.
A	*Acceptance again*: This time the salesperson seeks the prospect's acceptance of the proposed solution.

objection is successfully answered, the negotiation can continue until a mutually acceptable solution is reached. Objections can be handled in the following way:

1 Repeat the objection back to the prospect, to confirm that both the salesperson and the prospect understand each other, and the nature of the problem.

2 Isolate the objection; in other words, confirm that it is the only problem with the product.

3 Apologize for not having explained properly. This avoids making the prospect lose face, or feel silly.

4 If the objection is false (i.e. has no basis in fact) explain how the product actually meets the problem; alternatively, if the objection is real, show how the benefits of the product outweigh the disadvantages.

5 Confirm with the prospect that the objection has been overcome.

Objections should be distinguished from conditions; a condition prevents the sale going ahead. The commonest ones are as shown in Table 4.2.

Often, what appears to be a condition is actually a hidden objection. The prospect may have made a statement with the intention of putting the salesperson off, in order to cover up another objection which the prospect would prefer not to raise. Hidden objections need to be brought out into the open if the salesperson is to be able to answer them; this can sometimes be a difficult process, and relies heavily on the trust of the prospect. Salespeople can sometimes use the direct approach of simply saying, 'I get the feeling there's something else troubling you about the product – what's the problem?' Commonly the objection will be expressed as a desire to 'think about it'. In this case, the salesperson can say, 'Yes, I understand that. But just to clarify things for me, what is it you particularly want to think about?' Often this will lead to a statement of the real objection.

Objections can also be classified as real and false. A real objection is a genuine problem with the product; a false objection arises from a misunderstanding, or refers to something that has not yet been covered in the presentation.

TABLE 4.2 Common conditions

Condition	What the salesperson should do
The prospect has no authority to make the decision	Find out who does have the authority, and ask the prospect to make an appointment to see that person.
The firm has no money	If this is true, the sale cannot go ahead. In most cases it is not true; buyers will often say that the budget has run out as a way of getting rid of the salesperson. Astute salespeople will find out who has the authority to increase the budget, or will arrange for payment to be deferred into the next financial year.
There is no need for the product	Unless there is a need, no purchase will take place. This is a problem which the salesperson has caused by not properly identifying the needs in the first place.

Objections can sometimes be used for a trial close; the salesperson says, 'If we can overcome that problem for you, are we in business?' This can sometimes mean closing the sale early, but at the very least it brings out any other objections. As a general rule, it is advisable to deal with objections as they arise; leaving them all to the end of the presentation means that the prospect is sitting with negative feelings about the product for a long time. Objections must always be taken seriously; even if the salesperson feels that the problem is a small one, and the prospect is getting too concerned over a triviality, it may not seem that way to the prospect.

Closing the sale

Once all the objections have been answered, the sale can be closed. Closing techniques are ways of helping the prospect over the decision-making hurdle. Perhaps surprisingly, most people are reluctant to make decisions, even more so if they are professional buyers. This is perhaps because of the risks attached to making a mistake, but whatever the reason buyers often need some help in agreeing to the order. Salespeople use a number of closing techniques to achieve this; Table 4.3 has some examples.

TABLE 4.3 Examples of closing techniques

Technique	Explanation	Example
Alternative close	The prospect is offered two alternatives, each of which leads to the order.	'Would you like them in red or in green?'
Order-book close	The salesperson writes down each feature in the order book as it is agreed during the presentation.	'OK, you want the green ones, you want four gross, and your best delivery day is Thursdays. If you'll just autograph this for me, we'll get it moving for you.'
Immediate-gain close	The prospect is shown that the sooner he or she agrees to the deal, the sooner he or she will get the benefits of the product.	'Fine. So the sooner we get this paperwork sorted, the sooner you'll start making those savings, right?'
Puppy-dog close	The prospect is allowed to borrow the product for a while. In the same way as someone becomes attached to a puppy left in their care, the prospect finds out about the advantages of the product for him or herself.	Volkswagen used this close very effectively by allowing people to borrow Golf cars for 24 hours, rather than relying on the customary short test-drive.
Sales manager close	The salesperson says that he or she is unable to give any further discounts, but agrees to call the sales manager and ask for a further discount, provided the buyer agrees to go ahead immediately with the purchase if the discount is forthcoming.	This is useful when dealing with buyers who want to drive a hard bargain. The buyer believes that the salesperson has given away every possible discount. In fact, an astute salesperson will keep back a small extra discount in order to be confident of giving this to the buyer when the sales manager 'agrees'.

There are, of course, many other closing techniques. Salespeople will typically use whichever one seems most appropriate to the situation, although most salespeople have favourite closes that work for them.

Incidentally, salespeople usually avoid asking prospects to 'sign' the order. This has negative connotations because it implies a final commitment – people talk of 'signing your life away' or 'signing your death warrant'. It is better to ask people to 'OK that for me' or 'autograph this for me'.

The astute reader will have recognized that the above sequence of events ties in closely with the NASA model described earlier. During the face-to-face part of the salesperson's job the prospect's needs always come first, followed by an acceptance of the needs, followed by the presentation of the solution to the need problem. Acceptance of the solution, or rejection of it, determines whether the sale goes ahead or not.

Post-presentation activities

It would clearly be rude simply to pack up the order forms and leave immediately after making the sale, so it is good practice to stay for a few moments and discuss other matters, or at the very least to recap on the sale and make sure the customer is happy with everything. In most cases the customer has, so far, only bought a promise to deliver, so it is also a good idea to leave behind some information about the product, a set of contact telephone numbers, and copies of the documentation. This serves two purposes: firstly, it ensures that problems can be nipped in the bud because the customer can contact the firm at any time. Secondly, it gives the customer a sense of security and tends to reduce the incidence of cancellations. Buyer's remorse is the term for post-purchase regrets; some of these second thoughts come about because the buyer acquires new information or remembers something important which was not covered in the presentation, and some of them come from a feeling of mistrust which arises because the customer has nothing tangible to show for the commitment made at the close.

Sometimes salespeople are afraid that, by leaving information and contact telephone numbers, the customer will be encouraged to cancel. The reverse is the case. Customers who are able to telephone are:

- more confident that they don't need to
- able to do so if there is a problem, which means that the problem can be solved before the goods are delivered.

This is a continuation of the salesperson's role, which is to solve problems for people. This is shown diagrammatically in Figure 4.4.

As Figure 4.4 shows, the initial problem-identifying sequence at the opening of the sale leads to the presentation, which in itself produces more problems – the buyer is able to identify new problems, either those which are inherent in the organization's situation or those which are perceived as problems with the proposed solution being offered by the salesperson. These new problems are classified as objections, but in fact they are simply requests for further information, and further solutions. Closing the sale leads to the problem of buyer reluctance, which can be overcome by using techniques as outlined above. Immediately following the pres-

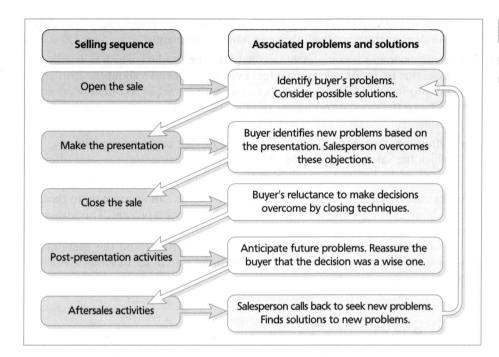

FIGURE 4.4

Problem-solving
matrix

entation, the salesperson or the buyer might anticipate future problems, but the salesperson should, in a subtle way, reassure the buyer that the decision was a wise one.

Finally, the salesperson should carry out aftersales activities such as calling back to the customer after delivery, in order to identify further problems which may need to be solved. In some cases the problems will have been caused by the new product or its delivery, but in other cases the buyer might have discovered new problems which the salesperson's company might be able to solve. This, in effect, brings the salesperson back to the opening of the sale.

◼ Aftersales service

Because the salesperson's main activity is solving problems, it would be reasonable for a salesperson to be proactive in seeking out problems to solve. Sometimes salespeople are nervous about going back to customers they have sold to, for fear of cancellations or for fear of having to deal with complaints. The reason for this is that salespeople need to maintain a positive outlook about the company, the products and themselves, and dealing with customer complaints may mean that the salesperson becomes infected with negativity.

In fact it is always worthwhile revisiting customers once the delivery of the product has been made. The reasons for this are as follows:

- If there is a problem, the visit offers the opportunity to rectify matters. Research shows that customers whose complaints are dealt with to their complete satisfaction become more loyal than those who didn't have a complaint in the first place (Coca Cola Company 1981). Perhaps salespeople should actually encourage customers to complain, so that they can demonstrate how well they can handle complaints!

● If the customer is completely satisfied with the product, which is usually the case, this helps the salesperson feel even more positive about the firm and the products. Satisfied customers can sometimes act as recommenders or will give the salesperson names of other people who might have similar problems.

● Often the customer will have identified a further problem or problems which the salesperson may be able to assist in solving. Repeat sales often result, and a longer-term relationship can develop.

In the case of sales to householders, the salesperson can drop round to the customer's home, perhaps with a bottle of wine as a thank-you present. This invariably starts the call off on the right basis. In the case of an industrial customer, the salesperson could make an appointment to see both the buyer and the users of the product to check that everybody is happy with the purchase. In either case, only good outcomes are possible.

▌ Negotiation

'You don't get what you deserve in this life; you get what you negotiate.' Negotiation is about coming to a mutual agreement under which each party is prepared to give up something in order to obtain concessions from the other party. The emphasis on negotiation that is so apparent at present has come about largely because of the emphasis on establishing long-term relationships between customers and suppliers, and is particularly important in major-account selling.

There are six characteristics common to all situations in which negotiation plays a part (Lewicki 1992). These are as follows:

1 There are two or more parties. Although people can negotiate with themselves, for example by saying, 'If I get this report finished by 12, I can justify having a relaxing afternoon', for purposes of selling, more than one party (individuals or organizations) are necessary.

2 There is a conflict of interest between some or all of the parties. What one party wants conflicts in some way with what one or more of the other parties want, so a solution needs to be negotiated in order to resolve the conflict.

3 The parties believe that they can get a better deal through negotiation than they would by simply accepting what the other party is offering. For example, if a salesperson believes that the buyer's offer really is final, and that the deal will be lost altogether if the offer is not accepted, there is no point in negotiating. Negotiation is almost always a voluntary process – any of the parties can say 'Take it or leave it!' at any time.

4 The parties would, at least for now, prefer to search for agreement rather than fight openly, capitulate entirely, permanently break off contact, or take the dispute to a higher authority. For example, a buyer and a salesperson may prefer to negotiate between themselves rather than involve the boss, because of the loss of face this would entail. Negotiation is common where

there is no fixed system (e.g. procedures or established rules) for resolving conflict.

5 Both parties are prepared to make concessions in order to make gains. When people negotiate, they expect a certain amount of give and take – there is an expectation that opening positions will shift, and that the parties will move towards each other.

6 Successful negotiations involve the management of intangibles as well as the resolving of tangibles. Intangible factors are the underlying psychological and sociological factors which influence the parties during the negotiations. For example, some buyers will seek the satisfaction of driving a hard bargain, whereas some salespeople are affected by a desire not to lose face. Equally, the parties may be concerned not to set a precedent – in other words, neither party would want any temporary concessions to be regarded as standard practice in the future. Intangibles can also include core beliefs, which may be so strong that aspects of the deal become non-negotiable.

The basis on which negotiation rests is that both parties will benefit as a result of the trade. In everyday terms, a shopkeeper would prefer to have money than have the goods on the shelves, whereas the customers would prefer to have the goods than to have the money. If this were not the case, trade would be impossible. The contract results at any point along a line drawn between the maximum amount of money the customers are prepared to pay, and the minimum amount the retailer is prepared to accept. In a Middle Eastern bazaar, the price would be subject to negotiation by the parties, with the shopkeeper trying to get the highest price and the customer trying to pay the lowest. In Western shops there is only an indirect negotiation, with the customer going to the retailer who offers the best deal; this can scarcely be called negotiation at all. In any negotiating situation, the parties need each other; they are interdependent. A salesperson cannot sell unless there is a buyer, but equally a buyer cannot buy unless there is a seller.

Negotiating follows eight stages, as shown in Table 4.4. Negotiation takes practice, and a considerable degree of empathy; good negotiators need to be able to judge other people's behaviour accurately and reliably, and do this in real time with the customer present.

Opening positions should be somewhat removed from the expected final position, since there must be room for negotiation. Negotiators cannot expect concessions unless they are prepared to give them. On the other hand, initial positions should not be too unrealistic, or the negotiation breaks down immediately.

One of the difficulties is that opposing parties may not be clear about what they want from the negotiations, and even if they are clear they may not want to be open about this. Obviously negotiation would move much faster if both parties were totally open and honest from the outset, but this is rarely the case since each party will want to maximize their own outcomes by giving away as little as possible in return for as much as possible. This is less of a problem if the relationship is likely to continue long term, since each party will know that the truth will become apparent eventually anyway.

Thus the parties must exchange information and make an effort to influence each other. They should work towards a solution that takes account of each person's requirements and optimises the outcomes for both (Fisher *et al.* 1991). There are two dilemmas which confront negotiators (Kelley 1966). Firstly, there is the dilemma of honesty. On the one hand, telling the other party everything about the situation may give the other party an advantage in the negotiations. On the other hand, not telling the other party the relevant information will lead to a stalled negotiation, which of course benefits nobody.

The second dilemma is the dilemma of trust. This concerns the extent to which the negotiator believes the other party. Total belief in the other party will probably

TABLE 4.4 Eight stages of negotiation	

Stage	Explanation
Preparation	Good negotiators set targets: what is the maximum they might achieve, what is the minimum they are willing to accept, and what is the most probable outcome. This may mean working out detailed costings. More importantly, the negotiator needs to work out what it is the other side is likely to want and be prepared to give – this avoids surprises in the discussions.
Discussion	Listening carefully to what the other party is saying usually gives a clue as to how to express a counter-offer, or even to what it is the person really wants from the negotiation.
Signals	Negotiators need to give clear signals when the discussion is going in the right direction. This encourages further movement and helps the negotiation to proceed.
Proposition	The proposition being offered needs to be fair and flexible. Nelson Rockefeller's business maxim was, 'Always leave something for the next guy.' In following this, he ensured that everybody wanted to do business with him, because they knew they would always benefit from it.
Presentation	It is essential to communicate effectively so that the both parties are clear about exactly what is on offer and what each is going to gain.
Bargain	Bargaining is about getting something back for what one is prepared to offer. If the other party says 'Can you cut the price another 5 per cent?' the salesperson should not just agree to do it. The salesperson needs to say 'OK, we'll cut it if you'll guarantee to order 20 per cent more goods.' In other words, salespeople should negotiate, not donate.
Close	At some point both parties will need to summarize their positions, and come to an agreement. This should be done once both parties are happy with the deal they are getting so the close need not be aggressive or manipulative.
Agreement	Any agreement made needs to be put in writing to ensure that there is no misunderstanding. Salespeople should also seek some kind of formal commitment from the other party, either in cash or as a contract.

The story goes that a young salesman quotes for supplying stainless steel rods at £4000 a ton, roughly double the spot-market price at that time.

'OK,' says the buyer, 'What would you say if I agreed to that price, made you our preferred supplier for all steel products, and gave you a contract for the next ten years? Oh, and just to sweeten the deal, we'll buy you a car of your choice.'

'Wow!' says the salesman. 'Are you kidding?'

'Of course I am,' said the buyer. 'But you started it.'

mean that the other person will take advantage, but total disbelief will again stall the negotiations. The extent to which the parties trust each other will depend on previous experience of each other, reputation and the present circumstances. Obviously the situation is greatly facilitated if the parties trust each other, and this has been recognized as a key element in establishing long-term relationships (Heumer 2004). Two elements in negotiation help here – perception of the outcomes and perception of the process. A perception that the outcome will be positive and beneficial for both parties increases trust, and a perception that the process is transparent and fair also increases trust.

Techniques of negotiation vary from one individual to the next, but the list shown in Table 4.5 gives a useful overview, and some interesting names, for some of the main ones. Some of these tactics are used by buyers, some by salespeople,

TABLE 4.5 Negotiating tactics

Tactic	Description and explanation
Act crazy	Moving around from one topic to another can sometimes disorient the other party and cause their carefully prepared position to collapse. This is a tactic sometimes used by buyers in traditional selling situations, where they want to confuse the salesperson.
Big pot	Here the salesperson quotes a high price initially, in order to have room to manoeuvre later. Equally, a buyer may imply that a very large order will be placed in order to negotiate a better deal.
Prestigious ally	Mention of an existing customer who has influence over the prospect may sway the sale. For example, a computer salesperson selling to a car-component manufacturer is more likely to get the sale if he or she is already selling to Ford.
The well is dry	The negotiator says that there is no further room for negotiation; the deal must either go ahead as it is, or not at all. This is a somewhat dangerous tactic, since the other party might well call a halt at that point; it is advisable to leave the door open, perhaps by appealing to senior management to allow a little more room for negotiation.

TABLE 4.5 *(cont.)*

Tactic	Description and explanation
Limited authority	This is similar to 'the well is dry'. Here the negotiator says that the deal has gone as far as she or he is authorized to take it. This can have the effect of producing a little more from the other party, or it could lead to a demand to speak to someone who does have the authority to negotiate.
Whipsaw!	This needs two negotiators on the same side: one to play 'good cop' and the other to play 'bad cop'. The bad cop tries to drive as hard a bargain as possible, then when that is rejected the good cop (the other negotiator) speaks privately to the other party and says, 'Maybe I can talk him round. Can we go just a little bit higher?'
Divide and conquer	This is very commonly used in industrial selling due to the large number of people involved in the buying process. The salesperson approaches each one in turn, separately, and gets some kind of agreement to go ahead 'provided the others agree'. Finally there is no-one left to veto the deal.
Get lost	Very common in the legal profession, the negotiator simply is unavailable for comment. This tactic is intended to unnerve the other party, who then may offer more than was intended in order to secure the deal.
Wet noodle	The negotiator simply doesn't respond to anything. This tends to make the other party improve the offer in the hopes of provoking a reaction and kick-starting the negotiation.
Be patient	Just being quiet and letting the other person keep talking will often lead them into persuading themselves.
Split the difference	Probably the most common bargaining tactic of all, 'Let's split the difference.' The person who first suggests it probably has the most to gain, so it is worth waiting it out to get an even better deal.
Play devil's advocate	The negotiator gives the other party some good reasons *not* to accept the deal. Often this will provoke the other party into justifying why the deal should go ahead – the tactic works by using reverse psychology.
Trial balloon	'I suppose you'd go ahead if we were to offer . . .' This type of statement allows the negotiator to judge whether the other party is open to an offer, without actually committing to making the offer.
Surprise!	The negotiator suddenly slips in some new information which puts everything else in a different light and re-starts the negotiation on different lines. Sometimes this is done in order to unsettle the other party, more often it is done to re-start a stalled negotiation.

some by both; some are acceptable bargaining ploys, some are somewhat dubious ethically and are intended to get the best deal in a one-off selling or buying situation.

Knowing which technique to use is a function of deciding the framework within which the negotiation is to take place. There are three major conceptual approaches to framing, as follows:

1 *Frames as cognitive heuristics*: A frame has been defined as a decision maker's conception of the acts, outcomes and contingencies associated with a particular choice (Tversky and Kahneman 1981). The framework is a mechanism through which the individual both thinks about the risks associated with the problem, and employs simple decision rules to arrive at an acceptable outcome (Neale and Bazerman 1991).

2 *Frames as categories of experience*: The frame is a broad definition of the situation that extends beyond decision-making risk. It also incorporates a wide variety of personal and situational factors which will affect the individual's definition of the problem (Roth and Sheppard 1995).

3 *Frames as issue development*: Under this paradigm, the frame is seen as a means of getting the views of both sides into one field of vision (Follett 1942). The frame develops as each party proceeds in the negotiation by defining their needs and wishes.

When frames are used as cognitive heuristics, the salesperson and the buyer know what is permitted in the negotiations and what is outside the scope of discussion. Some of the cognitive processes which have been examined in this context are shown in Table 4.6.

TABLE 4.6 Cognitive aspects of negotiation

Cognitive aspect	Explanation
Perceptions of losses and gains from particular outcomes	Negotiators will be considering the consequences of the various offers being made, and need to be careful to think through all the implications of any agreements made.
The decision makers' risk-taking or risk-aversion tendencies	Some negotiators are extremely cautious while others are prepared to take risks. At the extreme, either policy may result in a non-optimum outcome.
Anchoring	This describes how a particular reference point for a decision affects the decision. If negotiators are starting from widely differing reference points it becomes more difficult to reach a consensus.
Overconfidence	If the negotiators overestimate the likelihood of success this will affect their approach to the discussions. An overconfident negotiator will not make enough concessions, and will make too many demands.
Availability of information	In some cases this will involve the information which is being shared between the parties, but in other cases it will also mean external information which only becomes apparent part way through the process, for example if it transpires that the finance director will not approve the budget for the deal.
Isolation effects	This refers to the tendency for each party to ignore some of the information as irrelevant. Unfortunately, what is irrelevant to one party may be highly relevant to the other.

As categories of experience, frames have seven dominant forms (Gray *et al.* 1997). These are:

1 *Substantive*: What the conflict is about. When the parties use a substantive frame they have a particular disposition about the key issue or concern.

2 *Loss–gain*: How the parties view the risk associated with the particular outcomes.

3 *Characterization*: How one party views another. This can be shaped by previous experience, by reputation, or by experience as the negotiation unfolds. For example, a salesperson faced with someone with a reputation as a tough negotiator will operate within that frame of reference.

4 *Outcome*: The predisposition that each party has towards reaching a specific outcome. The evidence is that individuals who have a strong outcome frame are likely to engage in win–lose or lose–lose negotiations because they are unlikely to be prepared to compromise.

5 *Aspiration*: The broader aims which will arise from the negotiation. For example, a salesperson may appear to be concerned only with the immediate sale, but in fact has a longer-term aspiration of becoming the buyer's preferred supplier, or even of winning the current sales competition.

6 *Process*: How the parties will resolve the dispute. Individuals with a strong process frame will be concerned less with the negotiations than with ensuring that the right people are present, that the negotiation takes place in the appropriate place, and that proper procedures are followed.

7 *Evidentiary*: An individual with a strong evidentiary frame will require a large amount of supporting data to back up the decision.

From the viewpoint of the buyer–seller relationship, an understanding of the type of frame being used by the other party is extremely helpful in knowing how to negotiate. A buyer with a substantive frame will have very specific views about the discussion, and will probably be uncompromising. A buyer with a loss–gain frame will be most interested in the possible risks of buying the product, set against the likely rewards. A buyer with a strong characterization frame concerning the company or its salespeople will act accordingly – which is why corporate brand-building is important, as is good personal presentation on the part of the sales force. Buyers seeking a specific outcome will drive a hard bargain and may well be prepared to lose out altogether rather than settle for less than a perfect result. The aspirations of the buyer will always be an issue – as of course will the aspirations of the salesperson. Buyers with a strong process frame may wish to speak with senior people at the supplying firm, and may wish to ensure that all interested parties are present at meetings.

It should be noted that some sales managers have strong process frames, and may be specific in laying down how sales presentations are to be conducted. The problem with this approach is that it tends to ignore the differing buyer character-istics which the sales force will confront. It should also be noted that different frames might be used according to the nature of the problem under discussion.

When frames are viewed as a process of issue development, the focus shifts to patterns of transactional development, and the transformations which will occur both in the participants and in the nature of the conflict. For example, a long-drawn-out negotiation may start out as a straightforward argument about price, but as the situation develops the salesperson may want a concession on long-term contractual obligations which may then become the focus of the conversation. This may then lead on to a discussion about areas of responsibility and decision making in the relationship. At the same time, each party is developing a new view of each other and the relationship.

At least four factors, summarized in Figure 4.5, affect how the conversation is shaped:

1 Parties tend to discuss stock issues, which are concerns that are raised every time they meet. In selling negotiations, the stock issue is always price, but there may be other issues which come up every time at meetings.

2 Each party tries to make the best possible case for his or her views. One party might use facts and figures, another might use emotive arguments, and it is not uncommon for both parties to try to do all the talking and none of the listening. This is not good salesmanship. Partly this is because the negotiation can easily degenerate into simply refuting each others' arguments, and partly it is because salespeople should not make direct confrontations with customers. The number one rule of selling is 'Never interrupt a customer to make a point.'

3 Frames may be used to establish a formula. Lewicki *et al.* (1992) found that parties may first seek out a compromise which establishes a framework for the negotiation, then draw out from this a number of points of agreement. This leaves a specific set of issues which need to be discussed.

4 Multiple agenda items may also operate. While the parties have a number of major issues which need to be discussed, there will be lesser issues or secondary items which will need to be cleared up. It should be noted that the agenda is not necessarily overt – it may only exist in the heads of the participants.

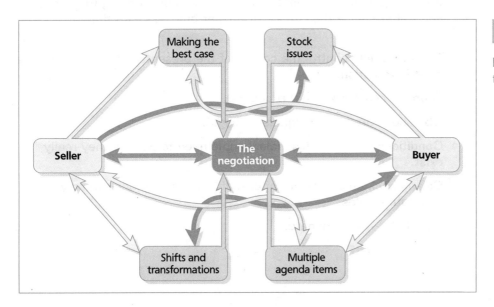

FIGURE 4.5

Factors in shaping the conversation

Knowledge of the frames that each party is using may be helpful in understanding each other and moving to operating from a similar frame. Given the usual power relationship between buyer and seller, it is more likely that the salesperson will be the one who shifts frame, but this is by no means always the case – many confident and charismatic salespeople are able to lay down the framework for the discussions from the outset.

Ultimately, the deal that is struck will depend on the relative strength of each party in terms of their firms' negotiating positions, and on the skills and charisma of the negotiators. The process is not a mechanical one; as pointed out at the beginning of this chapter, business is not done by companies, it is done by people. The chemistry between two individuals is at least as important as the final economics of the deal itself.

SUMMARY

Personal selling is about doing deals between individuals in order to solve problems for the purchaser. In some cases the problems themselves are relatively easily solved, in which case a traditional approach might be adopted, in other cases the firms concerned are looking towards a long-term solution which will involve long-term negotiation and a different approach to management.

The key points from this chapter are as follows:

- Ice breaking helps establish a human relationship for the sales process.

- Salespeople need to listen twice as hard as they talk.

- Establishing a reasonable level of trust is essential to selling.

- Salespeople must be honest – lies have a habit of being found out, and will prejudice the chance of further business with that prospect.

- Questions help control the course of the presentation as well as elicit information.

- People buy solutions, not products.

- Objections are buying signals in disguise.

- Conditions prevent sales; salespeople need to be sure they really exist.

- Calling back on customers after delivery of the goods can only help future sales.

- Negotiate – never donate.

REVIEW QUESTIONS

1 How might an ice breaking conversation help a salesperson later, during the negotiating stage?

2 Why are objections often considered to be buying signals?

3 What is the reason for isolating an objection?

4 If selling is about listening, why are closed questions used?

5 If it is the case that both parties will always gain from a trade, what is the purpose of negotiating?

REFERENCES

Anderson, E. and Robertson, T. S.(1995) 'Inducing multi-line salespeople to adopt house brands' *Journal of Marketing* 59 (2/Apr.): 16–31.

Blythe, J. (2003) *Essentials of Marketing Communications*, 2nd edn, Harlow: FT Prentice Hall.

Chu, W., Gestner, E. and Hess, J. D. (1995) 'Costs and benefits of hard sell', *Journal of Marketing Research* XXXII (Feb.): 97–102.

Coca Cola Company (1981) *Measuring the Grapevine: Consumer Response and Word of Mouth*.

Dion, P., Easterling, D. and Miller, S. J. (1995) 'What is really necessary in successful buyer/seller relationships?' *Industrial Marketing Management* 24(1): 1–9.

Fisher, R., Ury, W. and Patton, B. (1991) *Getting to Yes: Negotiating Agreement Without Giving In*, 2nd edn. New York: Penguin.

Follett, M.P. (1942) 'Constructive conflict', in H.C. Metcalf and L. Urwick (eds). *Dynamic Administration: The Collected Papers of Mary Parker Follett*, New York: Harper and Brothers: 30–49.

Gray, B., Younglove-Webb, B. and Purdy, J. M. (1997) 'Frame repertoires, conflict styles, and negotiation outcomes', *Proceedings of the International Association of Conflict Management*, Bonn, Germany.

Heumer, L. (2004) 'Balancing between stability and variety: Identity and trust trade-offs in networks', *Industrial Marketing Management*, 33(3/April): 251–9.

Kelley H. H. (1966) 'A classroom study of the dilemma in interpersonal negotiation', in K. Archibald (ed.), *Strategic Interaction and Conflict: Original Papers and Discussion*, Berkeley, CA: Institute of International Studies: 49–73.

Leigh, T. W. and Summers, J. O. (2002) 'An initial evaluation of industrial buyers' impressions of salespersons' nonverbal cues', *Journal of Personal Selling and Sales Management*, 22 (1/Winter): 41–52.

Lewicki, R.J. (1992) 'Negotiating strategically', in A. Cohen (ed.), *The Portable MBA in Management*, New York: John Wiley and Sons: 147–89.

Lund, Philip R. (1979) *Compelling Selling*, London: Macmillan.

McKenna, R. (1991) '*Relationship Marketing*', London Century Business.

Neale M. and Bazerman, M. H. (1991) *Cognition and Rationality in Negotiation*, New York: Free Press.

Roth, J. and Sheppard, B. (1995) 'Opening the black box of framing research: The relationship between frames, communication and outcomes', *Academy of Management Journal* (Briarcliff Manor): 94–8.

Schramm, W. A. (1948) *Mass Communications*, Urbana, IL: University of Illinois Press.
—— (1971) 'The nature of communication between humans', in W. A. Schramm and D. F. Roberts (eds) *The Process and Effects of Mass Communications*, Urbana, IL: University of Illinois Press.
Strong, E.K. (1925) *The Psychology of Selling*, New York: McGraw-Hill.
Tversky, A. and Kahneman, D. (1981) 'The framing of decisions and the psychology of choice', *Science* 211: 453–8.

ROYAL DUTCH SHELL

Royal Dutch Shell is one of the big seven oil companies, which between them control the vast majority of the world's oil production and retailing. Like the other majors, Shell, as the company is more commonly known, is a vertically-integrated company, controlling everything from initial exploration right through to the sales on the petrol forecourt.

Royal Dutch Shell is an Anglo–Dutch company, but it operates in a truly global environment – oil is extracted from the Middle East, Far East, North Sea, Gulf of Mexico and many other locations. Likewise, the company's petrol stations operate in most countries of the world. This makes negotiation complex, because the company needs to deal in many cultures and many languages, but also needs to have uniform standards in all its markets.

Two recent developments at Shell have highlighted the complexity of negotiation for the company. Firstly, the company is involved in a joint venture with PetroChina to construct an $8 thousand million gas pipeline across China. The second development is a new system for stock ordering for the retail stores, which is causing major changes for suppliers.

The pipeline agreement has proved problematical because most of the money comes from Shell. Shell's then company chairman, Sir Philip Watts, is quoted as saying, 'The company has to be very dogged about the terms expected because you're putting billions of dollars of Shell's money into it.' He still believed that a deal would be struck, however.

Under a framework agreement signed in July 2002, PetroChina owns half the pipeline, with Shell, Exxon Mobil and Russia's Gazprom each holding 15 per cent. The remaining 5 per cent is owned by Sinopec Corporation, China's second largest oil company. This means that the Chinese collectively own 55 per cent of the pipeline. PetroChina says that the pipeline was scheduled to begin pumping gas by the end of 2003, but by October of that year it had still not reached agreement with the foreign partners to invest in the project, nor had it agreed gas sales agreements with the end users. Part of the problem for PetroChina is that China is still a Communist country, so the Government will be setting the prices for the gas, and it had not yet done so.

Meanwhile, PetroChina was involved in talks with 35 final users, had signed deals to supply to Henan and Anhui provinces, and was talking about going ahead alone with the pipeline if the foreigners continued to be intransigent. Naturally, the foreigners see things differently.

The second development at Shell has come about because of the company's need to make its retail division more competitive. The company has 50 000 retail outlets spread across 125 countries, with total sales of $100 thousand dollars – which makes Shell one of the world's largest retailers. Obviously the bulk of the customers visiting the outlets are there primarily to buy fuel for their cars, but the Shell Shop network also carries newspapers and periodicals, drinks and snack foods, basic spare parts for cars such as windscreen wipers, hazard triangles and light bulbs, and in some cases even a limited range of groceries. In countries where it is legal to do so, the shops carry beer, wines and spirits, and all shops have a range of auto accessories such as deodorizing pads, compasses, map-reading lamps and, of course, road maps for the areas in which the shops are located. This wide range of goods means that the company deals with an equally wide range of suppliers, and consequently a very large number of salespeople.

Shell's response to the problem has been to introduce Category Management Business Solution. CMBS is intended to create a retail mindset within the company, so that, in the words of CMBS Programme Manager Norman King, 'By managing the retail business in a more disciplined fashion, Shell can use the huge number of daily customer visits as leverage. To achieve this, Shell needs to create a retail mindset. In practice this means instituting the right retailer agreements, building the retail network, and developing the retail brand.'

The raft of systems introduced by Shell now allow the company to break down sales activities to such an extent that it is able to sell the data to its suppliers for significant sums of money. 'With this information category managers can now undertake fact-based negotiation with suppliers which has resulted in some significant changes to pricing structures,' King says. These improvements include tiered rebates based on sales over a specific amount, which in many cases were not in the past paid by suppliers because the retailers did not have the detailed information to enable them to invoice for the rebates. Another outcome of CMBS is that the success, or otherwise, of sales promotions is calculated almost instantly, which means that Shell can insist on suppliers removing the stock items in the event that the promotion is not meeting expectations.

Moving its forecourt shops from being an adjunct to fuel sales to being retail outlets in their own right means that Shell is aiming to compete with mainstream retailers in a way that rival oil companies are unable to match. In an industry where the product itself will always remain largely undifferentiated, the forecourt shop is one area where Shell can stand out.

Case-study questions

1 How might suppliers respond to Shell's new retail systems, in terms of negotiation?
2 How would you categorize Shell's frame of reference in each of the negotiating situations outlined?
3 What power does Shell have in the pipeline negotiations?
4 What negotiating techniques does Shell appear to be using in the pipeline talks?
5 What problems might arise from the CMBS system, in terms of relationships with suppliers?

5

SELLING TO MAJOR ACCOUNTS

Learning objectives

After reading this chapter, you should be able to:

- Describe the differences between major-account and small-account selling.

- Explain the processes of managing key accounts.

- Describe the concepts underpinning research into key-account management.

- Explain why key-account selling techniques do not work on small accounts, and vice versa.

- Explain the differing role of the sales manager in a key-account environment.

■ Introduction

During the late 1980s and early 1990s a change in thinking about selling occurred. Up until then, there was an assumption that selling is selling, whatever the importance of the transaction. Researchers then realized that the selling techniques which work in small-account selling did not apply to major accounts, for a number of reasons.

This chapter outlines the differences between small-account selling and major account, or key-account, selling.

SUCCESS STORY – LEE IACOCCA

Lee Iacocca was the son of Italian immigrants, and was originally christened Lido. He changed his name to Lee because he thought it sounded more American. He was a hard-working teenager, because he had to be – he was the son of poor parents, and the Great Depression was on. In fact, his health was so badly affected that he was classified 4F during World War Two – too unhealthy to be allowed to die for his country.

Lee did well in college, in fact so well that he won a scholarship to Princeton. When he left Princeton in 1946, he got a job with Ford as a sales-man. He quickly became a sales manager, and in 1956 his district went from last place to first place for sales, following his innovative '56 for 56' campaign in which he sold new cars for $56 a month.

He acquired a reputation for thinking on his feet, and for listening to his customers. Ford put him on the committee responsible for developing the Mustang, and his skill at understanding what customers wanted meant that the car was a huge success. As a result, the Ford Corporation made him pres-ident, a post which he held for five years until he was lured away to Chrysler, where he spent the next five years turning the company round.

Lee Iacocca says that establishing priorities and being a problem solver are essential qualities for senior management. Also he uses his time wisely and encourages others to do the same – all of these are qualities he learned as a salesman, back in the 1940s and 50s.

Major accounts versus small accounts

A major account is one which possesses some or all of the following characteristics:

- It accounts for a significant proportion of the firm's overall sales. This means that the supplying firm is in a vulnerable position if the customer goes elsewhere. This in turn means that the supplier may be expected to negotiate significant changes in its methods, products, and business practices in order to fit in with the customer's business practices and needs.
- There is co-operation between distribution channel members rather than conflict. This places the emphasis strongly on good, effective channels of communication, with the salesperson in the front line.
- The supplier works interdependently with the customer to lower costs and increase efficiency. This again implies lengthy negotiations and frequent contact between the firms.
- Supply involves servicing aspects such as technical support as well as delivery of physical products. Servicing aspects will often fall to the salesperson, and because of the intangible nature of services, good communication is at a premium.

Because major accounts have these characteristics, the selling cycle tends to be very long. Selling to major accounts cannot follow the simplistic approach of finding out needs and closing which is used in traditional selling situations; it involves a much more drawn-out procedure. Buyers who are considering a major commitment to a supplier, either for a single large purchase or for a long-term stream of supplies, are unlikely to be impressed with a one-hour presentation followed by an alternative close (see Chapter 4). Major account selling will usually involve many decision makers and several sales calls by, possibly, a team of people from the supplying company. These might include salespeople, technical people and even finance experts. Also, the salesperson will need to sell the solution to his or her own firm, since major changes in products and practices are often needed.

This may seem obvious. After all, it seems unlikely that the same procedures used for buying a dozen boxes of copier paper would apply to buying a new factory site. The former probably only involves one buyer and one salesperson, whereas the latter will probably involve most of the senior management of the firm, and an equally wide range of people from the civil engineering firm hired to build the factory. The sale will not be completed in one call, and in many cases the salesperson will rarely, or never, meet the final decision maker. The quantity of information which needs to be exchanged will be much greater, so the process will need to go on for much longer. Communication between members of the selling team is also crucial; research shows that the strategic content of communication between team members has a critical role in sales outcomes (Schultz and Evans 2002).

Note that the size of the order is not the issue. The cash value of a sale is not relevant in deciding whether the account is a major account or not – what is important is that the account has strategic importance for one or both parties. For example, commissioning a new website at a cost of £5000 might be a major decision for a one-man business, whereas a supermarket chain's purchase of £100 000 worth of corn flakes would be a routine deal.

Traditional selling emphasizes objection handling, overcoming the sales resistance of the buyer, and closing the sale. This naturally tends to lead to a focus on the single transaction rather than on the whole picture of the relationship between the supplier and the buyer.

In itself, this may not matter for many purchases. A firm selling photocopiers, for example, or a double-glazing company, has many competitors who are supplying broadly similar products. This means that a quick sale is essential, since otherwise the buyer will be getting several quotes from other firms and will probably make the final decision based on the price alone. In addition, repeat business will be unlikely to materialize, and will be a long time coming if it does, so the salesperson is not looking to establish a long-term relationship with the buyer, nor is the buyer particularly interested in establishing a long-term relationship with the salesperson. Both parties are mainly interested in solving the customer's immediate problems, then moving on to other business.

From the viewpoint of the customer, making a major purchase differs in most respects from making a minor purchase. This is illustrated in Figure 5.1.

Because of the importance of the major account, the buyer will probably need to talk to other people, in meetings at which the salesperson will not be present. A slick sales talk will not help in these situations, because the buyer will:

- be unlikely to remember all the details of the conversation with the salesperson

- not have the motivation to try to sell the solution to the other members of the decision-making unit
- probably not have the necessary selling skills anyway.

What works in small-account selling will not work in major account selling.

There is some evidence that customers are less concerned about value in a small sale (Rackham 1995). Because the cost is relatively low in small purchases, and more especially the risk is low, buyers are less concerned about the cost–benefit payoff. In larger sales, the risk is high and so is the cost in most cases, and thus a concern for value for money becomes much greater.

TALKING POINT

Neil Rackham tells the story of two purchase decisions he made in the same day. In the first case he was buying a simple overhead projector. The salesman was an obnoxious individual of the old-fashioned fast-talking type. Rackham wanted to get the guy out of his office as quickly as possible, and since the overhead projector seemed to be a good one and the price was right, he gave the guy the order within five minutes and got rid of him.

In the second case he was considering buying $70 000 worth of computer equipment and software. In this case the salesman was pleasant and professional, but something about him seemed not quite right. Rackham didn't buy.

In the first instance, there was no likelihood of ever seeing the salesperson again. In the second case, Rackham would have been entering into a long-term business relationship. In small sales the seller is separate from the product – in large sales the seller is the product!

FIGURE 5.1

Factors in major accounts and their impact on buyers

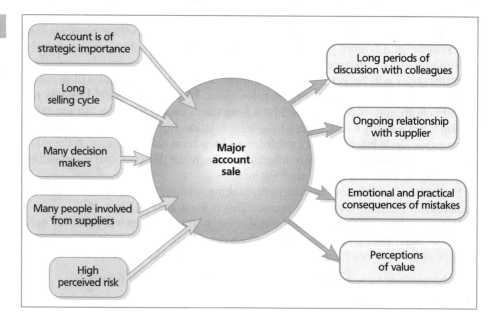

In a major sale there is an implication that the parties will be entering into a long-term agreement because there will be long-term technical support and other inputs. This can affect the buyer's perceptions considerably, since it is not only the immediate product that the company is buying. Buyers will be considering whether the other company is one with which they would like to be associated in the long term.

The risk which arises from mistakes is much greater in major account sales, because the buyer has to share the decision with colleagues. For example, a mistake on the part of fashion buyer when buying in swimwear can be covered up fairly easily – inappropriate goods, or over-ordered goods, simply go into the end-of-season sale. On the other hand, a mistake in ordering a new computer system is known throughout the organization. This affects the salesperson's ability to use emotional arguments in making the sale, because the buyer will need to talk to colleagues and will be unable to say, 'I think we should buy this because I like the salesperson.'

▌ Relationships in business

Business transactions may differ greatly from one another. At one end of the scale, there may be a one-off transaction involving relatively little decision-making and only limited contact between the buyer and the seller; for example, when the office manager needs to buy some emergency photocopier paper from a local office supplies company, and simply sends a junior member of staff out with some petty cash. At the other end of the spectrum a purchase decision might involve establishing a long-term relationship between the firms, operating at many levels and with frequent contact between members of both organizations. For example, a major insurance company might switch its business from IBM to Unisys, and consequently need to retrain its staff, establish a training programme for new staff, alter its internal systems, establish new protocols for dealing with its existing customers, and so forth. Such a relationship would be expected to continue at all levels within the organization for the foreseeable future, as new software and hardware are developed and introduced, and internal systems adapt to external environmental changes.

Within this complex relationship there will be distinct interactions between the parties; these are called episodes (Hakansson and Gadde 1992). The way each episode is handled will depend largely on the past history, if any, between the organizations. If the parties know and trust each other, the episode will be handled in a different way form the way it would be handled if the parties have no previous relationship, or have reasons for mistrust. The possible cases for handling episodes can be broadly categorized as follows:

1 *Simple episode with no previous relationship*: These episodes would involve simple purchases, often in small quantities, or regular purchases of basic raw materials which are of a fairly standard nature; for example, sales representatives buying petrol. Salesperson involvement by the selling company is minimal.

2 *Simple episode in a well-developed relationship*: Here the relationship facilitates the process; for example, a firm's relationship with its bankers

may mean that borrowing money becomes much simpler because the firm already has a track record. Salesperson involvement may be small or negligible.

3 *Complex episode with no previous relationship*: This type of transaction involves the most negotiation, because complexity in itself generates uncertainty and this is exacerbated by the unknown qualities of the other party to the transaction. Often these purchases are one-offs; for example, a power-generating company may only buy one hydroelectric dam in its entire existence, so there is no opportunity to build a long-term relationship with the civil engineers who build the dam. Salesperson involvement is very great, as both an instigator of the process and as a facilitator.

4 *Complex episodes in well-developed relationships*: Here many people from both organizations will need to interrelate (as in the case of the insurance company and the IT supplier mentioned earlier). Again, the previous relationship will inform the progress of events, and the nature of the interaction. Salesperson involvement is large, but mainly as a facilitator.

Investing in a long-term relationship will therefore almost certainly pay dividends in reducing transaction costs, since there is little or no time wasted on learning about the other party. It also reduces risk by reducing complexity. The difference between an investment and a cost is simple: a cost is expected to yield returns within the same accounting period, whereas an investment is expected to yield a stream of returns spread across several accounting periods.

Relationships clearly have at least some of the characteristics of investments. In the early stages of the relationship, the main costs of establishing the relationship will be most evident. In the first few years, outgoings are likely to exceed revenues for the selling firm. In one study, this situation prevailed for the first four years of the relationship, and the selling firm only moved into profit in the relationship after seven years. This means that it is far more profitable to retain and improve existing relationships than it is to seek out new ones, and it is well known that firms which expand too rapidly frequently encounter cashflow problems. From the purchasing firm's viewpoint, there are costs attached to dealing with a new supplier, particularly when the purchase is complex, and savings are likely to accrue over long periods.

Where relationships differ from most other investments is that the relationship is not transferable in the way that, for example, an investment in plant and machinery would be. If one firm acquires another firm and takes over its operations, the relationship may continue as part of the package, but this in itself poses an obstacle to implementing change.

One of the major advantages of establishing a relationship is the possibility for making adaptations. Classical economics assume that all products are identical, but of course this is not the case in the real world, and firms adapt their offerings in order to accommodate purchasers. To a lesser extent, purchasers sometimes adapt their requirements in order to take advantage of special offers from suppliers. An example of this is the Land Rover, which was originally designed in the late 1940s as a utility vehicle for farmers and landowners. The vehicle was designed around the availability of aluminium, which was then in oversupply in comparison to steel, which was strictly rationed. The rust-free qualities of aluminium quickly became a major selling point for the vehicle, but this was a side effect of the Rover car company's ingenuity in making use of a plentiful material to replace a scarce one.

From the seller's viewpoint, adaptation may take place in order to satisfy one purchaser's needs, or a group of purchasers. If the adaptation is intended to meet the needs of a group of purchasers, this is an example of segmentation and targeting. If the adaptation is intended to meet the needs of one purchaser, this is customization. Research shows that the commonest type of adaptation is in technological collaboration with materials suppliers (Hakansson 1989). Adaptations involving components, equipment and processes are less common. This means that technical salespeople may have a strong involvement in the process.

Knowledge-based adaptation gains in importance as development issues increase in importance. Buyers who encourage their suppliers to learn about their systems and applications of technology will give the suppliers the opportunity to make potentially useful suggestions; the downside of this is that the buyer becomes more committed to the suppliers, and may find it harder to switch suppliers at a later date, for example to take advantage of better deals elsewhere. In addition, the differences between supplier and purchaser are likely to lead to creative solutions for mutual problems.

Research shows that, at least in some cases, firms are not always aware of the extent of contacts made between themselves and their suppliers (Hakansson and Gadde 1992). In some cases, engineering staff might meet regularly to discuss technical issues, or marketing people might consider joint promotional campaigns, without necessarily bothering to notify other departments that this is happening. Some interactions occur informally – individuals might meet at seminars or trade fairs, or on training courses, or even on the golf course. The key-account manager is ideally placed to facilitate these contacts.

The result of this is that many long-term relationships between firms rely much more strongly on mutual trust than on formality. This approach is strongly evidenced in Japanese firms, where contracts are regarded as an adjunct to the business agreement rather than as its main pillar; Japanese executives spend a great deal of time establishing informal relationships with suppliers and purchasers, and try to create an atmosphere of trust before being prepared to do business. This can be frustrating for American salespeople, and to some Northern European salespeople, who are used to doing business at a much faster pace and even (in the case of Americans especially) involving their legal advisers from the outset. Partly this difference in attitude is rooted in the Japanese culture, which is strong on issues such as duty and honesty, and partly it is a result of the Japanese legal system, which actively discourages corporate lawsuits by making them expensive and extremely drawn out.

The Millman–Wilson (1995) relational development model is a tool for examining the initiation, growth and eventual demise of the relationship between firms. Linked to the product, process, facilitation (PPF) model of relational interaction (Wilson 1993), as shown in Table 5.1, it is possible to show that the types of problem being addressed and resolved by the partners in the relationship will vary according to the stage of the relationship.

The PPF model postulates that the nature of dyadic (two-sided) organizational relationships is directly related to the nature of the problems that the parties focus on resolving. In dyadic business relationships these problems are hierarchical, in that a more distant relationship between the parties will only generate problems related to products. The higher-order problems of process and facilitation will only become apparent as the relationship becomes closer.

The Millman–Wilson stages of relational development model describes the stages firms go through as the relationship achieves key-account status (Millman and Wilson 1995). In the pre-KAM (key-account management) stage, the firms do not have a relationship but are assessing whether there is potential for establishing key-account status. In the early-KAM stage the supplying firm might develop preferred-supplier status. In the mid-KAM stage the partnership builds further, consolidating the preferred-supplier status. In the partnership-KAM stage the firms develop a spirit of partnership and build a common culture, and the supplier locks in the customer becoming the external resource base. In the synergistic-KAM stage the firms share rewards and become quasi-integrated. The final stage is the uncoupling-KAM stage in which the firms disengage.

The combined KAM/PPF model categorizes the types of problem, and shows how these can be related to the stages that firms go through when establishing a key-account relationship. Table 5.2 shows the PPF strategies mapped against the stages of relational development model (Wilson 1999).

The strategic issues raised at different stages of the relationship connect with the firm's communication strategies, and particularly with the stated strategies of firms. In the early stages, communication might be dominated by outbound messages from the selling company, but in the later stages a true dialogue is likely to be the prevailing paradigm.

TABLE 5.1 The PPF model of problem characteristics

Problem category	Nature of problem
Product	Availability, performance, features, quality, design, technical support, order size, price, terms
Process	Speed of response, manufacturing process issues, application of process knowledge, changes to product, project management issues, decision-making process knowledge, special attention in relation to deliveries, design, quotes, cost reduction
Facilitation	Value creation, compatibility and integration of systems, alignment of objectives, integration of personnel, managing processes peripheral to customer core activity, strategic alignment

TABLE 5.2 KAM/PPF strategies		
Development stage	**Objectives**	**Strategies**
Pre-KAM	Define and identify strategic account potential. Secure initial contact.	Identify key contacts and decision-making unit. Establish product need. Display willingness to address other areas of the problem. Advocate key-account status in-house.
Early-KAM	Account penetration. Increase volume of business. Achieve preferred supplier status.	Build social network. Identify process-related problems and signal willingness to work together to provide cost-effective solutions. Build trust through performance and open communications.
Mid-KAM	Build partnership. Consolidate preferred-supplier status. Establish key account in-house.	Focus on product-related issues. Manage the implementation of process-related solutions. Build inter-organizational teams. Establish joint systems. Begin to perform non-core management tasks.
Partnership-KAM	Develop spirit of partnership. Build common culture. Lock in customer by being external resource base.	Integrate processes. Extend joint problem solving. Focus on cost reduction and joint value-creating opportunities. Address key strategic issues of the client. Address facilitation issues.
Synergistic-KAM	Continuous improvement. Shared rewards. Quasi-integration.	Focus on joint value creation. Create semi-autonomous project teams. Develop strategic congruence.
Uncoupling-KAM	Disengagement.	Withdraw.

Defining success in major account selling

All selling, whether major account or small account, has four basic elements which occur broadly in stages. These are as follows:

1 *Preliminaries*: The preparation and ice breaking stages. These tend to be less important in major sales.

2 *Investigating*: This is where the problem is identified and explored. In major sales this is much more than the simple collection of data.

3 *Demonstrating capability*: This is the stage in which the salesperson shows that he or she has a solution for the problem and has the capacity to put it in place. Because more factors are involved, this stage is much more complex in major sales.

4 *Obtaining commitment*: This is where the buyer commits to the solution being offered by the supplier. In small sales, this will usually mean placing an order, but in major sales there will be a number of other commitments which lead towards the final sale.

In small sales, defining the success or otherwise of a sales call is straightforward. If the buyer bought, the sales call was a success – if the buyer did not buy, the call was a failure. In major account selling, there will be several calls; in some cases there might be as many as 20 or 30 calls before a firm decision is made. This means that there is a problem in deciding whether the call was a success.

For example, a buyer might agree to a further visit from the salesperson. In some cases this could be a breakthrough (e.g. 'I'd like you to come back next week and tell the Board of Directors about this idea') or it could be a stalling manoeuvre (e.g. 'Give me a call in a couple of weeks and we'll get together again').

Rackham (1987) devised a four-way division of call outcomes to define whether the call had been successful. These are shown in Table 5.3.

The more detailed breakdown of possible outcomes outlined here means that salespeople and their managers can judge more easily whether the sales call has been successful. Of course, a sales call can be successful even if the salesperson's original objectives were not met. For example, if a salesperson visited a client aiming to arrange a presentation to the finance director and was told by the buyer that this would not be necessary because the firm was going to place the order anyway, this would hardly constitute a failed sales call. More subtly, a buyer might tell the salesman that the firm has no need for the product, but that one of their other supplying companies definitely has a need, and an appointment with their buyer can be made immediately. In this case, the sales call has been a qualified success.

TABLE 5.3 Defining call outcomes

Outcome	Explanation
Order	An unmistakeable intention to purchase, for example a signed order form. A customer saying, 'We're virtually certain to order from you' does not constitute an order, even though many inexperienced salespeople imagine that it is.
Advance	Any event which moves the sale further towards a decision. For example, the customer might agree to attend a demonstration of the product, might agree to a test of the product, or might agree for the salesperson to meet someone else within the firm.
Continuation	The sale process will continue, but no specific action has resulted so far. For example, a customer might say, 'It looks good. Come and see us next time you're in the area.' A continuation is certainly not moving the sale on, but the door is not closed either.
No sale	A situation where the customer has shown that no business will result. The customer actively declines the call objective; for example, if the salesperson had arranged the meeting specifically to discuss product specifications, and the buyer said, 'There's no point. We won't be going ahead with this any time soon, if at all.' This would constitute a no sale.

■ Preliminaries

In small-account selling, a typical preliminary is the ice breaker. This is a brief statement which places the meeting on a human level. Often salespeople are advised to look around the buyer's office and find something, such as a photograph or award, which can serve as a basis for establishing common ground. In practice, this approach may work well in some cases, but in others it will be counterproductive as the buyer talks to the tenth salesperson of the day about his fishing.

In major account sales, the salesperson may well be dealing with senior managers who are unlikely to want to waste time on general conversation. For this reason, many salespeople use an opening benefit statement to break the ice. For example, a salesperson might begin by saying something like, 'Mr Jones, I know you're a busy man, and you must be wondering whether it's worth spending 20 minutes of your time talking to me. But if I take 20 minutes of your time to show you how you can save your company £50 000, I'm sure you'd think that was time well spent.' This type of statement can seem very direct, but if it's handled well it can also seem businesslike and helpful. The problem with using this type of approach in major accounts is that there will be multiple visits to many people, so the 20 minutes is more likely to be 20 hours. Also, a salesperson who uses this line at every meeting will begin to sound extremely false.

Another problem with opening benefit statements is that they can lead salespeople to start talking about the product and its features and benefits far too early in the call, because the buyer becomes too interested and starts asking questions. In a small sale this would not matter, but in a major account sale it is fatal because the salesperson has not yet had time to build up the problem and increase the value of the solution.

In major account sales, and in fact in any sales, a good opening should establish who the salesperson is, the reason for the call, and the right to ask questions. For reasons of politeness, the opening should not be too blunt, of course; it may take several minutes to obtain permission to ask questions. Equally, the preliminaries are not where the sale is made, so salespeople should not waste too much time on them.

TALKING POINT

There was once a buyer who kept a picture of himself holding a huge fish on his desk. When salespeople called in to see him, they almost always commented on the fish, remarking on how proud he must have been to have caught it, and asking him about his hobby of angling.

'I hate fishing,' he would say. 'A friend dragged me along with him, he caught the fish, I was just holding it up so he could take the photo. The picture is there to remind me of how easy it is to waste a lot of time doing things you hate. So now can we stop wasting time and get to the point?'

This buyer was exactly the type to respond positively to a direct approach – and to be negative about the usual ice breaker favoured by many salespeople!

■ Using questions in major accounts

Having obtained permission to ask questions, the salesperson will be in a position to establish the need for the product. Customers have two types of need: implied needs and explicit needs (Rackham 1987). Implied needs are those which are inherent in the customer's situation, but which have not been expressed. Explicit needs are those which have been expressed by the customer, and relate to something specific. Implied needs may or may not be clear to the customer. For example, a customer may have a problem with an unreliable piece of equipment, but only be partly aware that this is a problem because he or she has no awareness that there is a solution available. Once someone points out that the unreliability is not merely something which must be endured, the customer may express a need to buy a more reliable machine.

This means that the questions that need to be asked are a little more sophisticated than just the open-or-closed dichotomy. Rackham (1987) suggests a four-way categorization of questions, known as SPIN (situation, problem, implication, need pay-off), for major account sales, as follows:

1 *Situation questions*: These are about the details of the customer's present circumstances. Much of this information could be collected before the first meeting through desk research, then confirmed at the meeting.

2 *Problem questions*: These are about difficulties and dissatisfactions which might be solved by the salesperson. Research shows that these questions are more strongly linked to major sales success than are situation questions. Experienced salespeople tend to ask more of this type of question.

3 *Implication questions*: Questions about the consequences of the problems, and possibly the solutions, that could make them urgent or severe enough to justify taking action.

4 *Need-pay-off questions*: These are about the benefits of adopting the proposed solution.

Figure 5.2 shows how the questions relate to each other. The purpose of the questions is to move the customer through the process of becoming aware of an

FIGURE 5.2   Examples of SPIN questions

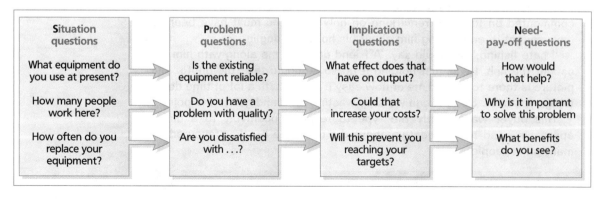

Situation questions	Problem questions	Implication questions	Need-pay-off questions
What equipment do you use at present?	Is the existing equipment reliable?	What effect does that have on output?	How would that help?
How many people work here?	Do you have a problem with quality?	Could that increase your costs?	Why is it important to solve this problem
How often do you replace your equipment?	Are you dissatisfied with ...?	Will this prevent you reaching your targets?	What benefits do you see?

implied need, through to expressing it as an explicit need, then upgrading the importance of the problem so that the buyer feels impelled to take action.

The process is driven by questions so that it is the buyer who is making the statements, not the salesperson. This has important psychological implications, since the buyer is not relying on a self-interested other party to make the arguments. As soon as the seller makes claims about the product, the buyer is in a position to raise an objection. The thrust of SPIN selling is to avoid objections rather than overcome them, because major sales are so complex that the potential number of objections is beyond the capacity of any salesperson to answer.

This classification of questions has been registered as SPIN by Huthwaite Research Group Ltd. The process of working through these questions and covering all the implications of the proposed solution is time consuming and will involve many people; this means that the one-call approach to selling which is typical of small sales will not apply to major accounts.

The way these questions are used varies between experienced salespeople and inexperienced salespeople, and also between successful sales visits and unsuccessful ones. These differences manifest themselves as follows:

- Situation questions refer to aspects of the customer's business, and are intended to provide the salesperson with background information which should be helpful in determining the buyer's needs. However, research shows that buyers sometimes find too many situation questions irritating, and experienced salespeople ask relatively few situation questions (Rackham 1995). This may be because situation questions are too general, and therefore an experienced salesperson will want to avoid them and get straight to the heart of the problem.

- Problem questions refer to specific difficulties the customer might be having. They are more strongly linked to sales success than situation questions, but as the sale becomes larger they become of lesser importance. This should not come as a surprise; the purpose of problem questions is to uncover implied needs, so if implied needs do not predict success in larger sales, problem questions will not help either. Problem questions are more often used by experienced salespeople (Rackham 1995).

- Implication questions seek to determine the consequences of a problem. The purpose of this type of question is to increase the importance of the problem in the buyer's mind. Often the implied need that the buyer sees is only part of a much broader picture; for example, the unreliability of a piece of equipment might be seen only in terms of how much it costs to fix it, rather than in the cost of lost production, the cost in terms of staff morale, the risk of losing customers because of unreliable deliveries, and so forth. The value of the solution has thus increased dramatically. The research shows that this type of question is most effective when dealing with decision makers as opposed to users or influencers. This may be because deciders have to see the whole picture, not the immediate problem.

- Need-pay-off questions focus the customer's attention on the solution rather than the problem, which creates a positive problem-solving atmosphere in which the salesperson is seen as an ally, not an enemy. Because the discussions are carried out in the form of questions and answers, the buyer, rather than the seller, talks about the benefits of the solution. The salesperson can talk about the product afterwards, but in fact the buyer is already sold on the idea.

Need-pay-off questions reduce objections. When a salesperson explains about a product, the buyer is likely to focus on what the product does not do rather than on what it does do. In small sales, this may not matter, because the problem being addressed is a simple one. In major sales, the problems are more complex and the solution is unlikely to provide a complete answer. Because the buyer knows this, the potential for objection raising is much greater, but by using need-pay-off questions the salesperson directs the buyer towards identifying which parts of the problem the solution will solve.

It is important to note that this is only helpful if the seller can meet the need. Using need-pay-off questions when the need cannot be met is counterproductive because it strengthens the need, thus making a sale less likely when the buyer finds out that the product cannot meet the need.

The other major benefit of need-pay-off questions is that they help the buyer to rehearse the necessary arguments for internal selling. Major sales require input and agreement from a large number of individuals in the organization. It is extremely unlikely that the salesperson will be able to talk to all the people involved in the decision, so the people he or she does see will need to have the ammunition to use with their colleagues (see Figure 5.3).

In Figure 5.3, the salesperson opens an initial dialogue, perhaps with a buyer or perhaps with an influencer. This meeting goes well enough for the buyer to arrange a meeting with an interested colleague. This colleague is doubtful, so arranges a meeting with a third colleague, this time without the salesperson being present. The third colleague asks the initial contact to have a three-way meeting with a senior decision maker, again without the salesperson being present. This meeting results in the senior person asking for a meeting with the salesperson.

This is not an atypical scenario, and is in fact simpler than the process might be in many cases. Note that the salesperson is not present at some of the most crucial meetings, and has no way of compelling the decision makers to make his or her presence necessary. This means that the various players need to be primed up beforehand, and need to be confident of their knowledge and able to express it well. Note also that, even in this simplified example, there have been a total of four meetings before the salesperson even meets the senior decision maker, and in many cases the decisions are made without the salesperson ever meeting the decider.

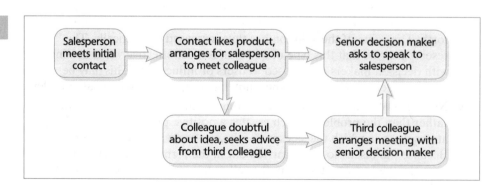

FIGURE 5.3

Word of mouth in major sales

In fact, the bulk of the selling activity happens in the salesperson's absence. The sale depends on the ability of the people in the buying organization to sell to each other; much of this type of discussion happens round the coffee machine, in corridors, or in the aftermath of other meetings. The salesperson would never have the time to attend all these meetings, even if the customer would allow it.

In small-account sales, the purpose of the sales presentation is to lead the customer from a recognition of the problem through to accepting a solution. In major account sales, the purpose of the sales presentation is to help the buyer think through the full implications of the problem and its solution. SPIN questions help this to happen, but only if the questions relate directly to the customer's problem. General questions about the company and its situation are of little help.

■ Features and benefits in major sales

Features are facts or information about a product's characteristics. Since a feature is a neutral fact, it does not help in persuading a buyer to buy. What persuades the buyer is the benefit the feature provides; the features of the product should provide the buyer with some advantage.

Salespeople, and marketers in general, are well aware that features in themselves are not very interesting. A long list of facts about a product does not in itself convey anything to a prospective buyer, and is probably tedious to listen to. A set of facts which relate to the buyer's problem will be far more interesting.

In major account sales, deep discussions about features tend to have a negative effect when used early in the sales process. This may be because the emphasis on features leaves the buyer able to raise objections, or it may be that the problem is not clearly defined at this stage, and is certainly not perceived as being of high importance. The exception to this general rule is when the salesperson is talking to users, who, not unnaturally, have a better understanding of, and interest in, features.

Later in the sale, buyers sometimes develop a great interest in the features of the product, since the problem, and consequently the solution, is complex. At this stage, the salesperson should bring in technical experts and others from the supplying company to provide the level of information the buyer needs.

Benefits can be divided into Type A benefits, which are those benefits which can help the customer or can be used by the customer, and Type B benefits which show how a particular feature meets an explicit need which has been expressed by a customer (Rackham 1987). For example, a customer might have expressed a need for a machine which will fit into a particular space in the factory. This would be a Type B benefit. The machine might also be more reliable than other machines; although the customer had not specifically asked for this, it is a benefit, and would be classed as a Type A benefit. Type A benefits work well in small sales, but do not work well in major sales, whereas Type B benefits show the opposite characteristics.

This is, of course, perfectly reasonable. Someone who is considering a major purchase will clearly not do so unless the purchase represents a significant solution to a known problem. In effect, the buyer is saying, 'This is what I want,' and the salesperson is saying 'We can give it to you.' On the other hand, in a small sale the problem may not be apparent until the salesperson points it out, so Type A benefits will predominate.

◼ Closing

In small-account sales, the close is generally believed to be the point at which the order is placed. Since the basic reason for any sales call in small-account selling is to create an order, this is perfectly reasonable. In major-account sales, the vast majority of calls, even the successful ones, do not result in an order, so a new definition is needed.

The key element in closing is establishing a commitment. In small sales this will be a firm order, preferably with a deposit cheque attached to it. In major accounts the commitment might be to agree to a feasibility study, or agree to a meeting with senior management, or an agreement to attend a demonstration of the product. Closing could therefore be defined as a behaviour used by the seller which implies or invites a commitment, so that the buyer's next statement implies or denies commitment (Rackham 1987).

In small-account sales, strong closing is usually helpful because it forces the customer into making a decision fairly quickly rather than spending a lot of time thinking about it. This allows the salesperson to make more calls, which eventually leads to more business. In major-account sales, speeding up the call will be counterproductive because the salesperson needs to spend time building up the importance of the problem; salespeople in this situation are extremely unlikely to wish that they could spend less time with the decision makers.

Another problem with slick closing techniques is that professional buyers, especially those at senior level, also read sales textbooks and know the closes. On the other hand, nothing is more irritating than a salesperson who cannot get to the point and ask for the order. In major sales, successful salespeople end the call by suggesting a commitment of some sort, though not necessarily an order. Having summarized the benefits of the product, the salesperson might say, 'Could I suggest that the next logical step would be for us to talk to your finance director about this?' The suggested commitment should follow these rules:

- The commitment should advance the sale in some way, moving closer to a final decision.
- The commitment should be the highest realistic commitment the customer can give.

The closing of major account calls depends largely on having realistic call objectives. If the salesperson is clear about the intended outcome of the call, he or she can ensure that the outcome is the one which is asked for at the end of the call.

◼ Managing major-account salespeople

From a sales-management viewpoint, major-account sales are almost entirely different from small-account sales. In small-account sales, the one-call sale is the norm; typically, sales managers operate on the basis that the more calls the salespeople make, the more sales will result; on the face of it, this is perfectly logical. If a salesperson has a closing rate of one in four (one sale for every four calls) then twenty calls will produce five sales, forty calls will produce ten sales, and twelve calls will only produce three sales. Therefore most sales managers apply pressure to their sales forces to make more calls.

In major-account selling this approach would be disastrous. Encouraged, or compelled, to call on more customers, the salesperson will inevitably begin to call on only those customers who can be sold to quickly and easily, in other words the smaller accounts. Sales managers therefore need to adopt a very different approach in managing these salespeople.

In major accounts, there appear to be three main approaches to success, as follows (Rackham and Ruff 1991):

1 *Entrepreneurial approach*: The sales manager acts as if his or her sales branch is a business in its own right. Accounts are treated as a marketplace of business opportunities to be seized upon and exploited. Entrepreneurial sales managers tend to use a hands-on approach and are often more directly involved in face-to-face selling than are other managers, and are competitive internally for resources, even stealing salespeople away from other sales managers within their own companies. Entrepreneurial managers have a strong business sense and good understanding of figures and profitability, especially their own contribution to the company's bottom line.

2 *Coalition builders*: These managers operate through networks of friends and contacts, both among customer accounts and within their own companies. Unlike the entrepreneurs, these managers operate behind the scenes and do not take a hands-on approach; any meetings they have with customers are aimed at building the relationship rather than advancing a specific sale. Often these meetings take place outside the work environment.

3 *Competitive strategists*: These managers operate by helping their salespeople to plan strategies which can be used against the competition. They spend relatively little time with customers, preferring to concentrate on knowing the competition and on planning approaches – they only become involved with the customers when there is a competitive element; for example where they know that a competitor is also likely to be asked to quote.

All three of these manager types tend to agree that coaching is an essential element in managing the major-account sales force. This is also true in small-account selling, but coaching has a very different focus in major-account selling. In small-account selling the emphasis is on developing the skills of the sales force, in other words helping salespeople become more proficient in using sales techniques such as objection-handling and closing. In major sales the emphasis is much more on strategy coaching, in which salespeople need help with deciding the next move in order to make a specific sale.

Practical problems also arise for the sales manager in assessing the effectiveness of coaching in major sales. In small sales, where the salesperson is perhaps making four or five calls a day, it is easily possible for the sales manager to accompany the salesperson for a day and observe what happens in calls. Corrections can be made to the salesperson's approach, and within a week or so the improvement in sales should become apparent. In major sales, the lead times between first contact with the client and the final agreement to the sale are likely to be very long indeed, often months and sometimes years; in those circumstances, coaching becomes difficult, to say the least. Improvements in methods may not show results for years, and therefore it may be difficult to motivate salespeople to make changes in their practices.

Effective coaching follows a set formula, with the elements shown in Table 5.4.

Improving sales productivity in major sales is even more complex. Sales productivity actually comes from two components: sales efficiency and sales effectiveness. Efficiency is about getting in front of the maximum number of prospects for the minimum cost; sales effectiveness is about maximizing the sales potential once in front of the prospects. Both elements are important, but small-account selling puts more emphasis on efficiency, whereas major account selling puts more emphasis on effectiveness. Small accounts place more emphasis on working hard, whereas major-account selling is much more about working smart.

In small-account sales, managerial involvement is not usually hands-on. The managers who are most successful concentrate on managing sales-team activities, but do little or no selling themselves and do not become involved directly with customers unless there is a major problem (Rackham 1995). In major-account selling, though, the sales manager is almost certain to become directly involved with the customer at some stage, if only because such a large commitment on the part of the customer demands that he or she should speak to the senior management of the supplier firm.

Sales managers should follow these principles when becoming involved in major sales:

- Only become involved when your presence makes a unique difference. The salesperson involved on the account is probably very deeply immersed in it, and will know a lot about the customer and the state of the negotiation; you cannot possibly know as much.

- Do not make sales calls on a customer unless your salesperson is with you. You could upset a delicate stage of the negotiation, or at the very least introduce new factors.

TABLE 5.4 Elements of effective coaching

Element	Explanation
Less is more.	Good coaches work with a few people in depth, or even on a one-to-one basis. They also work on a small number of issues at a time, rather than overload the individual with a large number of different elements. A good major-account coach will limit the number of accounts he or she is involved in rather than the number of individuals. This allows the opportunity to become familiar with each account in depth.
Strategic coaching is iterative.	The value comes from the coach having a repeated involvement in the strategy. This enables the coach to work in greater detail on the account, and to adjust the strategy as the account develops and the sale unfolds. The strategy cannot be set in concrete at the outset when dealing with major accounts.
Coaching is a motivational tool.	In small sales, salespeople quickly see the results of their efforts. Each week they will bring in sales, and in some cases they will be selling every day. It is only a matter of observing trends. In major accounts, sales may only happen once every few months, so coaching in between times helps to maintain the morale of the sales force.

- Before any joint call, agree on specific and clear selling roles with your salesperson. Again, control needs to be strongly with the salesperson who is responsible for the account, so it is essential to trust that person's judgement.

- Be an active internal seller for your salespeople. The solution arrived at for the client is likely to involve internal changes for the supplier, some of which will not be popular with the other people in the firm. They will need to be convinced, and the sales manager is the best person to do this.

- Always have a withdrawal strategy that prevents any customer becoming too dependent on you personally. Customers may prefer to deal with the boss rather than with the salesperson, but a sales manager cannot afford to spend all his or her time out of the office, selling to major accounts.

On of the biggest problems for the sales manager is that it is relatively easy to get people to work harder – extra incentives will usually motivate people to put in more hours, or otherwise increase sales efficiency. Increasing sales effectiveness, though, means getting people to work smarter, and since most people are working as smart as they know how to already, extra incentives will probably not help.

SUMMARY

Major-account selling and management is a relatively recent phenomenon, both in practice and in our understanding of how it differs from small-account selling. The advent of expensive, complex solutions which are aimed at expensive, complex problems has meant that salespeople have had to make changes in the ways in which they sell. The small-account techniques which worked in the 1920s will still work in the 21st century, but only for small accounts. Large accounts, and large problems, need a more detailed set of techniques.

The key points from this chapter are as follows:

- **Techniques used for small-account selling are counterproductive in large accounts.**

- **A major account is one which is of strategic importance to one or both parties, and which represents a major commitment in time and/or money.**

- **Coaching is of greater importance than motivation techniques.**

- **Major-account salespeople need to work smarter, not work harder.**

- **Need identification is not enough in major account selling. The salesperson also needs to explore all the implications of the problem.**

REVIEW QUESTIONS

1 Why might techniques used for major sales be counterproductive in small sales?

2 What is the purpose of implication questions?

3 What type of problems would a key-account manager be dealing with in the early-KAM stage?

4 Why should account managers avoid getting directly involved with potential customers in a key-account scenario?

5 Why would an emphasis on increased activity be counterproductive in key-account management?

REFERENCES

Hakansson, H. (1989) *Corporate Technological Behaviour – Co-operation and Networks*, London: Routledge.

—— and Gadde, L.-E., (1992) *Professional Purchasing*, London: Routledge.

Millman, A.F. and Wilson, K.J. (1995) 'Developing key account managers', *IMP 12th International Conference Proceedings*, Manchester Federal School of Business and Management.

Rackham, N. (1987) *Making Major Sales*, Aldershot: Gower.

—— (1995) *Spin Selling*, Aldershot: Gower.

—— and Ruff, R. (1991): 'The role of the sales manager in major sales', in R. Rackham (ed.) *The Management of Major Sales*, Aldershot: Gower.

Schultz, R.J. and Evans, K.R. (2002) 'Strategic collaborative communication by major account representatives', *Journal of Personal Selling and Sales Management*, 22 (1/Winter): 23–32.

Wilson, K.J. (1993) 'Managing the industrial salesforce of the 1990s', *Journal of Marketing Management* 9(2): 123–39.

—— (1999) 'Developing key-account relationships: The integration of the Millman–Wilson relational development model with the problem-centred (PPF) model of buyer–seller interactions in business-to-business markets', *Journal of Selling and Major Account Management* 1 (4/Summer): 11–32.

HEWLETT-PACKARD AND GLOBAL ONE

During the 1990s the world's telecommunications systems went global. The increasing use of satellite linkages, the advent of cellular telephones, the general increase in world trade, and the exponential increase in world travel all provided powerful drivers for the integration of the world's major telecommunications companies. During this period, British Telecom and AT&T formed a strategic alliance, and other national telephone companies entered into a scramble to create alliances, global joint ventures, and even mergers. Each new company or alliance was established with the intention of taking its share of the few hundred truly global customers who account for around 10 per cent of the world's telecom business.

One such joint venture was the creation of Global One by an alliance of Deutsche Telecom, France Telecom and Sprint. Global One was set up to provide telecommunications services to multinational corporations, private individuals and telecommunications companies worldwide. By the end of 1997 Global One had 3900 employees and a turnover of $1.1 thousand million, but it was still a small player in terms of the size of the overall market.

One of the obvious target companies for Global One was Hewlett-Packard. This company is a major player in the computer business, with a commercial presence in 120 countries. HP is a company which seeks to stay close to its customers, and does so by operating 35 call centres, 14 of which are in Europe. The company has a strong set of quality controls in place, and has no hesitation in imposing these on all its suppliers. Suppliers are evaluated on what HP calls the TQRDC method. The T stands for technical performance, the Q for quality of delivered product or service, the R for the supplier's capacity to react quickly, the D for delivery and the C for competitive cost. TQRDC creates a strong incentive for suppliers to improve their processes.

Until the mid-1990s HP, in common with other large multinationals, managed its own call centres. In 1994 the company invited bids for outsourcing its call centre management, as a result of finding the European market to be fragmented and uncompetitive, with the majority of telecoms organizations being government-owned. Relaxation of government restrictions and the privatization of telecoms systems allowed greater competition and co-operation, and HP had every intention of taking advantage of this. On the other hand, HP wanted to simplify its operations, so it wanted to appoint a single telecoms supplier to provide services on a worldwide basis.

Several other companies, including BT, entered the bidding but Global One came out with the contract. In the early stages of the relationship, Global One piloted a set of partial solutions, prior to implementing the global solutions HP were looking for. Meanwhile, HP defined a set of procedures and standards to evaluate the services offered on the basis of the defined specifications. The TQRDC indicators were evaluated weekly at joint meetings between HP and Global One, but Global One was proactive in looking for new ways of evaluating the outcomes, so the weekly evaluations eventually gave way to twice-yearly evaluations. The major account manager from Global One also facilitated greater direct interaction between engineering staff and managers at HP, and Global One, which offered greater flexibility and more rapid response. The perceived distance between the two companies has steadily shrunk as time has gone by – in some cases HP staff and Global One staff are closer to each other than they are to people in other divisions of their own companies.

Requests from HP to Global One are almost entirely filtered through the account manager or the sales support team at Global One. They then put a request for implementation through to the operations team, but from then on much of the communication between the companies bypasses the account manager. Since the account manager is based in the UK, and much of the interaction happens elsewhere in Europe, this is an inevitable consequence.

Both companies have had to make changes in the way they do business, and both companies have been able to learn from each other during the process. In the long run, the relationship is likely to continue, as both companies have a great deal invested in it; ultimately, the income stream from HP to Global One and the services Global One provides for HP are crucial to both companies' success.

Case-study questions

1 Having received the invitation to bid, how might Global One's key-account salespeople have ensured the success of their bid?

2 Why would Global One's key-account manager seek to increase interactions between HP staff and Global One staff?

3 Why might Global One have been innovative in finding new evaluation methods for their products? In other words, why not simply accept HP's systems?

4 How might Global One increase its business with HP?

5 What possibilities exist for Global One to use its experience when approaching other potential customers?

6

RECRUITMENT

Learning objectives

After reading this chapter, you should be able to:

- Explain theories of recruitment as they apply to sales management.

- Describe how to draw up a job specification and person specification for a salesperson.

- Describe the advantages and disadvantages of different sources of recruits.

- Explain the main issues in recruitment advertising.

- Conduct an interview for a sales post.

■ Introduction

The starting point for building a successful sales force lies in recruiting the right people at the outset. Although many other factors intrude into the equation (for example, motivation, training, remuneration and management style), the fact remains that none of these factors can operate successfully if the recruits are not suitable for the job.

James Nannen began his meteoric business career in a somewhat unusual manner. After graduating from college in the US, he hopped on a cargo ship to Australia and went to seek adventure and fortune.

On arrival, he soon drifted into a sales job, selling encyclopaedias door to door, because it was all he could get at the time. As a foreigner in a strange land, opportunities were few – but the work was there and he did it. Within a year he was the top salesman for Collier's Encyclopaedia Company in Sydney, and had been bitten by the sales bug.

He turned down Collier's offer to open a new sales office for them in Fiji, and returned to his native United States, where he worked as a salesperson and sales manager for Hallmark Cards and Proctor & Gamble. Eventually he started his own business, a speciality pet retailing store, and now owns 19 businesses including a mail-order business and a wholesale bird-distributing business. His secret of success? Hard work, of course, but also the courage to grab opportunities and seize the main chance. Nannen is a risk taker, but an intelligent risk taker; he knows where he is going, even if he is not always 100 per cent sure of how he will get there – but where he is at present is not at all a bad place.

Philosophies of recruitment

There appear to be three main philosophies in current usage regarding recruitment in sales. These are as shown in Table 6.1.

The third philosophy is true for some industries where the number of potential customers is very large, notably in the home improvement sector, or in financial services. Often these salespeople are paid on a commission-only basis; they will not be paid if they do not sell. There is therefore very little on-cost (the extra costs of employing someone; e.g. office space, training, pension, etc.) to recruiting large numbers, and the more salespeople there are telling the story the more sales will

Table 6.1 Philosophies of recruitment for sales

Philosophy	Description
Human-resources approach	Provided we can find out what it is we want recruits to do, we can find the right people to do it.
Warm-body approach	We have no way of predicting who can sell and who cannot so we recruit anybody and see whether they can do the job.
Throw it at the wall and see what sticks approach	The more people we recruit, the more sales we will get.

result. This is coming to be seen as a somewhat old-fashioned approach, but for many firms it still has merit. The major drawback of this approach is that it tends to result in the adoption of the selling concept (see Chapter 1) rather than a market-oriented approach. In the long run this will lead to inflexibility of approach and poorer customer service, unless the management of the firm is conscious of the problem and take steps to avoid it. There are also major problems regarding the motivation of salespeople, who rapidly become demoralized if they do not sell for even a few days, since they have no income if they do not make sales.

The second philosophy also has some merit. It is extremely difficult to predict who will sell and who will not. This is because many other factors enter the equation, and ability is only one of them. Many people have the ability to sell (some argue that everybody has some ability to sell) and someone who is of low ability but highly motivated will always outsell someone who has high ability but low motivation. Equally, training is an issue; the idea of the born salesman is a myth, just as the idea of a born dentist or a born truck driver would be ridiculous. Many salespeople can sell well for one company, then change companies and find that, in a new environment and with different management, they are unable to sell at all. The emphasis for firms adopting this philosophy needs to be on training and motivation, and also on careful monitoring of activity to ensure that salespeople are not dropping out of the picture. If, as is usually the case, this philosophy is combined with the third philosophy, training costs and motivational programmes are likely to be wasted on a large number, perhaps the majority, of new recruits. These issues are dealt with more fully in later chapters of the book.

The first philosophy is the one that is often seen as being the most scientific or professional, yet there is little hard evidence to support it. It is the approach about which most is written, and it is the approach that has attracted the most interest from academic researchers. Most sales managers are convinced that being able to predict who will sell will lead to more precise targeting of training and recruitment resources, which will lead to lower costs and an easier life.

Part of the reason for the credibility of the first philosophy is that it works well in other professions. If a firm is hiring accountants or factory workers it is fairly easy to decide what level of education would be needed for the job, what level of physical capacity, what types of previous experience would be useful and so forth. For salespeople, on the other hand, too many other factors affect performance. The main ones are as shown in Table 6.2.

Sales managers frequently complain about the quality of applicants for sales posts; there is a real foundation to this view, but there is also the possibility that

TABLE 6.2 Factors in sales-force performance

Factor	Explanation
Motivation	Salespeople work on their own for much of the time. It is very easy for them to become disillusioned and demotivated, and therefore not be able to sell. Since people are motivated by different things (see Chapter 8) performance can be very greatly affected by the type as well as the level of motivational factors.

TABLE 6.2 *(cont.)*

Factor	Explanation
Training	The ways in which people learn vary, and therefore training programmes need to be flexible; but since salespeople are working away from their peers and away from the office, misconceptions are less likely to be addressed in the early stages of the salesperson's career. This means that a basic misunderstanding might be perpetuated for years.
The product	If the salesperson does not believe in the quality and benefits of the product, this will have a serious effect on his or her credibility in front of prospects. This is not an issue for the company accountant or the factory worker, even though it might affect their morale.
The firm	Salespeople cannot afford to have doubts about the company they work for. Again, an accountant or factory worker who is dissatisfied with the firm might suffer some loss of efficiency, but for a salesperson this would be disastrous.
The customers	Salespeople spend most of their time with the customers. If, for example, a pharmaceuticals salesperson found doctors to be arrogant or too intellectual, this would have a serious effect on sales. Equally, salespeople often find themselves identifying with the customers rather than with the firm they work for.

TABLE 6.3 Personality factors and sales jobs

Personality factor	Relation to sales jobs
Emotional stability	The degree to which a person is neurotic or not does not apparently relate to whether he or she finds a sales career attractive or not.
Extroversion	More outgoing salespeople enjoy selling, training, recruiting and entertaining clients but do not like working with orders (i.e. paperwork).
Openness to experience	This personality characteristic correlates well with the travel aspects of selling (being out of town often, etc.) but these salespeople do not like working with orders.
Agreeableness	This trait is negatively associated with travel.
Conscientiousness	Highly conscientious salespeople enjoy the selling activity, meetings and conferences, but do not like to travel.

insufficient attention is being paid to the factors listed in Table 6.2. Obviously different personality types are attracted to careers in sales, and research by Stevens and Macintosh (2003) has identified some of the issues, as shown in Table 6.3. The researchers found that extroversion is the strongest factor in whether a salesperson finds a selling career attractive.

Planning for recruitment

Job analysis

Job analysis consists of identifying the tasks involved in carrying out a particular job. The purpose of the exercise is to ensure that the people who are recruited have the capacity to carry out the tasks involved, and also to ensure that recruits know what is expected of them. The analysis might be carried out for an individual post or for the department as a whole. If the latter, the information is used for manpower planning as well as for recruitment to particular posts.

The factors which affect job performance should also be taken into account. Typically these would include the following:

1 *The type of selling job*: The way a missionary salesperson acts is very different from the way an order-taker acts, and the requirements for a telesales job will differ greatly from those needed for a major account manager.

2 *The objectives of the job*: The role of someone who is taking over an existing territory from a departing colleague will differ markedly from the role of someone who is expected to market a new product line.

3 *The reporting relationship*: Salespeople who are expected to work on their own initiative will differ from those working within a bureaucratic hierarchy. Also, there is a difference between reporting to a sales manager (as would be the case in a large firm) and reporting directly to the managing director (as would be the case in a small firm).

4 *The role and tasks necessary to perform effectively*: Different companies require their salespeople to operate in different ways. For example, one firm might require its salespeople to generate their own leads, whereas another firm might have an effective telesales operation which generates all the leads.

5 *The environment within which the job operates*: This might include policies on sales, distribution and competitors. It includes both the external environment and the internal environment.

6 *Company regulations and policies*: These can range from simple rules about expense payments through to company ethical policies, for example on such issues as knocking the competition.

One of the difficulties of job analysis is collecting information about what existing staff actually do. For clerical or factory jobs, observation is relatively straightforward; apart from the inevitable change in behaviour that will occur when the staff member is aware of being observed, the observation itself is easily carried out. For salespeople, though, observation is more difficult since they work away from the firm for most of the time. Therefore it is more common to use questionnaires or time-analysis forms to assess the job. If data is collected from the entire sales force, it is possible that differences can be identified between high-flyers and the less successful salespeople; this will be useful in defining how the job should be done, as well as in defining how the job is being done. Self-reports of behaviour are notoriously unreliable, however. People often do not do what they say they are doing, either from a deliberate desire to deceive or because they have not really analysed what they do. Observation is much more effective and reliable, but is difficult to carry out in the sales environment (Rackham 1995).

Having analysed the job, the sales manager is in a position to consider man-power planning. This means taking a global view of the tasks facing the department as a whole; for example, identifying lead generation as one of the tasks involved in the company's selling activities might mean that individual salespeople are expected to carry out this function, or it might lead to the recruitment of a telephone canvasser (telemarketing operator) to carry out that function for the rest of the sales force. As another example, the manager might decide that the current sales force is composed of too many young, inexperienced people, and might therefore see a need to recruit an older person to act as a mentor. Manpower planning involves decisions on both the number of salespeople to be employed, and on the type.

Salespeople might be recruited for one of three general purposes. Firstly, the new recruit might be able to add some new skills to the existing mix of staff. It may be that a new product is being introduced, so that it would be beneficial to recruit someone with experience of the product category. Alternatively, someone with major-account skills or experience of selling to a particular customer group might be needed. If the vacancy has arisen because there is a need for specific skills within the team, this should become clear when the job analysis is carried out, and the necessary skills can be included in the job advertisement.

Secondly, a new recruit might be needed to replace someone who has left or retired. In the event of the post having become vacant because someone is leaving, it is advisable to look into the reasons why the person left: is there a problem which should be addressed? The following list of questions has been proposed by some recruiters as a way of analysing why the person left.

1 Who recruited this person?
2 Who trained this person?
3 Who motivated, or failed to motivate, this person?
4 Who controlled this person?
5 Ultimately, who failed this person?

The final question places the responsibility firmly on the management; although it could be argued that someone might join the firm who is not up to the job, this should, presumably, have been detected at the recruitment or training stages, rather than being left until the recruit leaves.

Thirdly, a recruit might be needed because the market is growing and the firm needs more salespeople to service it. If the vacancy arises because business is picking up, the sales manager should look at ways of improving the productivity of the sales force before committing to extra recruiting. Recruiting is, in itself,

There is a permanent shortage of salespeople generally, but in particular telemarketers are hard to find. However, one initiative, started in the United States, looks as if it might provide a solution.

Some telesales companies are hiring prison inmates to do their telemarketing. The prisoners get the same pay as they would on the outside, but the prison authorities deduct a percentage towards the inmates' room and food. The rest of the money belongs to the prisoner.

This captive sales force is unlikely to leave to work elsewhere, they learn a new skill which they can use when they are released, and of course the customers have no way of knowing that they are being called from a prison cell, so everybody wins.

expensive and salespeople are also expensive once hired; in the UK, it is estimated that the average salesperson on the road costs between £50 000 and £70 000 a year. In addition, unless the company is expanding geographically (i.e. moving into new areas or countries where the firm does not currently have a presence) increasing the number of salespeople will, at least temporarily, reduce the territory size for each existing salesperson. This may mean lower commission earnings in the short term, which may lead to resentment of the newcomers. This in turn might lead to experienced salespeople becoming dissatisfied and leaving the firm, or at least becoming demotivated in the short term.

Research by Barksdale *et al.* (2003) shows that there are two types of commitment to a firm. The first, continuance commitment, is based on economic issues such as salary and the availability of suitable alternative employment. The second, affective commitment, is based on feelings about the work itself, work colleagues, job satisfaction and so forth. If the salesperson is mainly bound by continuance commitment, he or she will leave as soon as a better-paying job comes along. Affective commitment is therefore likely to be more powerful in terms of staff retention.

Job description

Job descriptions contain the duties and responsibilities of the job, and the rewards that accrue from it. Performance measures should also be included; the job description forms the basis of the contract between the employer and employee, and should therefore be drawn up with considerable care. Employees would rightly feel entitled to refuse to carry out a task that is not included in the job description, so all aspects of the job should be included.

The job description is generated from the job analysis, and should include all the factors identified through the job analysis. Table 6.4 shows a checklist of duties and responsibilities.

Other issues to be included are the person to whom the employee will report (usually the sales manager, but in smaller companies possibly direct to the managing director) and some of the company's responsibilities to the sales person, for example providing market information about the territory.

Person specification

Having described the job, it is theoretically possible to describe the type of person who will be needed to do the job. In practice, this seems to be difficult to achieve, partly because there is little consensus among sales managers as to the type of person who would be most suitable for a selling job, and partly because the factors which are considered important are often difficult to measure. As noted in Chapter 1, one survey of sales managers showed that many of them mentioned communication skills, personality and determination as being characteristics they would look for in a recruit; unfortunately, these are rather difficult to define, and are often difficult to measure.

Mayer and Greenberg (1964) identified two qualities essential to selling: empathy and ego drive. Empathy is the ability to understand the customer's feelings, problems and needs; in effect, to be able to imagine oneself in the customer's shoes. Ego drive is the personal need on the part of the salesperson to make the sale. It is not necessarily linked to financial reward, rather it is about wanting to win. The problem with these two factors is that they are necessary but not sufficient. Many other factors may prevent a salesperson from selling, and equally some factors may enable a salesperson to sell successfully even when ego drive or empathy are weak.

TABLE 6.4 Checklist for a job description

Factors to be included	Description and examples
Sales tasks	The tasks involved in actually selling. For example, generate leads, make sales calls, sell products, negotiate specifications and delivery schedules, close sales, complete documentation.
Service tasks	The tasks involved in providing a service to the customers. For example, merchandising, train retailers' staff, follow up on deliveries, progress-chasing, complaint handling.
Management tasks	Those tasks described in Chapter 3. For example, journey planning, collecting and submitting market intelligence, collecting sales statistics, strategic planning and territory management.
Other tasks	The peripheral issues that surround selling. For example, attending sales meetings, representing the company, manning exhibition stands, maintaining the company property (sales kits, car, etc.), assist as necessary in training new recruits.
Authority	The limits of what the salesperson is allowed to commit the company to. For example, approving credit for customers, negotiating prices and other issues, and committing the company to expenditure on travel or hotel expenses. The job description should contain guidance on the upper limits of the salesperson's authority in these matters, although this may be contained in a staff handbook.
Performance measurement	The methods by which the salesperson's effectiveness in the job will be measured. For example, salespeople may be measured against achievement of sales targets, against profitability targets, against customer satisfaction targets, or against activity levels.

A more recent attempt to determine the qualities which lead to effective sales-person performance was a study by Krishnan *et al.* (2002) which found that self-efficacy (defined as the confidence an individual has in his or her ability to perform well in a specific task domain) has both direct and indirect effects of sales performance. Competitiveness, mediated by effort, also has a strong effect on outcomes.

Person specifications are likely to include the following factors:

1 Physical attributes such as state of health, physical disabilities, speech, appearance and, for some selling jobs, physical strength.

2 Attainments such as selling experience, educational qualifications, managerial experience and notable selling successes.

3 Aptitudes and qualities such as communication skills, self-motivation, intelligence and sense of humour.

4 Disposition in terms of optimism, maturity, sense of responsibility and so forth.

5 Interests and hobbies which may be of use in the job, or which may provide a suitable stress-relieving outlet. For example, it would be useful to employ amateur musicians to sell musical instruments.

6 Personal circumstances such as marital status, children, financial status, etc. In many countries there are legal problems in discriminating on the basis of marital status, since this can be construed as unfair and is, in most cases, irrelevant anyway. For salespeople, a stable home background is undoubtedly an asset, and managers often take account of spouses or partners when designing motivational exercises such as prizes or competitions.

Usually recruiters will specify which attributes of candidates are essential, which are desirable, and which are positively undesirable. Those who are lacking in the essential characteristics will not be shortlisted, and those who possess undesirable characteristics will also be filtered out. This leaves the recruiter in a position to choose between those who have desirable, but not essential, characteristics (see Figure 6.1).

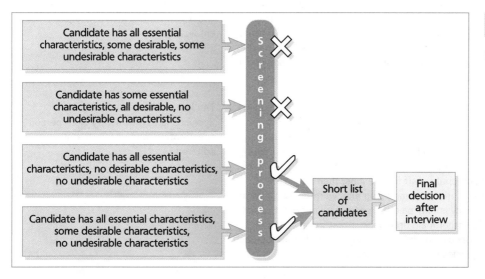

FIGURE 6.1

Filtering candidates

In Figure 6.1, the first candidate will be rejected for having some undesirable characteristics. The second candidate will be rejected for lacking some essential characteristics. The other two candidates will be shortlisted and interviewed, then a choice will be made between the two of them.

All recruitment methods seek to discriminate between applicants, but such discrimination must be fair, and must be seen to be fair. Broadly, equal opportunities legislation exists to ensure that job applicants are selected on the basis of their abilities, experience and qualifications and on no other factors. It is illegal in the UK to discriminate on the basis of gender, race or ethnic background; in the USA it is also illegal to discriminate on the basis of age. There are exceptions to these general rules. For example, it is legal to discriminate in favour of black people if the intention is to redress an imbalance in the proportion of black people employed by the firm. It may also be legal if the nature of the job is such that it requires people from a particular ethnic background, although this usually only applies to such jobs as waiters in Chinese restaurants. There is, of course, no reason why an employer should not require fluency in a particular language (for example Welsh or Gujurati) if this is essential to the job, but not if it is a ruse to discriminate against people of a different ethnic background.

◼ Sources of recruitment

Recruits can be obtained from the sources shown in Table 6.5.

TABLE 6.5 Sources of recruitment

Source	Explanation	Key to success in recruiting
Internal	The company's existing staff may be interested in a move to sales. This has the advantage that they will already be familiar with the firm's procedures, personnel, and policies. Internal candidates from other departments often bring useful skills in terms of their networking with other departments, and their knowledge of other aspects of the company's activities.	The key to success when recruiting internally is to ensure that the recruit really wants to transfer to sales, and understands clearly what the job entails.
Agencies	Recruitment agencies act as central clearing points for sales jobs. Applicants are pre-screened for suitability for sales positions, and are directed towards suitable vacancies. Although it is in the long-term interests of agencies to supply the most appropriate staff for the jobs, there is a clear temptation to send along any 'warm body' since the agency is only paid if a successful applicant is sent. The other main drawback is that many of the strongest candidates for sales jobs do not approach agencies in the first place.	The key to success when using agencies is to give a very clear person specification, and ensure that it is adhered to.

Educational establishments	Recruiting direct from universities or colleges is quite common for blue-chip companies. Unfortunately, many students have a low opinion of selling jobs (Donaldson and Thomson 1991), but this is to some extent moderated by the fact that many business students undertake work placements as part of their degree studies and will have some experience of sales. Often such recruits see selling as a stepping-stone to a marketing career, which may mean that they leave selling quite quickly.	The key to success is to offer good prospects for promotion.
Competitors	Recruiting from the ranks of the competition's sales force is an obvious way of acquiring salespeople who know the market and have experience of the product category. The drawbacks are that they may have a negative view of the firm's products (having spent considerable time making unfavourable comparisons between the firm's products and those of their former employer), and also they may not remain loyal to the new firm either. They may also have been trained in ways which are inappropriate or which the new firm might regard as unethical.	Applicants need to be carefully screened and trained.
Head hunters	Head hunters will, for a fee, search out suitable potential recruits who are not currently looking for a job. Normally, head hunting is only used for locating very senior people, since it is an expensive exercise both in terms of paying the head hunters and in terms of paying the potential recruits, who usually regard themselves as being in a strong bargaining position for higher remuneration packages.	Head hunters need to be briefed carefully, and also supplied with a list of possible targets for recruitment.
Government agencies	Jobcentres, in the UK, can be a useful source of recruits provided the company is operating on a warm-body philosophy of recruitment. Most government recruiting agencies deal with the unemployed; good salespeople tend not to be unemployed, since there is a chronic shortage of good salespeople.	Here, the sales manager needs to sell the applicant on the idea of accepting a sales job. Many applicants from Jobcentres will have no experience of sales, and may well believe that they are unable to sell.
Armed forces	Typically, career military people serve for a fixed term and retire in their middle to late forties. This means that they need new work, and the Army, Navy and Air Force have an internal careers service for re-locating these individuals into new jobs. Ex-military people often make good salespeople since they are trained to act on their own initiative, and to be self-disciplined.	The key to success here is good training programmes. Military personnel are used to the idea of very professional training.

TABLE 6.5 *(cont.)*

Source	Explanation	Key to success in recruiting
Professional associations	Organizations such as the Chartered Institute of Marketing have a practitioner's journal or news magazine which carries job advertisements. These can be very useful for targeting the right type of recruit.	The job must be very clearly described in the advertisement. Hype should be avoided.

Usually sales jobs are advertised in the press; research shows that 87 per cent of sales managers use national press, 69 per cent use local press, and 56 per cent use trade or professional journals (Jobber and Millar 1984). The same study showed that only 40 per cent use recruitment agencies, 8 per cent local radio, and 7 per cent recruit direct from higher education establishments. This research is now somewhat dated, and ignores the impact of the Internet. Most company websites now carry recruiting messages, so many applicants are recruited in this way.

Designing a job advertisement for the press is somewhat different from designing an advertisement promoting a product. The advertisement for a job is a sought communication, so the job seeker is likely to read most or all of the advertisements, and will respond to those that appeal the most. There is therefore less need for the advertisement to be eye catching, although it clearly helps if it is. The headline is the eye-catching part of the advertisement, so it should contain the most interesting aspect of the job. This is not necessarily the salary (see Chapter 1 for the factors which most interest salespeople about their jobs).

The more attractive the advertisement is, the more the firm will be able to pick and choose among applicants; therefore it is good practice to include all the main benefits of the job. Typically the job advertisement will contain the following:

TALKING POINT

Shopsmith Inc. is a company which manufactures woodworking equipment. Its salespeople need to be experienced woodworkers, both in order to explain the intricacies of the equipment and to have credibility with their hard-nosed, practical customers.

Shopsmith have a simple approach to sales recruitment. They recruit their customers. Obviously not all the customers would be interested in switching from carpentry to sales – but enough are. And the advantages are obvious. These are people who have direct experience of the equipment, who like the products, and who know how to use them. They are usually as well informed and skilled at carpentry as any of their prospects, and are eager to demonstrate their skill. Even the customers who do not become prospects are flattered to be asked, so nothing is lost.

- The type of person the firm is looking for.
- The main terms of employment – salary, holiday entitlement, hours of work, etc.
- A description of the firm and its products.
- Prospects for promotion.

Although it is important to make the job appear as attractive as possible in order to encourage applicants to respond, advertisers should avoid the temptation to make unrealistic assertions about the post. For example, earnings for sales jobs are usually quoted as OTE or on-target earnings. This is the amount the salesperson will earn if he or she hits the sales targets set for the territory, and it includes commission and bonuses. If it turns out that the target is unrealistic, or that the salary structure does not reflect the status of the job, the newly hired salesperson will simply look for a job elsewhere. Since recruiting, induction and training are expensive (not to mention the inevitable delay between hiring somebody and actually getting any productive work out of them), stretching the truth can prove to be an expensive waste of time.

Providing salespeople with a realistic view of what the job actually entails has a positive effect both on role clarity, which reduces stress, and on perceptions of training programmes (Barksdale *et al*. 2003). This research also found that an accurate preview of the job requirements also helped salespeople get the most from the training and induction programmes, since they knew what to expect and understood the importance of different aspects of the training.

■ Selecting applicants

Selecting the right applicant for the job is much more art than science. Although an applicant may fit the person specification, it is not unusual for errors to occur, usually through having made a mistake in the specification. Equally, it is extremely unlikely that the perfect candidate will appear. More often than not, the sales manager is faced with a choice of almost-suitable candidates, or sometimes with a choice of plainly unsuitable candidates but with no option but to hire somebody to fill a desperately needed position.

The selection tools available are shown in Table 6.6.

If the number of applicants is large, the recruiter needs to develop a shortlist. This will only include the most appropriate candidates, and has the advantage of reducing the overall time spent interviewing; it also avoids wasting the unsuitable applicants' time. The shortlist is developed by first rejecting all those candidates who lack the characteristics described as essential, then rejecting those who lack the desirable characteristics. This may result in all the candidates being rejected; if so, the manager must decide whether to re-advertise the post or to accept a compromise on the desirable characteristics and interview people who are, prima facie, not entirely suitable for the post.

Since interviews are widely used, and in fact are almost indispensable to the process since the applicant will probably have questions to ask, most sales managers need to develop interview skills. These are somewhat different from the skills needed to conduct a selling interview, since the sales manager is now in the position of being a buyer rather than a seller.

TABLE 6.6 Selection tools

Tool	Description
Application forms	If properly designed, the form gives an easy way to compare applicants, and also ensures that all the relevant information is readily accessible. The main drawback of application forms is that, like any other form, they are rigid; if the applicant has some special characteristic which is not asked for on the form it may be difficult to find out about it.
References	These are usually only of limited use for two reasons: firstly, the applicant will only supply names of people who are likely to give a positive reference, and secondly, recent lawsuits have made previous employers very reluctant to make negative statements about former employees. Since there are also legal risks in giving glowing references when these are undeserved, references are apt to be bland and relatively noncommittal, and therefore uninformative.
Interviews	Interviews should be interactive, and, ideally, should allow the candidate the chance to elaborate on what is contained within the application form and CV. Although widely used, interviews are not very reliable; it is too easy for a candidate (especially one who has sales training) to put on a good front for half an hour or so. 80 per cent of companies will interview candidates twice; in 80 per cent of cases it is the personnel manager and the sales manager who conduct the initial interview together; in 40 per cent of cases they make the decision together, in 37 per cent of cases it is the sales manager alone. In the other cases, marketing managers or other senior managers might become involved (Jobber and Millar 1984).
Physical or medical examination	This tends to be rare for selling jobs, although salespeople do need to be healthy and not suffering from depression or other psychological illness. Long periods working alone, perhaps suffering regular rejection by customers, will exacerbate depressive illnesses.
Psychometric tests	Tests of intelligence, aptitude and personality have become popular in recent years because they seem objective. In fact, they are usually very reliable at measuring what they are intended to measure; what they are not good at is predicting whether an individual will succeed at selling when in the field. The test is only as good as its ability to identify those factors important in performance (Perreault *et al.* 1977).
Role playing	Often candidates are invited to role play a selling situation. This gives the interviewer a chance to assess the candidate's performance in a selling situation; obviously this can only work with experienced salespeople.
Assessment centres	Occasionally a group of candidates will be taken to a hotel or conference centre for a day and put through a series of games, role plays and tests to determine their suitability. The advantage of the method is that it is very difficult for an applicant to maintain a false front for the whole day. The main drawback of the method is that it is expensive, but the cost is still a great deal less than that of hiring the wrong person. The technique is particularly valuable for detecting management potential.
CVs	Asking salespeople to supply a curriculum vitae (or résumé, in the US) allows the candidate the opportunity to sell themselves in a less structured way than would be the case on an application form. Salespeople will also occasionally send unsolicited CVs, which can be a good source of recruits as the candidate may well be particularly interested in working for the firm. On the other hand, there is a danger that the sender of an unsolicited CV is adopting a scattergun approach and sending out CVs to as many firms as possible. Such a candidate is unlikely to be committed to the firm, and may be having trouble finding work elsewhere.

The following is a checklist for interviewing:

1 The interviews should be conducted in a comfortable room where there will not be any interruptions.
2 There should be no physical barriers such as desks between the candidates and the interview panel. Physical barriers tend to result in a more formal, even adversarial, style to the interview which encourages role playing rather than honesty.
3 Candidates should be encouraged to talk about themselves – open questions should be asked, and every opportunity for expansion on the answers should be given.
4 The interview should open with some easily answered questions which will put the candidate at ease.
5 Interviewers should appear relaxed, and should encourage the candidate to relax also.
6 Interest in the candidates' responses will encourage further responses.
7 Probing questions are useful; asking, 'Why do you say that?' or, 'Can you explain some more about that point?' will elicit more information than a simple, 'Why?'
8 At the end, it is always useful to summarize the candidate's responses. This will sometimes elicit further information, and at the very least confirms that the candidate's responses have been fully understood by the interview panel.
9 The interview should not be allowed to degenerate into a cosy chat; it should remain a purposeful exercise.
10 Candidates should be told exactly what the job entails; there should be no unpleasant surprises when the successful candidate starts work.
11 If possible, references should be checked by telephone. This allows the referees to be more honest than they might be if they had to commit themselves in writing.
12 It is dangerous to rely on the candidate's unsupported word about their selling ability.
13 Body language can be a guide to the candidate's true feelings. Looking down and to the left often denotes lying, for example.
14 If possible, the candidate should be given a guided tour of the firm's offices and factories. This may provoke further questions on the part of the candidate, or at the very least give the candidate a clearer picture of the firm and its business.

Usually candidates will be offered the chance to ask questions of their own; this can also be a source of insight into the candidate's personality. Interviewers need to control the process, allowing sufficient time for the candidates to give of their best, but at the same time ensuring that the process does not run on indefinitely. It would not be fair on the other candidates to keep them waiting too long.

Finally, even if the candidate is one whom the firm would be particularly keen to recruit, it is unwise to stretch the truth about the job. There is really no point in recruiting someone who will simply leave when he or she finds out that the job is not what was expected.

▊ Getting a job in sales

Potential recruits into the selling profession need to be aware of what sales managers are looking for in a new recruit. Chapter 1 contains a list of characteristics that sales managers typically look for in a new recruit, and this should be considered carefully by any potential applicant for a sales job. Almost certainly at some point in the interview the sales manager will ask what the candidate believes are the characteristics of a good salesperson; the expected answer is that a good salesperson knows how to listen carefully.

Candidates should have some questions of their own ready; a useful phrase is, 'Will I have the opportunity to . . .' since this denotes keenness. For example, asking, 'Will I have the opportunity for further training?' sounds a great deal more committed than asking, 'What is the training like here?'

Since the job is about selling and negotiation, it is important that the applicant is prepared to demonstrate selling ability throughout the interview process: the ability to ask cogent questions, the ability to listen to what the interviewers are saying and respond in ways that lead to getting the job, and the ability to provide a solution to the firm's recruitment problem. Candidates should always remember that the firm is actually looking for somebody to employ – firms with no employees have no business, and in particular firms with no salespeople have no sales.

SUMMARY

The first step in building an effective sales force is to recruit the right people for the job. This is less easy than it sounds; factors other than ability dictate success in selling, and while this is true of other jobs as well, it is nowhere more true than in selling, where the employees are often working away from their colleagues and managers for long periods.

The key points from this chapter are as follows:

- It is hard to know in advance who will sell and who will not, although it is possible to know who has the ability to sell and who has not.

- Factors such as training and motivation probably have more effect on sales success than innate ability.

- Job analysis may result in reallocation of duties and responsibilities, and greater specialization, rather than in further recruitment.

- Interviews should be interactive, allowing the candidates to give of their best.

- Candidates should be told the bad aspects of the job as well as the good; this saves time and trouble in the long run.

REVIEW QUESTIONS

1 If it is difficult to know in advance who will sell and who will not, what is the point of drawing up a person specification?

2 What would be the advantages of advertising in the national press rather than in a professional journal or trade magazine?

3 Why might it be better to lose a good candidate by telling the truth about the job rather than gain a good recruit by covering up bad aspects of the job?

4 When should recruitment be avoided?

5 Given the relatively high levels of unemployment in Europe, why do companies need to make sales jobs attractive?

REFERENCES

Barksdale, H. C., Bellenger, D. N., Boles, J. S., and Brashear, T. G. (2003) 'The impact of realistic job previews and perceptions of training on sales force performance and continuance commitment: A longitudinal test', *Journal of Personal Selling and Sales Management* 23 (Spring): 125–38.

Donaldson, B. and Thomson, C. (1991) 'Recruiting graduates into sales', in *Preparing Marketing for the New Millennium*, Proceedings of the 1991 Marketing in Education Group, Cardiff: 340–53.

Jobber, D. and Millar, S. (1984) 'The use of psychological tests in the selection of Salesmen: A UK survey', *Journal of Sales Management* 1: 1.

Krishan, B. C., Netemeyer, R. G. and Boles, J. S. (2002) 'Self-efficacy, competitiveness and effort as antecedents of salesperson performance', *Journal of Personal Selling and Sales Management* 22 (4/Fall): 285–95.

Mayer, M. and Greenberg, G. (1964) 'What makes a good salesman?' *Harvard Business Review* 42 (Jul.–Aug.).

Perreault, W. D., French, W. A. and Harris, C. E. (1977) 'Use of multidiscriminate analysis to improve the salesman selection process', *Journal of Business* (Jan.): 50–62.

Rackham, N. (1995) *Spin Selling*, Aldershot: Gower.

Stevens, C. D. and Mackintosh, G. (2003) 'Personality and attractiveness of activities within sales jobs', *Journal of Personal Selling and Sales Management* 23(1/Winter 2002–3): 23–37.

AB LORENTZEN & WETTRE

The paper industry is large and diverse. The need for quality control is high because of the sheer variety of types of paper – and this is where AB Lorentzen & Wettre come in. This Swedish company, a subsidiary of industrial-door giant Cardo AB, provides quality-control and product-testing equipment for the paper industry. The products themselves are highly technical, and test moisture levels, permeability and other qualities of the paper itself. The company also produces special cutting equipment for taking samples, and provides a wide range of services to companies, including training in the testing of paper, and contract testing services for smaller companies who cannot afford to buy the equipment outright.

Overall, this means that L&W has a complex proposition for salespeople to handle. Added to this, the company wanted to expand into the UK, which compounded the recruitment problem. Recruiting in a foreign country is not a job for amateurs – different laws on recruitment, different customs and procedures, and different salary expectations create a minefield for the incoming firm.

L&W went to recruitment specialists Pinnacle Recruitment. Pinnacle specializes in both salespeople and engineering people, so was in the perfect position to find the necessary specialists. Pinnacle provides both temporary and permanent staff, even providing interim managers, and uses a sophisticated database of potential applicants to source candidates. The database automatically notifies the firm when candidates' details have been on the list for a while so that Pinnacle can check whether the candidate is still available and ensure that the details are correct before sending them out to the potential employer.

Rolf Turvall, vice-president in charge of personnel, agreed with Pinnacle that it would provide a combined search and advertising campaign aimed at finding a specialist sales manager and a service manager to deal with setting up the UK sales operation, which is based in Leicester. 'Pinnacle also provided us with full human resource support to enable us to recruit both candidates,' Turvall said later.

Graham Robson was appointed as sales and marketing director, and Colin Thompson was appointed as service manager. Both men are listed on Applegate's Top People in British Industry list.

Turvall has been delighted with the service he received from Pinnacle. The recruiters provided L&W with the same high level of service and comprehensive support that L&W provides for its own customers. The UK operation is small, but growing rapidly, thanks in no small measure to the professionalism of the recruitment agency and, of course, the people it found for the jobs.

Case-study questions

1 Why should a major company such as L&W need to employ an outside agency for its recruitment?

2 As the company expands in the UK, it will presumably need more salespeople. What are the pros and cons of using Pinnacle again?

3 How might the European Union affect the problems of cross-border recruitment?

4 What other methods of recruitment might L&W have tried?

5 How can a foreign firm minimize the risks of recruitment?

7

TRAINING

Learning objectives

After reading this chapter, you should be able to:

- Explain the main issues in designing a training course for salespeople.

- Describe ways in which people learn.

- Analyse a training programme and decide on suitable methods for its delivery.

- Evaluate training programmes.

- Describe ways of evaluating trainees.

- Design self-assessment methods for sales trainees.

Introduction

Salespeople spend most of their time working away from their colleagues and managers, and therefore away from sources of advice. An office-based worker can check information with a colleague, but a salesperson needs to have all the facts at his or her fingertips. Also, salespeople need to react quickly when faced with problems; if a customer has a particular problem, or raises a particular objection, the salesperson needs to respond to it on the spot. For these reasons, considerable time and effort is spent on training salespeople.

No-one has had more effect on the world's eating habits than W. K. Kellogg. He left school at 14 to work as a salesman for his father, a broom manufacturer. This early business training became useful four years later, when his older brother invited him to work at the Battle Creek Sanatarium, which he owned and operated. Dr John H. Kellogg was an expert in nutrition, and between them the brothers invented, and subsequently marketed, corn flakes. Will K. Kellogg set up a company to exploit the invention, using extensive advertising campaigns and a vigorous sales effort to spread the word about the nutritious and convenient breakfast food.

Nowadays, Kellogg's Corn Flakes, and many other breakfast cereals bearing the Kellogg name, are sold worldwide. It would seem that the Kellogg brothers did know something about nutrition, since Will Kellogg died at the age of 91. His vast fortune was left to the W. K. Kellogg foundation, a philanthropic institution based in Battle Creek, Michigan – the original location of the Sanatarium where the corn flakes were invented.

Ultimately, the success of corn flakes rested not only on the product itself (which might well have only ever been used as invalid food at the Battle Creek Sanatarium), but on Kellogg's salesmanship. His doggedness and understanding of how to sell to people persuaded hundreds of millions of people to change their breakfast habits – a remarkable achievement.

▌ Benefits of training

Offering a good training scheme for the sales force benefits the firm in several ways, as shown in Table 7.1.

The benefits to the salespeople themselves are equally valuable; better training means more successes, fewer rejections and more commission.

Training programmes can be long or short, depending on the product and the market. Table 7.2 illustrates the influences on this.

The role the salesperson is required to take on will also affect the length of training; missionary salespeople will take longer to train than order takers, and new-business salespeople will take longer than telephone canvassers. Most companies would regard training as an ongoing process, because markets are changing rapidly in most industries, and therefore salespeople will need continuous updating on techniques and products. New product training is probably the most common area of ongoing training, but even experienced salespeople need to hone their skills constantly to maintain a high level of expertise.

Training should be an ongoing process throughout the salesperson's career. This is especially true in the 21st century, when so much is changing; salespeople need to learn to adapt their approaches to changing circumstances, and will need to be trained in new techniques, new technology and new procedures for dealing with changing buyers. Sales-force perceptions of an organization's readiness to change will affect their attitude towards training and retraining (Chonko *et al.* 2002).

TABLE 7.1 Benefits of training

Benefit	Explanation
Improved sales-force performance	This is the most obvious benefit. Well-trained salespeople are likely to work more efficiently, close more sales and sell higher order values. Customer satisfaction is also likely to be higher; the salesperson *is* the company in effect, and customers obviously prefer to feel that they are dealing with a company which is professional and knowledgeable. There will also be fewer errors in orders and paperwork, which will also save resources.
Reduced costs	If the sales force is operating more efficiently, costs will fall; better closing rates means fewer call backs, fewer complaints from customers means less time spent troubleshooting.
Reduced staff turnover	Staff who are confident and who appreciate the support the company gives them are much less likely to leave for other jobs. This in turn reduces recruitment costs and, in the long run, also reduces training costs.
Improved motivation	Good training helps salespeople to stay motivated.
Reduced management input	Appropriately trained salespeople are much more capable of managing their own activities than are poorly trained people. This means that management can spend less time on supervision and problem solving with the sales force.

TABLE 7.2 Factors relating to length of training of sales staff

Factors indicating long training	Factors indicating short training
Complex, technical products: Salespeople need good product knowledge. At the extreme, for example in the defence industry, the products become so complex that teams of technical salespeople need to be brought in to back up the lead salesperson.	*Simple products*: If the product is simple (for example nails or screws), the customer probably understands it already anyway, and the salesperson only needs to know the added-value properties (e.g. special alloys used or specialist threads) in order to sell the product.
Industrial markets with professional buyers: The techniques used when dealing with professionals are likely to be more complex because professionals are likely to be more demanding and expect deeper product knowledge.	*Household, consumer markets*: Salespeople are usually only employed in these areas if the product is less well known or is of high value. Consumers are less likely to have an existing understanding of the products, and are therefore not in a position to ask awkward questions.
High order values (judged from the customer's viewpoint): Major account selling requires a higher order of skill (see Chapter 5) because the customer will need more persuasion of the value of the purchase.	*Low order values*: In small-account selling, the customer commitment is less, so concern about value for money is lower, and the value–cost relationship is more obvious. This, in turn, makes the salesperson's job correspondingly easier.

TABLE 7.2 *(cont.)*

Factors indicating long training	Factors indicating short training
High recruitment costs: If recruitment is difficult or expensive, training will help in retaining staff. Good training will also help in making the best of the staff already in post.	*Low recruitment costs*: If recruitment is cheap and easy, inefficient or ineffective staff can simply be fired and replaced.
Inexperienced recruits – for example, recruited direct from university: The less experience a salesperson already has, the greater the length of time needed to develop skills and knowledge.	*Experienced recruits from the same industry*: Although experienced recruits will need some training in company policies and in the differences between the products, they should already have considerable knowledge gained from their competitor analysis in their former role.

Typically, training falls into two categories: classroom training, in which the recruits are taught about the company and the products and may be given some grounding in sales techniques, and field training, which is an ongoing training programme carried out in front of real customers in the field. Field training is often the province of the sales managers, but classroom training can be carried out by other company personnel; in some cases, particularly in larger firms, there will be specialists who do nothing else but train salespeople. In some cases, firms are now looking to recruit graduates who have already received some form of sales training during their university careers (Mantel *et al.* 2002).

▊ Theories of training

The following are the principles underpinning a good training programme (Johnson *et al.* 1994):

1 A clear statement of what the training aims to do, how the individual can apply it to the job, and what benefits can be expected.
2 Clarity of presentation.
3 Planned repetition; this gives the trainee time to absorb what is being taught, and repetition helps to clarify the material and clear up misunderstandings.
4 Systematic review and follow-up to assess the effectiveness of the learning process.
5 Orderly development of the material. The material is presented in a coherent manner, rather than in the somewhat haphazard way that learning by experience offers.
6 Training should proceed at a suitable pace, allowing slow learners to keep up and faster learners to remain involved and interested.
7 The trainee should be engaged in the process as a participant rather than a passive receiver of knowledge.

People tend to learn best by performing the task, so most sales training programmes involve substantial field training, either by sending out *rookies* (trainees) with experienced salespeople, or by the in-at-the-deep-end approach of sending rookies out on their own fairly early in their careers. The latter method is indicated if there are plenty of possible customers for the product; the view is that a few mistakes (lost sales) won't matter. In industrial selling, though, it is often the case that there are fewer possible customers and therefore the loss of even one or two could be serious. In these circumstances it would be better to give rookies a long period of working alongside more experienced salespeople. The intention behind any training process is to enable the trainees to learn by other people's experience rather than by making their own mistakes; this means that shadowing an experienced salesperson will often be the most effective way of training someone in the field.

Trainees move through four basic stages in their skills development. At first, the trainee is *unconsciously unable*; although the individual does not possess the necessary skills, he or she is not concerned about this, and is unaware that this lack of skill is a problem. In the same way as a five-year-old child is unconcerned about being unable to drive a car, a rookie salesperson is unconcerned about being unable to ascertain a customer's needs.

The second stage, which is very quickly reached, is to be *consciously unable*. At this stage, the salesperson is aware of lacking the necessary skills for the job, and at this point becomes interested in being trained. This stage often occurs for experienced salespeople also; a failure to sell in a particular situation may make the individual aware of a need for further training in handling that type of customer.

The third stage is, or should be, reached immediately after the training programme. The trainee becomes *consciously able*, in other words has the skills and is aware of having them; this is the point at which trainees become most voluble about their skills, perhaps talking to friends and family about their new-found abilities.

The final stage is reached after some time in the field. The trainee, now a fully fledged salesperson, becomes *unconsciously able*, in other words uses the skills automatically, without conscious thought. For some people at this skill level, it seems incredible that other people do not have the same skills.

Since selling is essentially a skill, *practice* is a major element in the learning process. This is true of most learning; it is well known that children who have piano lessons but do not practise do not learn as well as do children who practise but do not have lessons. Some firms, notably IBM, carry out most of their training by practice, requiring their trainee salespeople to work in different departments of the

---

TALKING POINT

A junior salesman at IBM once made a major mistake which cost the company over £10 000. The young man decided that it would be better to resign than to wait for the company to fire him, so he went to his sales manager with his resignation already written out.

'What do you mean, resign?' the boss said. 'You're not going anywhere! It just cost us £10 000 to train you!'

company for a time in order to learn the work ethos and procedures for the whole company. This method results in a sales force which is well versed in all aspects of the company's activities, as well as providing the rookies with an initial network of contacts in different departments.

▮ Training programme

Salespeople will need to know about the following areas:

- The company's policies, objectives and overall business ethos.
- The company's products, and also competitors' products.
- Selling techniques for the industry concerned.
- Organizational issues such as paperwork and company procedures.
- For some industries, such as financial services or pharmaceuticals, legal or ethical issues.

The contents may vary according to whether the trainees are existing staff or new recruits. Because training is about taking people from their existing knowledge base to a different knowledge base, the individual's existing knowledge and skills will need to be taken into account when designing the training courses. A one size fits all approach is probably not the best use of the trainee's time or the firm's resources. For example, a recruit coming from a competing firm's sales force will probably already have considerable industry and product knowledge, and really only needs to be given a thorough training in company procedures and the company's business ethos. In practice, most recruits are likely to have some skills which can be recycled.

Research shows that UK companies vary their training programmes according to the trainees' existing skills level (Manolis 1985). This is shown in Table 7.3.

TABLE 7.3 Contents of training programmes

New-recruits training programme	Percentage of firms which include topic	Existing-staff training programme	Percentage of firms which include topic
Product knowledge	96%	Selling skills	76%
Selling skills	69%	New product information	57%
Sales administration	63%	Sales administration	54%
Company information	60%	Market/customer information	46%
Customer knowledge	47%	Company policy	23%
Market knowledge	44%		

Unless the firm is a large one, it may be difficult in practice to provide entirely tailor-made course for individuals, due to the economies of scale inherent in providing training for larger numbers. This is particularly true of classroom-type training. Field training, on the other hand, tends to take place on a one-to-one basis and is by its nature geared to the individual.

For new recruits, particularly those new to the industry, product knowledge is likely to be a crucial area. Salespeople must know and understand the products they sell in considerable depth – some firms even arrange for salespeople to have a period in the production department in order to have hands-on experience of making the product. In other cases, firms hire graduates with engineering degrees so that they already have a strong knowledge of the technicalities of the products they will be selling. Obviously product knowledge needs to be geared towards customer need – an overemphasis on technical jargon, or an emphasis on the wrong features, will not help sales. There is evidence that salespeople themselves regard product knowledge as the most important element in a sales training programme (Wilson *et al.* 2002).

There is frequently an overemphasis on selling techniques in many training programmes. Partly this is the fault of salespeople themselves. A natural desire to find a magic formula for closing sales quickly and easily can lead salespeople to demand new techniques, and many sales trainers and speakers promote the idea that magic techniques exist. In fact, such surefire closing techniques are unlikely to work because all customers are different and require different approaches. This is not to say that salespeople should not practise techniques, both in role plays in the classroom and in real situations with real customers.

Customer knowledge, and an understanding of what makes people buy, are clearly at the heart of any salesperson's success. Perhaps surprisingly, many firms leave the buyer out of their sales training (Puri 1993). Buzzotta *et al.* (1982) developed a ten-part approach to sales training, as shown in Table 7.4.

This framework provides a logical structure for the training process, and places much of the initiative on the trainees themselves. This encourages ownership of the learning, a key element in motivating people to learn.

The training given to rookies will usually need to include an element dedicated to unlearning some of the popular myths about selling. These are shown in Table 7.5.

TABLE 7.4 Ten stages of training

Stage	Explanation
Set sales-behaviour training goals	The aims of the training need to be made clear in terms of the expected behavioural changes of the trainees. These aims will vary according to the existing experience of the trainees and will depend on career aims, expected rewards and aspirations (Cron 1984).
Provide cognitive maps	A cognitive map is an organized, cohesive, meaningful description of the behavioural terrain through which salespeople must travel and in which they must exercise their newly sharpened skills (Buzzotta *et al.* 1982). Buzzotta *et al.* recommended four maps: the sales behaviour, the buyer behaviour, Maslow's hierarchy of need, and a communication model.

TABLE 7.4 *(cont.)*

Stage	Explanation
Develop sizing-up skills	These enable salespeople to analyse their own behaviour, their customers' behaviour, and the relationship between the two. The analysis of the interaction between the salesperson and the buyer is basic to understanding the selling process.
Translate sizing-up skills into an action plan	Understanding the interplay between buyer and seller enables the salesperson to refine his or her skills. In particular, this will involve questioning, probing, developing and obtaining commitment.
Practice these improved techniques	Most sales training courses include role-playing exercises in which the new skills can be practised. Obviously the classroom situation differs somewhat from real life, but role-play is powerful in developing unconscious ability.
Provide feedback on the salesperson's behaviour	Feedback is essential to the learning process. Salespeople need to know what they have done wrong, but more importantly they need to be told when they have done the right thing. Each salesperson may also need an in-depth analysis of specific areas of strength or weakness, such as opening, obtaining commitment or raising the value of the sale.
Set individual goals	The salesperson needs a set of goals to take out into the field at the end of the training period. These are learning goals, rather than sales goals.
Draw up a detailed, step-by-step guide to achieving the goals	Trainees need a 'road map' to enable them to achieve the goals. Knowing which stages to pass through on the way to success is extremely useful, since it enables trainees to stay on course.
Review results and modify plans if necessary	Deviations from the training road map should be corrected as soon as they are detected. Note that the deviation should be corrected from the new position. For example, if a trainee has failed to reach a given sub-goal of the programme by a specific date, catching up is unlikely to be possible. He or she needs to reschedule the programme to take account of the missed date.
Research the results	A post-mortem examination of the outcomes of the training programme should be undertaken. Were the results as expected? Were the goals the right ones, and were they achieved? What new goals might be appropriate?

Sometimes these myths can be very difficult to dislodge. Salespeople who believe, for example, that selling is about trickery and conning people into buying can cause a great deal of damage to a firm's reputation before they can be stopped; those who believe that the route to success is through fast talking can also cause problems for themselves and others. Equally, salespeople need some training in overcoming these myths when they are believed by customers.

In fairness, most professions look completely different from the inside compared with how they look from the outside. Selling is no exception.

TABLE 7.5 Popular myths about selling

Myth	Description
Salespeople are born not made	As with any other field of endeavour, it is true that some people are better suited to selling than others. Most people can be trained to sell; conversely, virtually nobody can sell from birth. The myth is widely held, perhaps because a well-trained salesperson becomes unconsciously able, and therefore makes the process look natural. The same is true of champion athletes, and yet it is patently obvious that this is the result of long and strenuous training.
Salespeople are good talkers	In fact, the reverse is the case. Successful salespeople are good listeners, able to understand and respond to a customer's needs; salespeople who do all the talking merely irritate, or bore, the customers.
Selling is about tricks and techniques	Although some techniques are appropriate, they rarely work consistently. Customers are individuals, with individual needs (they are a lot like people in that respect) and therefore a tailored approach is needed, rather than a prepared script.
Good salespeople can sell anything	Successful salespeople are those who believe in the product they are selling. If the salesperson believes the product to be inferior, he or she will not be credible to a customer.
Good salespeople could sell sand to the Arabs	A good salesperson would not even try to do this. The customer would not need the product (unless, of course, it was a specific grade of sand for some specific purpose).
People do not want to buy	Organizations and individuals need products in order to survive and prosper. Often they need help in making choices, and this is the role of the salesperson.

Training methods

There are several options for training, each with its advantages and disadvantages. Trainers should therefore try to determine which is the appropriate method for the skill or knowledge which is to be imparted. In general, people learn better when they are actively involved in the process rather than passively sitting in a classroom. Table 7.6 shows the most commonly used methods of training, with their advantages and disadvantages.

Ultimately, the training method must match up with what has to be learned. Table 7.7 gives some guidelines on which method would be best suited for teaching each aspect of selling; it should be noted that this guide is not intended to be prescriptive. Much also depends on the learning styles of the trainees, and the available training skills within the firm.

TABLE 7.6 Advantages and disadvantages of training methods

Method	Advantages	Disadvantages
Classroom lecture	Lectures are a low-cost method of imparting factual information to large groups. They work best for teaching facts about the company history, company procedures and product knowledge, but can also provide a framework for trainees. Trainees are able subsequently to fill in the details, studying by other methods.	Lectures do not engage the trainees, most of whom have trouble remembering the content. In common with other mass teaching approaches, lectures also tend to be rigid and do not adapt to unusual situations or the individual needs of trainees.
Role playing	These exercises give the trainees the opportunity to test skills and practise such things as selling technique. Role-playing can be very useful in identifying the more common weaknesses in selling techniques. It is extremely effective if the session is video recorded so that trainees can observe themselves in action.	Role plays are artificial, and therefore demand a degree of acting ability on the part of the trainees. Sometimes the person playing the role of the buyer might be deliberately obstructive in a way that a real buyer would not be; situations are thus often not realistic.
Discussion groups	As a way of sharing experience, discussion groups are difficult to beat. They are therefore very useful in training experienced salespeople, and in allowing rookies to learn from experienced salespeople.	The exercise can degenerate into swapping anecdotes. Leadership of the discussion group, and in particular laying down appropriate terms of reference, is a difficult but essential process if the exercise is to work.
Field visits	The sales manager, or other experienced salesperson, accompanies the trainee on calls. The main advantage is that the training is geared exactly to the trainee's needs.	The disadvantage of field visits is that they cost a great deal in terms of the sales manager's time. Also, the sales manager may not be a skilled trainer, and the experience may be intimidating or demoralizing for the trainee.
Training films and videos	Some very good films are available, showing common mistakes as well as good practice. The advantage is that the information is conveyed in a memorable and engaging way. Films are best used as a supplement to lectures or written materials.	The main disadvantage is that the films are passive; trainees can easily drift off and lose concentration. Also, some training films are poorly made or only apply to a specific industry.
Programmed learning	Packages of material are provided for the trainees, to be studied at their own pace. The cheapness and flexibility of the medium are its main advantages.	Trainees may simply shelve the material, unless some way of assessing their knowledge of the material is available. Programmed learning is also poor for teaching skills.

TABLE 7.7 Training objectives and methods	
What is to be learned	**Method by which it could be taught**
Product knowledge	Lectures, demonstrations in the factory, hands-on experience of either making or using the products
Selling skills	Role plays, field visits, film/video
Sales administration	Lectures, programmed learning, field/office visits, working alongside administrators
Company information	Lectures, programmed learning, factory/office visits
Customer knowledge	Lectures, programmed learning, field visits, film/video
Market knowledge	Lectures, programmed learning, field visits

Since selling is a skill, training only works if the knowledge and skills gained are put into practice. A five-stage formula for field training has been suggested (Lidstone 1986):

1 Tell the trainees what to do.
2 Show them how to do it.
3 Make them practise what they have been told and shown.
4 Assess the outcome of what they do and show them how to correct errors.
5 Make them keep on practising.

The old adage that practice makes perfect is never more true than in selling.

■ Delivery of the training course

The question of who should deliver the course and where it should be delivered is one which depends largely on the resources available to the company. Ideally, specialist trainers should be used, and a dedicated training centre should be made available; in practice, for most firms, these options are too expensive. Also, in firms which do follow this route, the tendency is for the field sales managers to become distanced from the training process, with a consequent loss of realism in the training (Honeycutt *et al.* 1994).

On the other hand, good salespeople (or good sales managers) do not necessarily make the best teachers; they have often become unconsciously able (see earlier) and have difficulty in remembering what it was like to be consciously unable.

Table 7.8 shows the location and trainer options. In most cases, firms are likely to use a combination of approaches. An initial training course provided by a specialist trainer, either in-house or at an external location, followed by field training under a sales manager or experienced salesperson is probably the most common pattern. This means that sales managers themselves need to be trained in teaching methods, as well as motivational, managerial and communication skills.

Often such training courses are run by business schools or specialist training consultants. Techniques used are similar to those used to train salespeople.

TABLE 7.8 Trainers and locations

Trainer	Location	Advantages	Disadvantages
Internal specialist	Internal	Knowledge of the firm and its markets, knowledge of teaching techniques, convenience of location.	Cost is high.
External specialist	Internal	Convenient location. Only paid for when needed, so usually cheaper.	May not have specialist knowledge of the firm and its markets.
External specialist	External	Cost is relatively low, considering the specialist knowledge which is being made available.	Lack of fit to company's needs. Sometimes experienced salespeople feel suspicious or dismissive of outside experts. Inconvenient location.
Experienced salesperson/ sales manager	Internal	Low cost. Up-to-date with company's policies, procedures, markets, etc.	May not have sufficient ability to teach. May teach bad habits as well as good. Also means taking a successful salesperson away from selling while the training course is on.

■ Assessment

Assessing the trainees' retention of the skills and knowledge gained from the training can be carried out by examination, by written work, by observation of their activities or by self-assessment.

Examinations tend to be a poor way of assessing learning. As tests of memory they can be useful, but more often they become tests of how fast the candidates can write; also, the correlation between the ability to remember facts and the ability to apply them in practice is tenuous to say the least. Also, examinations have unfortunate associations for many people – the fear of failing engendered by school examinations produces a similar feeling when faced with other examinations. A more enjoyable way of achieving a similar result would be to hold a television-style quiz with teams of trainees competing against each other for a prize.

Written reports or coursework are less threatening to the salesperson, but are unlikely to reflect the reality of the job. They can be very useful in teaching salespeople about the markets and competitors – for example, asking trainees to produce a report on the activities of a competitor, with particular emphasis on the strengths and weaknesses of their selling approach, might be a potent way of ensuring that the trainees go off and find out about the competition, even if the finished result is not necessarily a good way of assessing their knowledge.

Observation of the trainee in action can take place in the classroom during role-play sessions, or in the field in front of customers. The advantage is that the trainee is being assessed in as real a situation as can be contrived; the disadvantage is that it takes up a great deal of managerial time.

Self-assessment is a much-neglected area of training. A self-assessment exercise allows the trainee to reflect on his or her performance, and formulate ways of improving, without the embarrassment of involving the sales manager or trainer. Figure 7.1 shows an example of a self-assessment form which a rookie, or even an experienced salesperson, might use after leaving a presentation.

Such a self-assessment form gives the salesperson automatic feedback, a checklist for the future, and a reminder; if there are any 'No' boxes ticked, this gives the salesperson a very clear idea of which areas need to be improved upon. Some sales forces would need to assess against other issues; a major-account salesperson might include areas such as networking and call backs.

Any self-assessment system must be simple for the trainee to use, must give instant feedback, and must actually assess the areas that it purports to assess. Trainees need to know what the assessment criteria are; in the case of the form in Figure 7.1, this is simple because the answers are yes-or-no types, and the activities listed are clearly understood by the trainee. It is much more difficult to design self-assessment packages which test a trainee's understanding; the usual route is to offer multiple-choice questions followed by lengthy explanations of why each answer is right or wrong. This is a specialized area of writing, usually only undertaken by professionals, and is usually only used in the context of programmed-learning courses.

For any type of assessment to work, there must be feedback, and this should be given as quickly as possible. In the case of observation of activities, the feedback is often given immediately after leaving the sales call. Most salespeople and sales managers are familiar with the concept of the kerbside conference, held sitting in the salesperson's car after leaving the client's premises. Delays in giving feedback

FIGURE 7.1

Self-assessment
form

	Yes	No
Did I shake hands with the prospect?		
Did I ice break?		
Did I ask open questions to ascertain the problem?		
Did I ask closed questions to lead towards a close?		
Did I find out all the customer's needs?		
Did I confirm the needs back to the customer before offering a solution?		
Did I offer a solution which fitted the needs?		
Did I explain the benefits of the product?		
Did I confirm that each benefit met a specific need?		
Did I confirm that the prospect understood what I was saying?		
Did I confirm that the product met the needs before I quoted a price?		
Did I negotiate on the price?		
Did I try at least three closes before leaving?		
Did I complete the paperwork in the customer's presence?		
Did I leave the door open to return at a later date?		
Did I cement the sale?		
Did I arrange another appointment?		
Did I find out who else I need to talk to about the product?		
Did I ask for referrals?		
Did I leave documentation and samples/brochures with the customer?		

will only mean that the salesperson will forget what the assessment was all about, and will concentrate on the bottom line – i.e. the grade received – rather than on the comments, which are, of course, the important part of the assessment.

Assessment is also useful in determining future training needs. The sales force can be assessed individually or collectively and conclusions drawn about weak spots in the team or in individuals. Training exists to fill the gap between what the salesperson already knows and what he or she should know; assessment can be used at both ends of the process to determine the change brought about by the training.

◼ Evaluating the training course

The costs of training are easily determined, but the benefits may not be immediately apparent. As with other marketing endeavours, the first step in evaluating the effectiveness of the activity is to set realistic, measurable and specific objectives.

Using the list of benefits of training set out in Table 7.1, it is possible to identify ways in which the company might evaluate the success, or otherwise, of the training.

1 *Improved sales performance*: It should be possible to measure increased sales, increased order values, increased customer satisfaction and so forth. These measures are a necessary part of sales-force management in any case (see Chapter 9) and therefore improvements should be readily identifiable. The trainees themselves should be able to identify which improvements are due to the training, and which are due to other factors.

2 *Reduced costs*: Again, proper monitoring of sales-force costs should enable the manager to determine whether a reduction has occurred. The difficulty this time is that the reduction may be due to other factors (seasonality, changes in the market, etc.) and this may very well cloud the issue.

3 *Reduced staff turnover*: This is easy to measure, but difficult to allocate causality to. A reduction in staff turnover might well have occurred due to improvements in motivational tools (see Chapter 8) or simply because those who were dissatisfied have left, leaving only those who are happy with the job. Possibly the trainees themselves might be able to ascribe causality to their satisfaction; in any case, those who leave should be given leaving interviews at which some of the causes of dissatisfaction might be identified (see Chapter 6).

4 *Improved motivation*: Motivation comes from many areas. Trainees might be able to ascribe a value to training in this respect, but objective measurement would be difficult.

5 *Reduced management input*: This can frequently be identified. The manager should be able to determine the degree to which salespeople need management intervention in the sales process, and be able to identify any reduction. A possible factor to be aware of is that salespeople might be reluctant to ask for help if they have just been on a course to deal with the specific problem; 'I ought to know this,' could be a factor in not asking for help when it is needed.

Knowing what has changed is not the same as setting objectives, however. Objectives imply that the manager has considered in advance what the training course should achieve, and has developed a benchmark. Performance below the benchmark level would indicate that the course has failed, performance above the benchmark would indicate that the course has succeeded. This type of objective setting is difficult in practice, since the value to the company of the outcomes might be hard to integrate. For example, the company might be of the opinion that training should improve motivation, improve sales performance across a range of measures, and should reduce management input. Improvement in motivation is difficult to quantify in financial terms, but perhaps comparison could be made against the cost of other motivational tools. The question remains, though, to what extent should an increase in motivation be traded off against a reduction in management input? Which is the more valuable, and what can realistically be expected?

For most firms, this problem is too complex and time consuming to warrant much consideration; in effect, the solution becomes more expensive than the problem, so managers will view training simplistically, as a way of improving sales performance that is easily targeted and measured.

SUMMARY

Training is an expensive part of acquiring an effective sales force, since the trainees are not engaged in any productive activity during the period of training, and indeed are absorbing resources instead. Nonetheless, there is really no way of avoiding expenditure on training. Those who view training as expensive should, perhaps, consider how much more expensive it would be to have an ignorant sales force.

The key points from this chapter are as follows:

- Training offers many more benefits than just an increase in sales.

- Training is an ongoing process.

- People learn better by doing than by listening.

- Unconsciously able people sometimes have difficulty in teaching, since they forget that other people do not already have the skills.

- A teaching programme tailored to the individual works best, but is difficult to design and expensive to deliver.

- Practice makes perfect.

- Self-assessment is cheap, effective and non-threatening for the trainees.

- Feedback should be given as quickly as possible.

- Evaluation of the effectiveness of the training can only take place if clear objectives are set.

REVIEW QUESTIONS

1 What training methods might be most appropriate for refreshing the selling skills of experienced salespeople?

2 What length of training course is indicated for a kitchen-fitting sales force? Why?

3 What length of training is indicated for a computer-software sales force? Why?

4 Who might be better trainers: those who are consciously able, or those who are unconsciously able? Why?

5 In what ways might feedback from participants help in designing future training courses?

REFERENCES

Buzzotta, V. R., Lefton, R. E. and Sherberg, M. (1982) *Effective Selling Through Psychology*, Cambridge, MA: Ballinger.

Chonko, L. B., Jones, E., Roberts, J. A. and Dubinsky, A. J. (2002) 'The role of environmental turbulence, readiness for change, and salesperson learning in the success of sales force change', *Journal of Personal Selling and Sales Management* 22 (4/Fall): 227–45.

Cron, W. L. (1984) 'Industrial salesperson development a career stages perspective', *Journal of Marketing* 48 (Fall): 41–52.

Honeycutt, E. D. Jr., Ford, J. B. and Tanner, J. F. (1994): 'Who trains salespeople? The role of sales trainers and sales managers', *Industrial Marketing Management* 23(1): 65–70.

Johnson, E. M., Kurtz, D. L. and Scheuing, E. E. (1994) *Sales Management Concepts, Practices and Cases*, New York: McGraw Hill.

Lidstone, J. (1986) *Training Salesmen On The Job*, 2nd edn, Aldershot: Gower.

Manolis, C. K. (1985) 'Sales force management in British manufacturing industry: An empirical investigation', M.Sc. thesis, University of Strathclyde, Glasgow.

Mantel, S. P., Pullins, E. B. Reid, D. A. and Buehrer, R. E. (2002) 'A realistic sales experience: Providing feedback by integrating buying, selling and managing experience', *Journal of Personal Selling and Sales Management*, 22 (1/Winter): 33–40.

Puri, S. J. (1993) 'Where industrial sales training is weak', *Industrial Marketing Management* 22: 101–8

Wilson, P.H., Strutton, D., and Farris, M.T. (2002) 'Investigating the perceptual aspects of sales training', *Journal of Personal Selling and Sales Management* 22 (2/Spring): 77–86.

ESTEEM SYSTEMS PLC

During 2002 Esteem Systems plc sold over £27m of IT products and services. The heart of the business is configuring server-based solutions; a complex market with a high growth rate.

The company was started by Richard Doyle in 1985. Richard, a former account-ant turned salesman, was formerly employed by Systime, and was determined not to make the same mistakes he had seen there. He did not want his company to be vulnerable to a single point of failure; for example by relying on a single supplier or being overly dependant on outside funding. Richard's ability to learn by other people's mistakes is not, of course, the only talent he has brought to running the business, but it certainly helps. Richard started out with only enough capital to cover the first six-months' running costs, so he needed to grow the company fast and solidly. A chance conversation while he was on his honeymoon gave him the clue – talking to a fellow diner in a restaurant at the resort, the conversation turned to business. 'I was offered this advice,' he says. 'The only way to make any serious money is to employ a lot of good people. The alternative is to stay small.'

Richard decided that the way to ensure that he was employing good people was to train them thoroughly, and also to share the wealth. 'Even experienced people should attend regular training,' he says. 'There are three wins that you get from attending a course. One is that you learn something new from the tutor. Two is that you learn something new from the other people on the course. Three is that you are reminded of something that you once practised but have now forgotten.'

Esteem operates two incentive schemes. One awards employees shares in the company based on their seniority and length of service, while the other is a profit-related share scheme. The first scheme rewards loyalty; David Cumberworth, an account manager with the firm, says that calls from head hunters seem less attrac-tive as one builds up shares in the company. The second scheme rewards people for hitting targets and for working as a team to generate profit.

Much of the training is contracted out to Sales Sense, a training consultancy which specializes in training salespeople who work in technically complex envi-ronments. Sales Sense trains salespeople in essential skills and habits (a basic course), selling to major accounts, managing accounts in an ongoing relationship, negotiating skills and selling knowledge.

Esteem spends an average of £2000 per employee per annum on training, and regards this as money well spent. The policy of prioritizing training has paid off – the company has doubled its sales in the last 18 months, and has an enviably low staff turnover. Richard Doyle is convinced that his policies have enabled his company to survive in a competitive market – and his staff obviously agree.

Case-study questions

1 Why might Esteem plc have contracted out their sales training?
2 What advantages are there in training staff rather than hiring in experienced people who have been trained elsewhere?
3 Why does Esteem offer two incentive schemes?
4 What benefits accrue from the Sales Sense courses?

MOTIVATION AND REMUNERATION

Learning objectives
After reading this chapter, you should be able to:

- Evaluate differing theories of motivation.
- Describe ways of tailoring motivation to the individual.
- Explain how a salesperson's remuneration works.
- Explain the difference between motivation and remuneration.
- Explain the role of commission in remuneration.
- Develop sales competitions and other motivational devices.
- Administer systems for payment of expenses.
- Devise appropriate bonus systems.

■ Introduction

Motivation and fair pay are clearly important to any employee in any industry. Motivation is what makes people want to work; remuneration is what compensates them for doing so. In the selling context special conditions apply: salespeople carry out most of their work away from the office, and out of sight of their colleagues. In those circumstances it becomes easy for the salesperson concerned to feel isolated, and occasionally for morale to slip. Sales managers therefore give a great deal of attention to motivation issues, since they are unable to supervise the salespeople directly for more than a tiny fraction of the time.

Penny Neff had a somewhat unconventional start to her working life. In school her best subjects had been music and agriculture – in fact, she was the first girl to enter and win the Future Farmers of America talent contest. Everybody thought she would become a farmer – but no, she turned to her other talent, music, and became a professional singer and composer. She made her living by writing, producing and performing advertising jingles. This was fun, but didn't pay enough for Penny – so she went into the hotel business.

She began as a desk clerk, but rapidly moved into sales. By the time she was 30, Penny had risen from sales manager to national director of sales and finally vice-president of a major hotel chain. At this stage she left to find new challenges, and went to work for oil billionaire 'Bud' Adams Junior. Here she learned the skills of negotiating major deals, and also the power of professional team building.

At age 34 she returned to hotels. She divides her time between team building, and negotiating major deals with large corporations and travel agents. Her attention to detail is part of what makes her a great leader; for example, she once rode the buses that her staff would use to get to work in order to assess the problems they might encounter on the way, and to judge how far each person might have to walk in bad weather. She believes in building results-oriented sales teams, and has built a successful career, and a substantial personal fortune, from taking over troubled hotels and turning them round. A very different career from that of farmer or professional musician!

Motivation

Motives are the reasons why people take action. A motive can have both strength and direction, and can be positive or negative; that is to say, a person can be motivated to do something, or motivated to avoid doing something. Motivation may also be internally generated, from within the person (for example hunger), or externally generated, from the environment (for example a social invitation).

Within the context of employing salespeople, motivation becomes important because the salespeople are working away from the supervision of the sales manager. Therefore, if they are not motivated to work, it is likely that they will not do so, and so an understanding of motivation is an important element in the sales manager's education.

The level to which one is motivated will depend on the following factors:

- The desirability of the end goal.
- The ease of achieving the end goal.

One of the problems with studying motivation is that it cannot be inferred from behaviour. For example, a young man may be at a concert in order to hear the music, or he may be there because his girlfriend likes the band and he wanted to give her an enjoyable night out. He may even be there because he plays in a band himself and he wants to see what the competition is doing. His motivation is therefore subjective and not available to the observer.

A further complication arises because motivation is rarely simple. Few actions take place as a result of one motivating force; in the example above, several motivations are probably at work, and some of these may not even be apparent to the man in question. It may be that he likes the band, and also wants to impress his girlfriend, but is also avoiding having an evening in with his brother whom he dislikes.

Motivations may come from many sources, and because it is usually impossible to satisfy all one's emotional and physical needs at once, researchers have tried to determine the extent to which individuals categorize and prioritize their needs. Henry Murray's early attempt to classify psychological needs resulted in a list of 20 basic needs. These are: succorance, nurturance, sentience, deference, abasement, defendence, infavoidance, harmavoidance, achievement, counteraction, dominance, aggression, affiliation, autonomy, order, rejection, sex, understanding, exhibition and play (Murray 1938).

Virtually all of these needs have implications for salespeople and sales managers. The need for rejection is used by salespeople when they urge customers to reject competing brands in favour of the company's brand; the need for nurturance is emphasized in home-improvement selling situations; the need for sentience is appealed to in selling encyclopaedias. The need for dominance is used when negotiating; allowing the customer to think that he has won the argument is a good way of closing a sale.

Murray's list is probably not definitive. There are probably many other needs which are not included in the list. Not all the needs will apply to everybody, and the needs may have differing priorities for different people. Also, some of the needs on the list conflict with each other; for example, dominance and deference. It should also be pointed out that Murray's list was developed as a result of his clinical experience rather than as the result of a research programme, so much of the evidence for the list is anecdotal rather than empirical.

Researchers have therefore tried to establish whether there are certain needs that everyone has in common, and whether these needs can be prioritized for most people. The best-known example of this approach is Maslow's hierarchy of need (Maslow 1970).

Maslow's hierarchy of need

According to Maslow, people have survival needs (food, shelter, clothing), the need to belong to a group, the need to earn the esteem of the group, the need for aesthetic fulfilment, and finally the need to self-actualize or to become a particular type of person and fulfil ambitions. These needs are given in order of achievement, and the theory is that an individual will not be interested in higher-level needs if the lower-level needs have not been satisfied.

The hierarchy of need theory postulates that people will fulfil the needs at the lower end of the pyramid before they move on to addressing needs at the upper end, but in practice it is really only a difference of emphasis. The exceptions to the hierarchy of need theory are so numerous as to render the theory doubtful; a tramp might well prefer to satisfy belonging needs by sitting in the open air with his friends rather than seek shelter for the night, for example. Equally, an artist might skip meals in order to satisfy aesthetic needs. In other words, there is little doubt that the needs exist, but considerable doubt that they form any kind of hierarchy.

For most people, however, the theory is a reasonable one and at least gives an indication of which needs will be uppermost in the individual's mind. Once a salesperson has assured his or her basic survival needs, these cease to be motivators; the individual will then be moving onto esteem needs, or belonging needs. For this reason sales managers usually have a battery of motivational devices for salespeople to aim for.

For rookies, the award of a company tie might address the need to belong. For more senior salespeople, membership of a millionaires' club (salespeople who have sold more than a million pounds' worth of product) might address esteem needs. Many sales managers offer prizes for salespeople's spouses or partners. This can be a powerful incentive since salespeople often work unusual hours, and thus have disrupted home lives; spouses or partners are sometimes neglected in favour of the job, so a prize aimed at them can help assuage the salesperson's natural feelings of guilt.

Table 8.1 illustrates some of the incentives commonly used, and maps them against Maslow's hierarchy.

TABLE 8.1 Sales incentives

Incentive	Description	Relationship to Maslow's theory
Company ties/scarves	A tie/scarf (or other clothing, such as a jacket) with a company logo on. This enables the salesperson to show his or her association with the firm.	This relates to belonging needs; the tie/scarf or other clothing shows that the salesperson is part of the larger group.
Salesperson of the month award	The highest-achieving salesperson is given a small prize and a round of applause at the monthly, weekly or annual sales meeting.	This addresses esteem needs. The salesperson is given a tangible mark of the esteem of his or her managers and colleagues.
Ladder of achievement	Salespeople are ranked according to their achievement; those at the top of the ladder fight to stay there, those near the bottom fight to rise up. Ladders of achievement foster competition between the salespeople.	Ladders of achievement operate on self-actualization for those near the top, who want to be the best, and on esteem for those nearer the bottom. There is, however, a risk of those at the bottom becoming demoralized due to feeling excluded from the group.
Flowers or wine sent to the salesperson's partner	If the salesperson has made a special effort, the reward is directed to the partner of the salesperson. The intention is to recognize the contribution made by partners to the salesperson's welfare and efforts.	This works on aesthetic needs and also on esteem – the salesperson's standing with the partner is often greatly improved by these measures.

Millionaires' club	This is a club for salespeople who have sold a million pounds' worth of business (or whatever sum is appropriate for the industry – it could be a billionaires' club in some industries where order levels are high).	This can operate on self-actualization, or on belonging needs. Salespeople will try to enter the millionaires' club in order to achieve an ambition; equally, belonging to the club says a lot for the salesperson's professional skill.
Holidays, meals out and weekend breaks	Achievers are given a weekend away, a holiday or dinner for two at a good restaurant. This also often equates to a reward for partners.	This type of reward addresses aesthetic needs, and also esteem needs because the partner appreciates the reward. Rewards which involve the spouse or partner can be very powerful motivators.
Competitions	Competitions can be run at intervals through the year, for example to increase effort during a quieter time of year.	These appeal to the individual's esteem needs, and in some cases to self-actualization needs, if the individual has a strong desire to win.
Promotion	Promotion should always be based on merit rather than merely filling vacancies.	A promotion is concrete proof of the esteem of the manager for the salesperson concerned.
Sales meetings	The purpose of a sales meeting is to motivate the sales force. Exchanging information is a secondary function, and is sometimes not addressed at all in the meetings.	Meetings work on the salesperson's sense of belonging, and the desire to be part of a team (even though salespeople generally work as individuals, not as team members).
Accompaniment in the field	Although the sales manager usually accompanies the salesperson for the purposes of training, it can be motivational to be given special attention.	This is very much connected to the needs for belonging and esteem.

For salespeople, striking a balance between home and work is as important as it is for any other employee. Boles *et al.* (2003) found that work–family conflicts are not significantly related to satisfaction with the work itself, or to relationships with colleagues, but there is a significant negative correlation with pay levels. In other words, if there is a conflict between work and family, it often relates strongly to a dissatisfaction with salary. Interestingly, the same study found that work–family conflict often relates to the supervisor (the sales manager), and to promotion issues. There are differences between men and women on these issues, since men appear to believe that promotion compensates to an extent for the job making inroads on home life, whereas women tend to consider time constraints and lack of promotion opportunities as being more frustrating. The fact that men and women appear, in general, to have different feelings about work–family conflict is not news, but it is significant in that sales managers need to be aware that what works well for men may not work well for women. For example, a weekend away on a stress-management course might be an excellent idea for many male

> **TALKING POINT**
>
> One sales manager hit on a very effective way of motivating his top sales-people. He bought a Porsche, then each month allowed the top salesper-son to drive it.
>
> 'They love the idea of taking the boss's Porsche off him,' he said. 'And all the other guys want to take it away from last month's winner, so it's a perpetual-motion machine.' The only drawback is that he only gets to drive the Porsche himself for one weekend a month – but that's a small price to pay.

salespeople, but for many female salespeople it might be regarded negatively because it increases work–family conflict.

There are other motivational tools available to sales managers, some of which are idiosyncratic; a good sales manager will usually be on the alert for new methods of motivating the sales force, and will tailor the approach to the individual. There is more on this later in the chapter.

Herzberg's dual-factor theory

A few years later than Maslow, Herzberg published his dual-factor theory of motivation (Herzberg 1987). Herzberg started out as a medical researcher, and became interested in the possibility that some factors might be motivators, whereas the lack of others might be demotivators, and the two groups might not necessarily overlap. As a medical man, he called the second group the 'hygiene' factors, since their absence would cause the 'disease' of demotivation.

Herzberg found that factors such as fair pay for the job, reasonable working conditions and a good relationship with the boss were basic to staff contentment, but that more of those things would not motivate staff to perform better. Motivators were found to be such things as the esteem of colleagues, deserved praise from the boss, and promotion. Motivators would tend to be subjective, i.e. specific to the individual.

Table 8.2 shows some typical hygiene factors and motivators for salespeople. Since motivation is subjective, the lists in Table 8.2 are not necessarily mutually exclusive; some people clearly are motivated by money, others would prefer not to be promoted due to the extra responsibility involved.

The importance of Herzberg's findings lies in the classification of job-related factors as either hygiene factors or motivators. The most controversial aspect of the theory is the inclusion of salary as a hygiene factor; the implication is that people are not motivated by salary, but are demotivated by a lack of it. Herzberg has been criticized by sales managers for this, since their experience shows that sales-people are often motivated by commission, but Herzberg argues that commission represents a recognition of success, and that motivation derives from the recognition not the money. There is certainly strong anecdotal evidence for Herzberg's view that money is not a motivator, since many people work extremely hard at tasks for which they receive no pay whatsoever (for example amateur actors, charity vol-

TABLE 8.2 Hygiene and motivation for salespeople	
Hygiene factors	**Motivators**
Respectable and practical car	Greater freedom of action; e.g. the ability to grant credit to customers or offer special discounts
Salary and commission	Competition prizes
Supportive manager	Esteem of colleagues
Supportive and efficient office staff	The work itself; the challenge of the job
Prompt reimbursement of expenses	Recognition of achievement
Job security	Promotion

unteers and amateur sportspeople) and in many cases would refuse payment as this would compromise their amateur status.

From the viewpoint of the sales manager, Herzberg's theory has major implications. Firstly, the nature of the job itself is a stronger motivator for most people than the salary, and in fact many people work for lower salaries than they could earn elsewhere, simply because they like the job and the working conditions. Secondly, the level of hygiene factors must be at least adequate, but issues such as job enhancement or greater autonomy in working practices are likely to motivate people more. Thirdly, cash bonuses and commissions work because of the recognition and esteem of colleagues, so such rewards need to be given publicly, for example in sales meetings. This is contrary to normal practice, in that staff earnings are usually confidential. While basic salaries should remain confidential, it is common in sales management to publicize bonus earnings, as a way of giving the salesperson recognition and also as an incentive to others.

Conflict between members of the sales team can act as a demotivators, especially in team-selling situations where the salespeople work closely with each other. In some cases this can lead to salespeople leaving a successful team, so it is important to ensure that lines of communication are kept open and team members feel able to discuss issues with one another (Dixon *et al.* 2002).

Vroom's expectancy theory

Expectancy theory (Vroom 1964) assumes that the salesperson's motivation to exert extra effort is linked to his or her expectation of success. The theory is based on three concepts, as shown in Table 8.3.

For example, if promotion is important to the individual, and it is clear that increasing sales performance will lead to promotion, then the individual will seek to make those extra efforts which he or she believes will lead to improved sales performance.

TABLE 8.3 Concepts of expectancy theory	
Concept	**Description**
Expectancy	The degree to which the individual believes that increased effort will lead to increased performance.
Instrumentality	The extent to which the individual believes that improved performance will be rewarded.
Valence	The value placed on the reward being offered.

Expectancy theory is useful in assessing the possible downside of some motivational tools. For example, if a salesperson is low on the ladder of achievement and believes that it is not possible to rise up the ladder, the result will be demotivation. Equally, if an individual sees no hope of winning the sales competition, perhaps because the more experienced salespeople are sure to generate the most sales, he or she is likely not to make any effort to win. For this reason, the more astute sales managers try to design the competitions so that each salesperson has a chance of winning something, even if only a minor prize; if the sales force is a small one, it may even be possible to ensure that the prize that each individual is most likely to win is also the prize that is most likely to be seen as desirable. For example, if a sales manager has a rookie who has not been performing well, but who likes to travel, the prize for the salesperson showing the most improvement in sales could be a weekend in Paris. The rookie would be in the best position to win such a prize, and at the same time would value the prize itself.

Expectancy theory shows that motivators can have a positive or negative effect; a motivator that is not valued, or one which is perceived as being unattainable, is likely to cause a reduction in motivation.

◼ Managing motivation

The key point in motivation is that different people are motivated by different things (Shipley and Kiely 1986). For this reason, managers need to tailor the motivation package to the individual, which will result in multidimensional packages rather than single motivators (Demirdjian 1964). Obviously this can lead to some extremely complex motivational packages, which can be counterproductive since there is no point in having a scheme which is too complex for anyone to understand.

One way around this difficulty is to segment the sales force, offering different incentive schemes to different groups. An early attempt to do this was the division of the sales force into four groups by Mossien and Fram (1973). The groups were trainee, salesperson, senior salesperson and master salesperson. Unfortunately these groups are defined by their job titles, not by their personalities. In 1982, Ingram and Bellenger identified three types of salesperson, defined in terms of their responsiveness to different motivators. These types were as follows:

- *Comfort seekers*: These salespeople are likely to be older, less educated and with high incomes. Comfort seekers are looking for job security, and respect and liking from their colleagues and managers, so they respond best to verbal encouragement and being asked to mentor junior colleagues.

- *Spotlight seekers*: This group has lower incomes than the first group, but like to have highly visible pay and bonuses, and they are concerned with extrinsic rewards such as prizes and status awards such as millionaires'-club membership.

- *Developers*: These are younger salespeople, with good incomes and often with young families to support. They seek opportunities for personal growth, though not necessarily promotion. Developers respond well to the opportunity to go on training courses, and to opportunities for career development.

The difficulty with segmenting the sales force is that sales-force members work together, and therefore know what incentives are being offered to each other. Any system for offering different incentives to different people must be transparent, and must be seen to be fair. In this respect then Mossien and Fram model works much better than the Ingram and Bellenger model.

Lack of motivation results in poorer performance in presentations, lower activity levels, rising absenteeism (which can be difficult to identify when salespeople are out of sight), higher staff turnover and poorer customer service. Lower motivation also leads to an increase in complaining by staff, and sometimes even in negative statements to colleagues; this can affect rookies badly, and spreads the demotivation, as well as making the sales manager's job harder.

In many cases, the management of motivation is more about the avoidance of demotivation. Demotivating influences are as follows:

- Poor working conditions.
- Poor reporting procedures.
- Unfairness in rewards or in other ways.
- Lack of promotion opportunities or career progression.
- Lack of individual involvement and participation in decision making.
- Lack of incentives.
- Poor internal communications.

Working conditions, for salespeople, will usually mean their cars and the equipment supplied to them. Many employers allow salespeople to choose their own vehicles, within a price range, and this has the advantage of giving the salespeople a degree of control over their working environment.

Reporting systems need to be fair, comprehensive, and not too arduous; most people prefer to be doing the job they were hired to do rather than filling in forms or writing reports (see Chapter 10).

Rewards need to be fair, and also need to be seen to be fair; part of the function of sales meetings is to allow the salespeople access to information about each others' activities. This enables them to see that the people who win the prizes, or who earn the most commission, are the people who are the most active and successful at selling.

Promotion opportunities may not always be easy to arrange, particularly in a small firm. Part of the problem, for any firm, is that having too many tiers of management tends to lead to bureaucratic rigidity and too much overhead. On the other hand, not having enough senior posts leads to a lack of opportunity, which encourages the more able people to look elsewhere. This dilemma can sometimes be partly resolved by creating senior-salesperson posts, where the more experienced people are paid more in exchange for taking more responsibility, for example helping with the training of rookies and occasionally deputizing for the sales manager.

Sometimes managers are reluctant to involve individuals in decision making, perhaps due to a fear that the individual will make decisions based on personal gain. Management can be seen as a clearing house for pressures, and giving one group the opportunity to apply more pressure may seem perverse. Salespeople, on the other hand, have a very direct interest in increasing the company's business, and can usually be trusted to give useful opinions and ideas on how this is to be achieved. Also, involvement in decision making will help to foster team spirit and solidarity. Internal communications need to be as transparent as possible; salespeople lead a solitary life which can lead to paranoia about the company's decision making.

Overall, motivation is about rewarding effort and success. Motivation should not be confused with avoidance. Adverse outcomes (pain or other undesirable effects) will not necessarily lead to a positive behavioural activity; in other words, threatening somebody will not necessarily make them do what you want them to do. Despite widespread use of the cautionary tale in selling, where the adverse outcomes of not taking a particular course of action are stressed, the motivational effects are uncertain at best.

The reason for this is that rewards can only be obtained by following a specified course of action, whereas pain can be avoided in many ways. Burris F. Skinner (1953) demonstrated that rats could be taught to push buttons in complex patterns in order to obtain food, and could also learn to avoid electric shocks. The main result of these experiments was that the rats were inventive in the ways they avoided the shocks, but did not necessarily engage in the behaviour the shocks were intended to induce.

Human beings are, of course, not rats. People are likely to be far more inventive than a rat would be. For example, if salespeople are told that failure to sell will result in dismissal, some will go out and make sure that they sell, others will fake a sale (which mysteriously cancels later) and others will simply look for another job. In all cases the results are likely to be negative; salespeople who are desperate to sell often seem nervous in presentations. Prospects are likely to perceive this as nervousness about the product on offer, or as evidence of dishonesty. Obviously bogus sales or wholesale resignations are not in the company's interests either.

When designing a motivational exercise, sales managers should try to imagine what would happen to the salespeople who fail to reach the objective; for example, if a ladder of success is drawn up, sales managers should ensure that those at the bottom of the ladder do not perceive the ladder as a punishment designed to shame them into greater effort.

Research into sales-force motivation has been extensive, since it is a key aspect of management. Doyle and Shapiro (1980) found that the most important factors in motivation were:

1 *Nature of the task*: This alone accounted for more than 33 per cent of variation in sales-force performance.

2 *Personality of the salesperson*: Salespeople with a high personal need for achievement perform better than those with a low need for achievement. This accounted for 21 per cent of the variation in achievement.

3 *Pay structure*: Only 11.8 per cent of the variation between individual performances was due to variations in payment systems; i.e. the mix between salary and commission.

Since management has control over two of these factors, and can influence the third by careful selection and training, motivation has a lot to do with the quality of the sales management.

Walker *et al.* (1979) found that increased financial rewards are more valued by older salespeople, and, not surprisingly, those who are married with large families. Higher-order rewards such as career advancement, promotion or simply a sense of achievement are more valued by younger salespeople and those with higher levels of education. It should be noted that this research is now nearly 30 years old, and therefore should be treated with caution – cultural shifts and a general rise in the national standard of living and education are likely to have distorted the attitudes of salespeople. Interestingly, a study by Churchill and Pecotich (1982) found that salespeople with higher levels of pay were actually less satisfied than those with lower levels of pay – perhaps due to a lack of challenges.

A study by Donnelly and Ivancevich (1975) found a positive relationship between role clarity and job performance. In other words, salespeople who understand exactly what they are supposed to achieve and also know how they are supposed to achieve it are less likely to leave and more likely to achieve the expected outcomes. This may seem obvious, since it is true of all employees, but for salespeople the situation is different since they are expected to operate on their own initiative in so many areas of their daily lives. An anchoring framework therefore acquires a greater importance than it would for someone who is working in an office, in easy reach of the manager should any problems arise.

Sujan (1986) proposed that motivation to work harder is, in many cases, less important than motivation to work smarter. Working smarter is more likely to occur when salespeople attribute their failure to poor strategic planning, whereas salespeople who are motivated by extrinsic rewards such as bonuses and prizes are more likely to work harder. Working smarter comes from wishing to influence customers and from wanting to become better at the job. Sujan refers to this as attribution theory, since it derives from salespeople's attempts to attribute failure to specific behaviours.

Factors affecting motivation are shown in Table 8.4.

Leadership on the part of the sales manager will affect morale and motivation. Much of the emphasis on leadership has been about the born leader, and undoubtedly some individuals appear to be endowed with a natural charisma which allows them to dominate or persuade. Some of the elements which go to make up a charismatic leader are appearance, confidence, intelligence, knowledge, experience, innovation, determination, articulateness, persuasiveness and empathy. Research has been inconsistent as to which of these traits predominate in great leaders, however.

TABLE 8.4 Factors affecting motivation

Factor	Explanation
The job itself	Autonomy, variety and a lack of strict discipline are the factors which attract many people to a career in sales. Hackman and Oldham (1975) and Becherer *et al.* (1982) created a formula for measuring motivating potential. This is: $$\text{Motivating potential} = \left(\frac{\text{skill}}{\text{variety}} + \frac{\text{task}}{\text{identity}} + \frac{\text{task}}{\text{significance}} \right) \times \text{autonomy} \times \text{feedback}$$ The problem with this type of formula is that it is almost impossible to attach objective values to the various components.
Accurate feedback	Sales tasks and effort only have an indirect effect on sales performance. Therefore it is essential that feedback is both accurate and timely, since this has a positive effect on both job satisfaction and job performance (Bagozzi 1980).
Motivated people	The intrinsic drive and need for achievement of some salespeople is a major factor in achievement. This type of motivation may be expressed as a function of the salesperson's economic, social and self-actualizing needs (Demirdjian 1984).
Participation	Salespeople show a greater commitment when they are involved in decision making. Management by objectives is often helpful in these situations, since staff are judged on outcomes rather than on processes.
Being part of the company	Commitment to the company and to colleagues will lead to a belief that the sales effort will make a real contribution to the welfare of others. Because salespeople are usually away from the company offices, it is easy for them to feel like outsiders, so it is even more important to make them feel included than would be the case for other employees.
Morale	Morale is the total mix of feelings an individual has towards the company or the job. Since so much of an employee's life is taken up with work, these feelings can have a profound effect on the overall well-being of the individual. Good morale is a hygiene factor rather than a motivator, however.
Discipline	Too strict a discipline is likely to be counterproductive, especially as there is no way to enforce it when salespeople are on the road, but a good manager will lay down some general ground rules. In particular, issues such as dishonesty, appearance, and delivery of paperwork in good time and in good condition should be covered, otherwise the situation becomes anarchic.
Monetary rewards	Basic salary (and even commission) are probably hygiene factors, but bonuses and cash prizes can be excellent motivators. A useful device is to pay cash prizes in actual banknotes rather than a cheque, but note that income tax in the UK, at least, will still be payable.
Good management	Factors such as coaching, evaluation, understanding and selling skill on the part of the manager all contribute to motivation. Managers should be supportive and knowledgeable about the job in order to earn respect.

Power theory is concerned with the establishment of authority over the sales force (French and Raven 1959). Power arises in the following ways:

1 *Legitimate power*: This is based on the individual's position in the organization. As the appointed sales manager, the manager will have this type of power.
2 *Reward power*: This derives from the manager's ability to reward the sales force by providing incentives or pay rises.
3 *Coercive power*: The ability to punish subordinates, for example by dismissal or by withholding rewards.
4 *Expert power*: This type of power is based on the subordinate's respect for the sales manager's skill and knowledge.
5 *Referent power*: This originates in the leader's charisma or inspirational abilities.

There is a relationship between these sources of power and the level of job satisfaction (Busch 1980), but it turns out that legitimate power is not as strong as might be expected (Comer 1985). Most sales managers would agree that managers need to earn respect rather than command it on the basis of their position in the firm, however.

Blake and Mouton (1964, 1978) distinguishes between five different types of leadership, as shown in Table 8.5.

TABLE 8.5 Leadership types

Type	Explanation
Impoverished management	These managers are low on both task achievement and concern for people. There is minimum effort to ensure that the work is done, and little concern for the staff well-being. These managers only maintain enough activity to keep from being fired.
Authority-obedience management	These managers are highly task-oriented, and require their people to produce results at whatever cost. These managers are likely to take a carrot-and-stick attitude to managing staff, rather than the more subtle approaches available.
Country-club management	Under this type of manager, being in work is like being at a country club. People concern is high, task orientation is low: such managers are reluctant to pressure people, on the assumption that higher job satisfaction will, of itself, lead to greater productivity. This may not always be the case, of course.
Organization-man management	Effective performance and job satisfaction are balanced so that the outcomes are satisfactory for both the organization and the employees. This probably represents the majority of middle-performing managers.
Team management	100 per cent commitment is expected from the group, but it is coupled with care and concern for the employees. These managers are usually extremely effective, combining maximum task orientation with strong people concern, but in practice this outcome is extremely difficult to achieve.

Stroh (1978) divided leadership styles into five separate types. These were as follows:

1 *Autocratic*: This is a style where the manager issues orders, with the threat of punishments or the promise of rewards to back up the commands.
2 *Democratic*: Here decisions are made as a result of collective consent of the group. This management style is characterized by meetings and votes of staff.
3 *Consultative*: The manager consults with all interested parties, then makes the final decision.
4 *Paternalistic*: The manager works to develop a common culture. This type of manager often uses the phrase 'one big happy family'.
5 *Laissez-faire*: This system works best with individuals who are able to control their own working patterns effectively. It works best with major-account salespeople and with high-commission direct salespeople such as home-improvement salespeople.

Stroh's research showed that the paternalistic, laissez-faire and autocratic styles were not very effective. The democratic and consultative styles appear to provide the best outcomes for salespeople, but it should be noted that the least successful approach is to try a combination of different styles, since this only leads to confusion. Therefore it is almost certainly better for a manager to adopt a style which he or she finds suitable and natural rather than to try to adopt a style which does not come naturally, since the resulting lapses into his or her true approach will simply confuse.

Remuneration

Remuneration is compensation given in exchange for work done. It is not motivation, it is merely fair recompense, and in Herzberg's terms is a hygiene factor. Remuneration includes salary, commission, bonuses, expenses and fringe benefits such as cars, pensions, holiday entitlement, subsidized meals and other payments in kind.

Typically, salespeople are paid partly by commission and partly by salary, although some salespeople (missionaries, for example) are paid by salary only, while others (home-improvement salespeople, for example) are usually paid by commission only. Table 8.6 shows the advantages and disadvantages of each method.

Although it is commonly supposed that a commission-only salesperson will be highly motivated to work hard, since otherwise he or she will not earn any money, this is not necessarily the case. Salespeople who are paid solely by commission will sometimes decide that they have earned enough for this month, and will give themselves a holiday; the company has very little moral power to compel them to work, since there is no basic salary being paid. Conversely, a salesperson who is paid salary only may feel obligated to work in order to justify the salary, and is more likely to carry out tasks which are not directly related to winning an order. For example, a salary-only salesperson is more likely to carry out aftersales follow-ups and technical services than a salesperson who feels under pressure to bring in more orders.

Herzberg (1987) says that the payment method must be seen to be fair if demotivation is to be avoided; the payment method is not in itself a good motivator. Salespeople are out on the road for most of their working lives and do not see what other salespeople are doing; whether they are competent at the job, whether they are getting some kind of unfair advantage, even whether they are working at all. In these circumstances a commission system does at least reassure the salesperson that extra effort brings extra rewards. The chart in Table 8.7 shows the trade-offs between a mainly commission-based package and a mainly salary-based package.

Making an exact calculation is, of course, somewhat complex and most firms end up offering a similar package to that found throughout the industry.

Salespeople's response to the remuneration packages falls into five categories (Darmon 1974):

1 *Creatures of habit;* Those who have determined the amount of money they need to live on, and who earn up to that level.

2 *Satisfiers*: Those who only perform at a level which ensures that they will not be fired.

3 *Trade-off-ers*: Salespeople who allocate their time between work and leisure according to some formula of their own; they are not influenced by the prospect of earning more money.

TABLE 8.6 Advantages and disadvantages of remuneration mixes

Method	Advantages	Disadvantages
Salary only	Gives the salesperson a sense of security. Ensures that the company knows exactly what the payroll will be. Ensures that salespeople think long term rather than being tempted to make quick sales to earn commission.	Does not reward extra effort. May be seen to be unfair by harder-working salespeople.
Commission only	Ensures that poor salespeople are not a drain on the company's resources. Rewards effort very directly. Is usually seen to be fair. Links the cost of the sales force directly to the amount of business done.	Usually results in high staff turnover, since most salespeople have occasional dry periods. May be seen as motivating by punishment; no sales means no food on the table. Sometimes results in high earners relaxing, since they can earn enough to live on in only a few days' work. Also tends to be expensive for the firm, because salespeople expect high earnings to compensate for the risk they are taking.
Mix of salary and commission	Can be tailored to suit the company's circumstances. Gives the salesperson a measure of security, with a measure of incentive.	Difficult to gauge the right proportion of salary to commission. Individuals may feel differently about what is the appropriate mix. Poor salespeople can prove expensive. Difficult to budget for sales-force salaries.

4 *Goal-oriented*: Those who seek to achieve their targets. For these individuals, money is only seen as a recognition for achievement.

5 *Money-oriented*: These individuals seek to maximize their earnings at whatever cost to their social lives, families or health.

The main difficulty in designing a compensation package lies in ensuring that these differing types of salesperson are all catered for and motivated. Goal- and money-oriented salespeople are more likely to be moved by a stronger commission element in their pay; trade-off-ers and satisfiers are more likely to be motivated by salary, since they may feel an obligation to work harder to justify the salary.

Commissions, and bonuses, might be based on sales value, on sales volume, or on profit. Sales value is easy to calculate, but may result in salespeople giving away discounts too easily in order to increase their sales. The same is true of sales volume schemes; these also suffer from the problem that salespeople may feel that they lose out when prices increase, because they have a harder job to sell the same number of units as before. In other words, their workload increases without a corresponding rise in income. Profit-based systems are harder to calculate, and rely on the salesperson trusting the company's financial people to be fair about what constitutes profit and what does not.

For example, a salesperson selling power tools to garages might believe that profit is the difference between what the tool costs and what it is sold for. The company's finance director might consider that the costs of running the salesperson's car also needs to be taken into account – and will probably also want to include an allowance for corporate overheads. These figures are impossible for the salesperson to check. On the other hand, calculating commission on the basis of the profitability of the deal does focus the sales force on an appropriate target, relevant to the corporate strategy.

TABLE 8.7 Choosing the right pay package for salespeople

Mainly salary	Mainly commission
Where order values are high	Where order values are low
Where the sales cycle is long	Where the sales cycle is short
Where staff turnover is low	Where staff turnover is high
Where sales staff are carefully selected against narrow criteria	Where selection criteria for staff are broad
For new staff, or staff who have to develop new territories	For situations where aggressive selling is indicated, e.g. selling unsought goods
Where sales territories are seriously unequal in terms of sales potential	Where sales territories are substantially the same

Bonuses

A bonus is a one-off payment made to recognize the achievement of a specific goal or target. There is some conceptual overlap between commission and bonuses, because bonuses tend to be motivators rather than hygiene factors; also, bonuses are used at the discretion of the sales manager and can be used flexibly for adjusting the motivational direction of the sales force to suit different situations.

For example, during an exhibition (see Chapter 12) the sales manager might offer a bonus based on the number of enquiries dealt with. This encourages salespeople to deal with the enquiries, even though most of them will not result in sales and even those that do will not result in sales for the individual salesperson who initially deals with the enquiry. Another example might be a one-off bonus to a rookie for achieving a first sale.

The focus of selling activity has moved towards producing profits rather than sales revenue, and in this context bonuses have become more relevant to the reality of selling. Since the profit on a deal is difficult to calculate accurately while the deal is actually being done, end-of-year bonuses are common in industries where profitability is the criterion for selling success.

Bonuses cannot completely replace commission, especially if they are to be paid annually; reward needs to follow behaviour as quickly as possible if it is to be effective. They should be used mainly as instant rewards for hitting targets, and should be seen as tangible recognition of achievement rather than earnings. Having said that, bonuses are also used to correct imbalances in the remuneration scheme, and to ensure that a salesperson is compensated for extra effort even when this effort falls outside the rules of the commission structure.

It is also important to set appropriate thresholds for bonuses. If the threshold is too high, salespeople will assume that they cannot win the bonus whatever they do; if it is too low, they are likely to relax, secure in the knowledge that the bonus is already in the bag. A further problem with bonus schemes arises if the customers become aware of them. A recurring problem for some companies is that buyers know that the salesperson is keen to win a bonus, and will therefore be vulnerable to a more aggressive negotiating stance.

Fringe benefits

Most occupations carry some fringe benefits; these are rewards or compensation which are not directly related to pay. Often it is the fringe benefits which make the difference between a salesperson accepting a job or not, and between a salesperson staying with a company or not. The main fringe benefits which salespeople might enjoy are shown in Table 8.8.

There are many other possibilities; the key to success in offering fringe benefits is to offer something which is cheap for the company to provide but which has greater benefits for the staff member. Some fringe benefits, such as company cars, still have tax advantages in most countries, despite the tendency of successive governments to tax such benefits. Others, such as pension funds, are positively encouraged by governments and are given substantial tax breaks.

TALKING POINT

When SAP, the German software giant, opened its offices in Jermyn Street, London it turned out that they were above Quaglino's, a world-famous restaurant. One salesman joked that it would make a great staff canteen – so SAP investigated, and discovered that Quaglino's were prepared to offer a special deal for SAP staff.

This turned out to be cheaper than running a dedicated staff canteen (an expensive operation in central London) so Quaglino's really was, for a while, the staff canteen.

TABLE 8.8 Fringe benefits

Benefit	Explanation
Non-contributory pension fund	A pension fund to which the employer makes all the payment, so that the employee does not contribute. Especially for older salespeople or for those with families, a pension is a valuable benefit; from the employer's viewpoint, it reduces staff turnover as, despite legislation which requires it, pension funds are not easily transferable from one scheme to another.
Company car	Although a car is a tool of the trade for salespeople, the standard of car represents an important fringe benefit. There is a great deal of difference between a BMW and a basic Ford, and the salesperson driving the BMW would be reluctant to lose it by leaving the company.
Discounts on own purchases	In some companies, it is appropriate for the sales force to be offered substantial discounts if they buy the company's products for their own use. Examples might include life insurance, bank loans, timeshare properties, houses, home improvements, cars, consumer durables or food products.
Private use of company facilities	Some firms have holiday homes or accommodation in major cities which can be used by staff; some firms even have yachts or other facilities used to entertain clients. These can sometimes be made available, perhaps at weekends, for staff use.
Private health care	This is a substantial benefit to the employee, and one which would almost certainly encourage loyalty. It is also good for the employer, because it is likely to reduce absenteeism through sickness.
Share options	Many companies allow their employees to acquire shares in the firm either cheaply, or as a performance-related bonus. This has the advantage that the employee acquires a direct interest in the firm's performance, and reduces the possibilities of conflict between the employee and the firm.

Expense payments

In the course of the job, salespeople will incur out-of-pocket expenses. Most of these (petrol, hotels, taxis, business entertaining, etc.) can be easily calculated and reimbursed, whereas others (lunches, telephone calls made from home) may be harder to assess.

From the company's viewpoint, such expenditure presents a dilemma. On the one hand, the salesperson's job is probably impossible without incurring some expenses. On the other hand, no company can afford to give its staff a free rein in spending company funds. Invariably salespeople think that the company is too tight fisted; equally invariably, the company finance director thinks that the sales force is too lavish. To avoid conflict, strict guidelines need to be laid down, but sales managers need to allow some leeway for the unexpected, and also to allow salespeople some autonomy in making decisions on the ground. If a salesperson judges that paying for lunch in an expensive restaurant will mellow the client enough to swing the deal, this should be allowed.

The criteria for establishing the rules are as follows:

- The system should be fair and should be seen to be fair; expenses actually incurred should be reimbursed in full and promptly, but expense accounts should not be padded so that they become an extra source of income.

- The system should be flexible to allow for regional variations and exceptional circumstances. Selling is not always a tidy, mechanical process, so expenditure incurred when building goodwill may not come to fruition for several years.

- The rules laid down should be simple and unambiguous.

It is important that salespeople should not feel demotivated by a refusal to pay expenses. In the event that an employee has broken the rules, the sales manager needs to decide whether the infringement is serious enough to warrant refusing to pay out; if at all possible, it is better to pay out and warn the employee that payment will not be made in future rather than risk demotivating the salesperson by refusing to reimburse the expenses.

■ Problems in assessing performance

Assessing sales-force performance is not as straightforward as it might at first appear. Table 8.9 shows some of the problems associated with assessment of pay and performance, with some suggested solutions.

TABLE 8.9 Problems of assessing performance

Problem	Explanation	Suggested solution
Evaluation basis	Evaluation on sales turnover is straightforward, but misleading – salespeople can increase sales greatly by heavy discounting, which cuts profits.	A formula for a quick assessment of the profitability of a deal might be worked out, or perhaps a combination of commission on sales value and bonus on profitability might be possible.

TABLE 8.9 *(cont.)*

Problem	Explanation	Suggested solution
Cancellation of orders	Sometimes customers will cancel orders, which means that the commission will not be payable. This is extremely frustrating for the salesperson, especially when the cancellation results from delivery or service problems which are not the salesperson's fault. Waiting for orders to be paid for may mean long delays between doing the work and receiving the reward.	Commission can be paid out on invoiced orders, or can be paid half on receipt of the order, half on payment of the invoice.
Bad debts	If payment is never received for the goods, salespeople will often feel that they should be paid the commission anyway; it is a commonly held view that the salesperson is not responsible for poor credit risks or poor credit management.	In fact, this is not strictly the case. The salesperson is often in the best position to judge whether a prospect is trustworthy or not. Failure to recognize this may mean that the salesperson is concentrating on his or her own position vis-à-vis meeting quotas rather than concentrating on the company's best interests.
Team selling	In some firms, particularly where major accounts are involved, several people are likely to be involved in the same sale. Allocating rewards thus becomes complex.	A suitable set of rules for deciding on the split of commission needs to be established and agreed upon by the staff members concerned. In some cases it may be appropriate to allow staff to allocate bonuses to each other, although this tactic needs to be used with care if conflict between team members is to be avoided.
House accounts	Some companies have subsidiaries which trade with each other. Often these accounts will still need aftersales support, but usually do not attract commission.	Either a special sales team should be established to deal with these accounts, or a suitable system should be developed for recompensing salespeople for time spent servicing these accounts.
Size of orders gained	In key-account selling, an order may be a very long time coming, but large when it arrives. This means that the salesperson may have little or no commission for a long time, but suddenly become entitled to a huge reward.	Emphasizing the salary element of the remuneration package will help, but also bonuses for achieving targets in the course of making the sale can help. The same problem arises for highly seasonal businesses such as travel and tourism or the toy industry.
Telephone and mail order sales	Incoming telesales or mailed-in orders may be the result of the salesperson's efforts, but may be credited to good advertising, exhibition activities, or any one of several other marketing communications activities.	Good communications between the salesperson and the manager are the key here. If the sales manager is kept informed about which customers the salesperson is working on, it should be feasible to allocate the orders to the right commission account.

Ultimately all performance-related pay schemes will suffer from the same basic problem; the trade-off between having a simple, easy-to-follow system that fails to cover all eventualities, or a complex system which covers the possible permutations of effort but which gives no clear guidelines as to what is expected of the staff. A degree of discretion and a sense of fair play are essential attributes for successful sales managers.

One of the difficulties of recruiting salespeople is the problem of explaining the commission system and the likely earnings in advance of an interview. Job adverts need to carry some indication of potential earnings, yet it would be cumbersome to describe the system in great detail. In most cases firms quote a figure relating to on-target earnings (OTE, also sometimes known as opportunity to earn) which allows the salesperson to gauge the potential of the job. Some employers become tempted to inflate the OTE figure in order to attract applicants; this is a danger-ous practice, since the successful applicant will very quickly find out that the figure has been exaggerated, and is likely to leave, or at least become demotivated. Either of these outcomes is seriously counterproductive.

SUMMARY

Remuneration and motivation are linked, but not identical; while both aspects of reward are concerned with meeting the salesperson's needs, the needs they address are different. It could be said that remuneration is more about meeting the salesperson's basic survival needs (and about maintain-ing a high standard of living) whereas motivation is about meeting the sales-person's higher-order needs.

The key points from this chapter are as follows:

- Motivation is what makes an individual want to work; remuneration is the individual's compensation for working.

- Needs are not necessarily met in strict order, but a salesperson who is not earning enough to keep food on the table is unlikely to be concerned about winning a sales competition.

- Management of motivation often consists of developing strategies to avoid demotivation.

- Salespeople are individuals, and need to be treated as such whether in terms of motivation or in terms of remuneration.

- Bonuses should be used as one-off recognition of achievement, not regarded as part of the salesperson's salary.

- Performance-related pay systems are extremely unlikely to be perfect, and those that are close to perfection are likely to be complex.

- OTE figures should not be exaggerated; it is counterproductive in the long run to do this.

REVIEW QUESTIONS

1 If money is a poor motivator, why are salespeople usually paid commission, while other employees are not?

2 As cars are often offered as prizes on quiz shows, why should salespeople regard a car as a hygiene factor?

3 Why do sales managers often give prizes and rewards to salespeople's partners?

4 What is the difference between a bonus and a commission, in terms of motivation and remuneration?

5 Why might a salesperson prefer to win a company tie, value £5, than be paid an extra £50 in commission?

REFERENCES

Bagozzi, R.P. (1980) 'Performance and satisfaction in an industrial salesforce: an examination of their antecedents and simultaneity', *Journal of Marketing* 44 (Spring): 65–77.

Becherer, R. C., Morgan, F. W. and Richard, L. M. (1982) 'The job characteristics of industrial salespersons: relationship to motivation and satisfaction', *Journal of Marketing* 46 (Fall): 125–35.

Blake, R. R. and Mouton, J.S. (1964) *The Managerial Grid*, Houston: Gulf Publishing.
—— —— (1978) *The New Managerial Grid*, Houston, TX: Gulf Publishing.

Boles, J. S., Wood, J. A. and Johnson, J. (2003) 'Interrelationship of role conflict, role ambiguity, and work–family conflict with different facets of job satisfaction and the moderating effects of gender', *Journal of Personal Selling and Sales Management* 23 (2/Spring): 99–114.

Busch, P. (1980) 'The sales manager's bases of social power and influence on the salesforce', *Journal of Marketing* 44 (Spring): 91–101.

Churchill, G.A. and Pecotich, A. (1982) 'A structural equation investigation of the pay satisfaction–valence relationship among salespeople', *Journal of Marketing* 46 (Fall): 114–24.

Comer J.M. (1985) 'Industrial sales managers: Satisfaction and performance', *Industrial Marketing Management*, 14(4): 239–44.

Darmon, R.Y. (1974) 'Salesmen's response to financial incentives: An empirical study', *Journal of Marketing Research* 11 (4/Nov.): 418–26.

Demirdjian, Z.S. (1984) 'A multidimensional approach to motivating salespeople', *Industrial Marketing Management* 13(1): 25–32.

Dixon, A. L., Gassenheimer, J. B. and Barr, T. F. (2002) 'Bridging the distance between us: How initial responses to sales team conflict help shape core selling team outcomes', *Journal of Personal Selling and Sales Management* 22 (4/Fall): 247–57.

Donnelly, J.H. and Ivancevich, J.M. (1975) 'Role clarity and the salesman', *Journal of Marketing* 39 (Jan): 71–4.

Doyle, S. X. and Shapiro, B.P. (1980) 'What counts most in motivating your salesforce?', *Harvard Business Review* 58 (3/May–June): 133–40.

French, J. R. R. and Raven, B. (1959) 'The bases of social power', in D. Cartwright (ed.) *Studies in Social Power*, Ann Arbor, MN: University of Michigan Press.

Hackman, J.R. and Oldham, G.R. (1975) 'Development of the job diagnostic survey', *Journal of Applied Psychology* 60: 159–70.

Herzberg, F. (1987) 'One more time: How do you motivate employees?' *Harvard Business Review* 65 (5/Sept.–Oct.): 109–20.

Ingram, T.N. and Bellenger, D.N. (1982) 'Motivational segments in the salesforce', *California Management Review* 24 (3): 81–8.

Maslow, A. (1970) *Motivation and Personality,* 2nd edn, New York: Harper & Row.

Mossien, H. and Fram, E.H. (1973) 'Segmentation for salesforce motivatio', *Akron Business and Economic Review* (Winter): 5–12.

Murray, Henry A. (1938) *An Exploration in Personality: A Clinical Experimental Study of Fifty Men of College Age*, London: Oxford University Press.

Shipley, D.D. and Kiely, J.A. (1986) 'Industrial salesforce motivation and Herzberg's dual-factor theory: A UK perspective', *Journal of Personal Selling and Sales Management* 6(1): 9–16.

Skinner, B. F. (1953): *Science and Human Behaviour*, New York: Macmillan.

Stroh, T. F. (1978): *Managing the Sales Function*, New York: McGraw-Hill.

Sujan H. (1986) 'Smarter versus harder: An exploratory attributional analysis of salespeople's motivations', *Journal of Marketing Research*, XXIII (Feb) 41–9.

Vroom, V. H. (1964) *Work and Motivation*, New York: John Wiley.

Walker O. C., Churchill, G. A. and Ford, N. M. (1979) 'Personal characteristics of salespeople and the attractiveness of alternative rewards', *Journal of Business Research* 7(1): 25–56.

FRAM AND SONY

FRAM oil filters are known worldwide. The company was founded over 70 years ago by two chemists, Frederick Franklin and Edward Aldam, on the back of their discovery of an easy-to-replace oil filter. At first, sales were slow and the filters were hand assembled and sold to motorists as replacement parts, but in 1934 the chemists hired a salesman, Stephen B. Wilson, who persuaded the major motor manufacturers to fit the filters as original equipment.

In due course, the company developed a large number of other systems for protecting cars, using the slogan 'Pay a little more now – or pay a lot later' to emphasize the advantages of maintaining vehicles properly.

Products are sold through automotive distributors who act in the same way as sales agents. They take title to the products, but act as salespeople for the company. FRAM therefore needed to come up with an incentive scheme which would motivate both the FRAM salespeople and the distributors in order to move the products out to the end customers. FRAM called in incentive specialists Cascade Promotion to structure a programme, and Cascade decided to link the promotion to Sony electronic products.

The programme, called 'Rugged road', was designed to achieve three main objectives. The first aim was to move FRAM products through warehouse distribution channels. The second aim was to motivate the counter staff at the automotive distributors to recommend FRAM products rather than competing products. The third aim was to provide the FRAM sales force with a powerful selling tool to encourage distributors to stock FRAM and to buy extra amounts.

The FRAM promotional base was about protecting the car from the kind of tough conditions many motorists put the car through, such as high-speed, long-distance driving, stop–start driving in heavy traffic, driving off-road and so forth. The incentive programme operated on five levels, featuring 13 different promotional products, all produced by Sony. Each product was chosen on the basis that it fitted with the theme of the promotion, for example Sony's weatherproof cordless phones. Counter staff won certificates for each FRAM product sold, and could redeem the certificates against products. Distributors' sales forces were given certificates for opening new accounts and also for increased sales.

The result? Almost 14 000 certificates were redeemed against Sony products in a three-month period, representing £7 million worth of extra sales. The total cost of the entire incentive programme came to approximately 4 per cent of those extra sales – a remarkable return on investment for FRAM.

Case-study questions

1 What might have been the effect of using the particular products as motivational prizes?

2 Why not simply give the salespeople cash?

3 What needs might the incentive scheme have addressed for the counter staff?

4 What needs might the scheme have met for the distributors' salespeople?

5 Why might this scheme have been more successful than an advertising campaign aimed at consumers?

9

FORECASTING AND BUDGETING

Learning objectives

After reading this chapter, you should be able to:

- Explain the use and misuse of computers in sales and sales management planning.

- Explain some of the issues surrounding database management.

- Explain the role of forecasting and budgeting in the planning process.

- Describe the main forecasting methods used by sales managers.

- Describe some of the problems of forecasting.

- Explain the issues surrounding territory design.

■ Introduction

Most business planning is undertaken using computers, and the sales process is gradually becoming more and more dependent on the rapid availability of information. Computers have enabled a greater range of factors to be taken into account when planning, making the models more comprehensive and more accurate in terms of ability to predict outcomes.

Predicting the future is a common activity of managers, and most people are capable of doing it, with varying degrees of accuracy. The purpose of developing a forward view of the firm's selling activity is to ensure that deviations from the plan can be corrected, and to ensure that resources are available at the right times to meet the company's overall objectives.

For financial purposes, forward planning is usually enshrined in the form of a budget. This should show what funds are coming in, what funds are going out, and the timing of these incomes and disbursements. In the selling context, part of this budgeting of resources encompasses the management of individual sales territories.

■ Principles of forecasting

The aim of a sales forecast is to produce an accurate figure for the company's future sales; in practice, this is extremely difficult to do, and all forecasting suffers from a greater or lesser degree of inaccuracy (Battersby 1968). Because of this, sales forecasting is better carried out as a continuous process rather than a once-a-year exercise. Figure 9.1 illustrates the elements in the process.

In the diagram, the forecast calculations are based on conditions within the industry, conditions within the country and conditions within the firm. Each of these elements is taken into account, and the forecast itself is developed. The forecast is then compared on an ongoing basis with actual results, and the findings are fed back into the company conditions and the forecasting calculation. It should be noted that the forecast itself will affect performance; once a forecast has been made, the sales force will feel under pressure to achieve it, or if the forecast is perceived as being too easy to achieve, the sales force may relax a little. Prophecies often become self-fulfilling due to these factors.

The conditions within the industry, country and firm are themselves the results of other forecasts, which can also become self-fulfilling, particularly in the case of large firms with substantial market shares.

Forecasts may be short term (perhaps for two or three months ahead), medium term (perhaps for a year or two ahead) or long term (for periods of three years or more). Short-term forecasts are usually used for tactical planning, for example to schedule production or to plan leave allowances for salespeople. Medium-term forecasts are of most use in budgeting; it is important to be as accurate as possible in medium-term forecasting, because an underestimate of demand might leave the company unprepared to meet the needs of its customers, and an overestimate of demand might leave the company with unsold stocks. Some company directors do not understand that salespeople are there to manage and direct demand rather than create it; therefore some sales forecasts are actually generated by directors who want to force salespeople to sell goods whether there is a need for them or not.

Long-term forecasts are used to develop strategic plans. Some industries habitually predict demand for ten years or more into the future, particularly those industries which rely on large investments in capital equipment; some fast-changing industries such as the electronics industry regard a year as a long time and may not predict demand for a given product more than three years or so in advance. In general, these concerns belong with the board of directors. The sales manager might have the task of contributing to a long-term forecasting exercise, but is unlikely to have sole responsibility for it.

The main users of sales forecasts are as shown in Table 9.1.

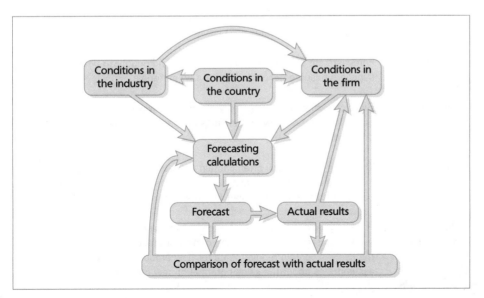

FIGURE 9.1

Sales forecasting as a process

Rules of sales forecasting

According to Donaldson (1998) sales forecasting should follow five basic rules, as follows:

1 Distinguish between hard and soft data. Hard data can be objectively assessed; past sales records, published statistics or other verifiable sources of information. Soft data are subjectively assessed; for example, research conducted into opinions or attitudes. Both are useful, but in different ways: hard data are useful for finding out what happened, soft data arej202 useful for understanding why it happened.

2 Use as few variables as possible and distinguish between dependent and independent variables. The dependent variable is related to a number of independent variables; for examples, sales level (dependent variable) is linked to sales-force activity levels, sales-force skill, marketing activities, market conditions, national economic conditions and a host of other factors. If all the independent variables were to be included, the forecasting process becomes hopelessly complex and prone to error – the errors which

TABLE 9.1 Users of sales forecasts

User	Ways of using the forecasts
Production	The forecasts are used to plan deliveries of raw materials, schedule the workforce in terms of hiring or arranging overtime, schedule purchases of plant and equipment, and arrange maintenance schedules. Similar considerations apply to service industries.
Distribution	Scheduling of delivery runs, availability of transport, arranging for just-in-time deliveries, and arranging warehousing and transhipment facilities.
Personnel	Forecasts are used to predict manning levels, training needs, staff development and management issues.
Purchasing	Forecasts are used to schedule deliveries and negotiate deals with suppliers based on expected use of raw materials.
Finance	Since the sales force is the only department which generates income, other departments rely on the sales forecast to be able to predict their own budgets.
Marketing	The sales forecast will often contain caveats about necessary marketing expenditure to achieve the forecast. Also, the marketing people will have a strong input into the development of the forecast.
Research and development	R & D demand is likely to be for long-term forecasts, which can be used to dictate the launch timing of new products. Sales forecasts may themselves contain requirements for new product launches, or assumptions about the sales potential of new products.

arise from using too few variables are probably less serious than those arising from using too many variables. Trying to forecast too many dependant variables is also dangerous because it leads to overloading the system and creating too much work.

3 Use the indicators that have proved most reliable in the past. Housing starts tend to be good predictors for the construction industry, for example.

4 Identify appropriate time relationships. There will often be a lag in the effects of a change in an independent variable, and this will not necessarily be obvious to the observer. For example, it is fairly obvious that a change in the number of new home starts will affect demand for bricks almost immediately, but the impact on sales of curtains and soft furnishings may take some time to follow on.

5 Do not use variables which cannot themselves be forecast. For example, it is almost impossible to forecast the persuasiveness of salespeople, or to predict outbreaks of war.

Use of hard data is likely to lead to a more accurate forecast than the use of hunches or guesswork. The data are used to build a model of reality which can be used to predict outcomes. Model building is problematical in that there exists a trade-off between making the model complex enough to reflect reality (which makes it difficult to produce and maintain) or making it simple enough to be easily produced and comprehensible, but probably a poorer predictor because it leaves out too many variables. Because models will tend to suffer from one or other of these failings, or even both of them, managerial judgement will usually come into play. Some research (Mathews and Diamantopoulos 1986) suggests that the accuracy of such models is increased by managerial adjustment, even though such adjustment is inevitably subjective.

▋ Collecting information

Much of the information used in forecasting will be collected via management information systems or market research (see Chapter 10). Much of it will be collected by and from the sales force itself; this should be extremely beneficial, since the salespeople are closest to the customers. However, information gathered in this way suffers from the following problems:

- Salespeople would always rather make a sale than collect information.
- Salespeople may not be objective; research shows that results using sales staff varied considerably from those obtained using outside researchers (Fouss and Solomon 1980).
- Collecting, or even recording, information takes time which might be better spent selling.
- Some accounts may be given more attention than others – for example, the most vociferous customers, or the last ones to be visited, may be given greater weight than others.
- Customers may not give the salesperson the unvarnished truth; the differing role of researcher and negotiator is almost certain to lead to bias.

Marketing Intelligence (Mintel) reports are widely-used in many industries. These reports are produced by using traditional survey methods and sources of secondary data – methods which are easily available to any firm in the industry. What makes Mintel successful is that the firm carries out very large surveys, with between 1000 and 6000 respondents. The investment in research is huge – and yet Mintel reports sell for around £1000.

Spreading the cost in this way allows firms to access high-quality, detailed information at a fraction of the cost of carrying out the research themselves.

Objective market research methods tend to be more expensive, but have the advantage of being, usually, more accurate. In some industries the leading firms pool their resources to buy basic market research collectively. This has the advantage of minimizing the cost for individual firms, and any extra research can be carried out separately if the firm wants to gain an information advantage. Since each firm will be collecting the same information about, for example, market shares, it seems obvious to collect the information only once – this is less irritating for the customers in the industry, who would otherwise be asked the same questions four or five times, and cuts the cost dramatically.

Consensus methods involve asking interested parties (the sales force, the marketing department, the sales managers) to make predictions about future sales, based on whatever factors they as individuals feel are relevant. The predictions are then integrated in some way to produce a single forecast.

The main advantages of this system are as follows:

- Those involved in creating the forecast are also those who will have to make it a reality.
- The forecast is prepared by those who are closest to the customers, i.e. the sales force.
- Involvement in producing the forecast makes the salespeople feel more involved in the company's aims and objectives.
- Preparing the forecast makes the salespeople consider wider issues, and think long term rather than focusing on the next sale.

Often consensus methods are operated poorly; it is not unusual for boards of directors, or even marketing managers, to forecast that next year's sales will be 10 per cent higher than this year's, purely on the basis of wishful thinking. Equally, salespeople may be reluctant to commit to a forecast which might not be achieved, so some underestimating might well take place.

Several qualitative methods are available for estimating future sales. Firstly, the firm can use a jury of expert opinion approach (Peterson 1990). This involves setting up a committee of executives with the brief of developing a sales forecast. The committee then exercise their best judgement in developing a consensus about future sales. This is probably one of the oldest forecasting methods, but suffers from a lack of objectivity and also the possibility of bias due to office politics. In most cases the jury will be interdisciplinary, drawing its membership from marketing, sales, production, accounting, market research and so forth. Written justification for the estimate is sought from each committee member, and the composite view is agreed on as a result of meetings.

A similar approach was developed by the Rand Corporation, and named the Delphi technique. Delphi is more often used to develop long-term forecasts, and involves assembling a panel of experts from both inside and outside the firm. Membership might be drawn from leading academics, members form private research foundations, industry leaders and so forth. Delphi differs from the jury of expert opinion approach in that the jury members are kept apart and form their opinions independently. Each member prepares a forecast which is submitted, then a report is prepared which amalgamates all the individual forecasts. This is then circulated to the members of the panel, who are invited to amend their predictions on the basis of the composite report. The process continues until a reasonable consensus is reached.

The major advantage of Delphi is that it eliminates the group pressures caused by a committee meeting. It also removes any problems arising from office politics, since the members do not necessarily know who else is on the panel. The main drawback is that it can be somewhat expensive and time consuming – the experts are expensive to hire, and the reiteration of the process can take some time, since the experts are likely to be busy people who have other calls on their time.

A third commonly used method is the sales-force composite approach. The basis of this is that each salesperson is thought to be the best person to estimate sales on his or her own territory. Salespeople are invited to estimate future sales on their own territories, and these forecasts are then combined to achieve an overall estimate for the company or division. The difficulty lies in ensuring that salespeople are honest about their estimates. If they fear that they will be punished or disadvantaged if they fail to meet the estimated figures they may underestimate. On the other hand, overconfidence might lead to overestimating (van Rycke 1986). It has been suggested that some form of bonus might be offered based on the accuracy of the forecast (Gonek 1978) but this might lead to overachieving salespeople being penalized, or to resentment by salespeople whose estimates are thrown out by events beyond their control.

Sales-force composites work best if the sales force is given some training in making forecasts, if the sales managers are involved in reviewing the estimates, and if the salespeople are assured that the estimates will not be used as a stick with which to beat them (Cox 1989). If these conditions are met, salespeople are more likely to accept the quotas allocated to them, since they have had a major role in their preparation.

A more formal approach based on the marketplace is the survey of buyer's intentions method. This works well if the buyers are clearly defined and limited in number, which is the case in most industrial markets. Various levels of sophistication are apparent in these surveys, but they all have the advantage of being based on direct responses from the market. The group of buyers will be approached and asked what their buying intentions are for the next year, and a composite forecast will be developed from this.

The drawbacks are, of course, considerable. In a major-account situation the buyers are unlikely to know what their needs are for the next year, for example.

Also, people do not always do what they say they are going to do. Thirdly, if buyers knew in advance what they were going to buy, there would be no need for a sales force. Finally, some buyers may overestimate their future needs in order to extract concessions form the company.

The drawback of all consensus methods is that they often amount to no more than educated guesswork. In addition, consensus is often time consuming to achieve, and can sometimes be led by one or two powerful voices, who may or may not be objective in their assessment.

With all forms of sales forecast, it is usually better to forecast sales by item rather than by sales revenue. The reason for this is that it removes the problem of handling inflation (price increases) or discounting (price reductions). In some firms, sales forecasts are estimated in profit terms, which may be even more realistic.

Actual performance should be checked against predicted performance. Many firms only compare last year's figures with this year's, thus comparing where they used to be with where they are now. While this is an interesting comparison, and often gives rise to self-congratulation, the comparison should really be between where the firm is now and where it ought to have been by now. The reasons for this are as follows:

- The market itself may be growing, in which case an increase in business is only to be expected, and is not necessarily due to any greater efficiency or effectiveness.

- A small increase in business may be pleasing, but competitors may have made large increases over the same period, thus capturing a greater market share.

- The world is changing rapidly, and comparison only with last year's figures does not give sufficient warning of new factors entering the equation. A deviation from projected figures may indicate some change in the marketplace which would not necessarily be apparent if comparison is only being made with the previous year's figures.

■ Analysing information

Analysis of objective information (hard data obtained from management information systems or quantitative market research) falls into two categories. Firstly, data can be analysed by time-series techniques. Time series assumes that the only independent variable is time. Sales figures are compared with the previous month or previous year, and variations in the figures over time are explained purely by the seasonality factor. In some cases time and seasonality might in fact be the major variables in sales; for example, a toy manufacturer will make most of the year's sales in January, when stores order for the following Christmas, and make most of their deliveries in October and November. Firework manufacturers make most of their sales ahead of public holidays, and barbecue manufacturers make most of their sales in winter and early spring ready for delivery in early summer.

One of the problems of using a time series method is that occasional blips in the figures can distort the following month's forecast. The simplest way of smoothing out these blips is to use a moving average. A moving average takes the average of the preceding, say, six months, each month adding in the new month's figures and deducting the first month's figures. Table 9.2 shows an example of this.

Figure 9.2 shows the same values graphically; this method of display shows how the smoothing has taken place.

The variations in sales can still be seen, but the anomalies (such as the exceptionally high figures for April and November, or the exceptionally low figures for August) have less effect on the overall trend.

One of the problems with a straight moving average is that the average includes figures which are some months old; response to any changes in the marketplace will need to be rapid, so it is likely that more recent figures will be more relevant. To overcome this problem, greater weighting can be given to the more recent figures by using a technique called exponential smoothing. The actual calculations are usually carried out by computer, and the weightings can be applied as a matter of professional judgement on the part of the manager. If recent figures are given a higher weighting, the curve will be less smooth; if given a lower weighting, the curve will be less responsive to market shifts.

TABLE 9.2 Example of a moving average

Month	Sales figures (£000s)	Moving average (to end June)	Moving average (to end Jul.)	Moving average (to end Aug.)	Moving average (to end Sept.)	Moving average (to end Oct.)	Moving average (to end Nov.)	Moving average (to end Dec.)
Jan.	238	*						
Feb.	342	*	*					
Mar.	328	*	*	*				
Apr.	492	*	*	*	*			
May	381	*	*	*	*	*		
Jun.	278	343	*	*	*	*	*	
Jul.	405		371	*	*	*	*	*
Aug.	206			348	*	*	*	*
Sep.	321				347	*	*	*
Oct.	334					321	*	*
Nov.	508						342	*
Dec.	307							347

* months which are included in the calculation

An extension of exponential smoothing is the Box–Jenkins technique (Box and Jenkins 1976), which applies different weightings to different parts of the time series. Here the computer takes earlier parts of the time series and weights them against known sales from later parts of the time series. The weighting that provides the best fit is calculated, and this is used to forecast future sales over the next time series. The technique produces a much more accurate forecast than that generated by exponential smoothing, particularly for short-term and medium-term forecasts.

As computer programs become more sophisticated, such analyses will become more accurate and sophisticated. The drawback with time series is that the relationship between sales and time is a tenuous one. Time series ignores other factors, such as changes in the industry, changes in the sales force and its motivation, and changes in the marketplace. If sales deviate from the expected figure, these other factors need to be called into play to explain the deviation, so a more accurate forecast would be generated if such factors were included in the first place.

Causal methods

Causal methods develop from time-series approaches, but try to establish the causes for sales increases and decreases. The basis of the approach is to try to predict changes in the dependent variable from changes in one or more independent variables. This relies on having independent variables which can themselves be predicted with some accuracy. In this case, time is not regarded as the

FIGURE 9.2

Smoothing effect of calculating a moving average

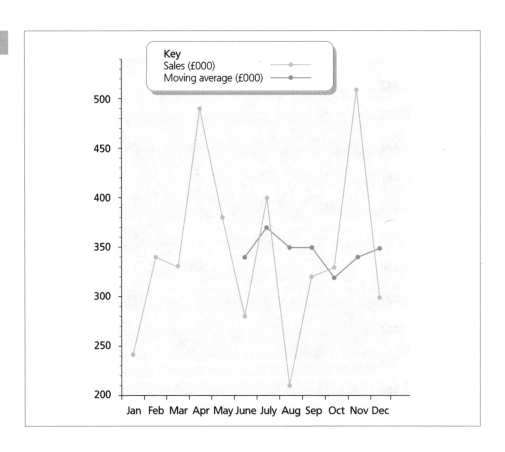

sole independent variable; the time series which shows seasonality (for example, increased sales during the summer months) may be unreliable if the summer is abnormally wet. A causal relationship (sales increase during fine weather) would be more accurate, but this time the prediction would be based on the long-range weather forecast rather than on the month.

Using more than one independent variable increases the accuracy of the forecast, provided the right variables are chosen; in some cases, the variables will show clear relationships, but the causality will not be clear; statistical analysis abounds with variables which change very closely alongside each other, but which have no discernible connection. Multiple linear regression, using computer packages such as SPSS or Minitab, can perform the calculations, but the sales manager must ensure that the interpretation of causality, and the interpretation of the final figures, makes some kind of sense.

Diffusion models

When new products are first launched into the market, there are no past sales on which to base predictions of future sales. For this reason, various models have been developed which seek to illustrate the innovation diffusion process. Diffusion theory assumes that social factors, communication factors, product factors and time are related in a complex manner which generates diffusion over time. Social factors apply as much in industrial markets as in consumer markets.

Everett M. Rogers (2003) classified customers for innovations as follows:

- *Innovators*: those who like to be first to own the latest products.
- *Early adopters*: those who are open to new ideas, but like to wait a while after initial launch.
- *Early majority*: Those who buy once the product is thoroughly tried and tested.
- *Late majority*: Those who are suspicious of new things, and wait until most other people already have one.
- *Laggards*: those who only adopt new products when it becomes absolutely necessary to do so.

Rogers' research was carried out among farmers, so the research is based on industrial selling; there is no reason to doubt that the same results would apply to consumer markets, however.

Innovations themselves can be classified as follows (the list is in order of technological distance from existing products) (Robertson 1967):

- *Continuous innovations*: Those which represent a small incremental improvement on an existing product; the new model.
- *Dynamically continuous*: Those which represent a considerable change over the existing product, offering new benefits in a new package.
- *Discontinuous*: Those innovations which bear little or no relationship to what has been available before, and which will change the way the customers run their lives. For example, the home video recorder has made a radical change in people's lives, changing TV viewing habits, affecting cinema attendances, and changing the face of the advertising industry.

Some products are adopted faster than others, and of course some innovative products are quickly superseded by even newer models. Typically, the fashion industry and the consumer electronics industry are very fast moving, so measures of the expected rate of adoption will need to be put in place and then carefully monitored to correct for any deviation.

Communication can be formal or informal, sought or unsought. Formal communication is, at least in part, the province of personal selling; the product is taken out to the customers and demonstrated. Informal communication is likely to follow, via word-of-mouth between potential customers; innovation theory demonstrates that some people are more influential than others in this process, so identifying and contacting the influentials will help the process along. This needs to be built into the model.

Sought communications are those where the potential customer seeks out the information (Blythe 2003). In personal selling, this will happen where the customer contacts the firm for information, or approaches the salespeople on an exhibition stand. Unsought communications are those where the company goes to the customer, and in innovation diffusion it is likely that this form of communication will predominate in the initial stages, with sought communication becoming more prevalent as the late majority and laggards seek out the product.

▮ Budgeting

Having produced the sales forecast, management can develop a budget for the next year's operations. A budget is the financial guideline which controls expenditure; the projected income shown in the sales forecast needs to be divided up between the various departments responsible for its achievement. In most cases, this process will be carried out by the firm's accounting and finance people, to the accompaniment of heads of departments demanding their own slice of the cake. The sales department is in the same position as all the other departments; each department regards itself as being crucial to the firm's success, and indeed salespeople would have nothing to sell if it were not for the production people, they would have no administrative back-up were it not for the finance people, and no marketing support were it not for the marketers.

Producing the sales budget means balancing alternative ways of spending the money. In most cases, this means making an economic choice; deciding to spend money on one aspect of the sales process means having to cut back expenditure on something else. Deciding what can safely be cut from the budget is as important as deciding what should be supported. For example, setting up a telesales operation may save money on salespeople's expenses, since they will spend less time cold calling, but this alone will not justify the cost. A telesales operation must be justified on the basis that it will increase time spent actually presenting products. Equally, the money spent setting up the telesales operation might be diverted from increasing the incentive programmes for the salespeople, which might have a detrimental effect on motivation, which in turn might decrease selling activity.

Basic budgeting follows four possible philosophies. Firstly, the objective and task approach can be used. This involves setting objectives and deciding on the appropriate amount of money to apply to achieving the objectives. This method is attractive, in that it allows for very clear cost–benefit analyses to be undertaken; it is difficult to apply, unfortunately, because it is difficult to assess how much money and other resources will be needed to achieve the objective. For example, competitive response or other changes in the market can seriously affect the planning.

Secondly, the percentage of sales approach is commonly used. This method involves setting the budget as a fixed percentage of sales, perhaps 10 per cent. There is a fatal flaw in the conceptual basis for the approach; it is based on the false idea that sales create promotional expenditure, and usually results in less being spent on selling activities when sales fall, thus reducing sales further. It does have the advantage of being simple, and is usually the basis for setting commission payments for salespeople; it is favoured by finance directors, who find that it makes the calculations simpler.

The competition matching approach involves spending the same as the competition. This has the advantage of ensuring that the firm does not lag behind its competitors in terms of expenditure, but it also means that the firm is allowing its budgets to be set by its enemies. The other major problem with this route is that competitors are, naturally, unlikely to be forthcoming about revealing the details of their budgets.

Fourthly, there is the arbitrary approach whereby a senior executive, usually a finance director, simply says how much can be allowed within the firm's overall budgets. This suffers from the major disadvantage that it does not take account of how the firm is to achieve the objectives. This is left as an exercise for the sales manager, and leaves many questions unanswered.

The sales budget needs to be broken down as shown in Table 9.3. The figures shown are for illustration only; each firm's situation is different, and should be treated accordingly.

Although it is difficult to do, sales managers need to regard the sales force as an investment. The expenditure made on the sales force should, ideally, be linked to a return on the investment, and experience over a number of years should enable sales managers to make a reasonable estimate of what the return will be for a given investment. This will enable the necessary trade-offs between investment in the

TABLE 9.3 Elements of the sales budget

Element	Explanation	Possible percentage of budget
Employment costs	Salaries, wages, employer's contributions to pension schemes, etc.	60%
Travel	Costs of running the sales-force – cars, overnight stays in hotels, train or air fares, etc.	15%
Motivation	Incentives, competitions, sales conferences, bonuses, etc.	15%
Miscellaneous expenditure	Telephone costs, office expenses, sales support.	10%

different elements to be made. It is always tempting to try to cut back on administrative overhead; if this is to be effective, the manager must ensure that it is the administration itself which is streamlined, not merely the number of administrators that is cut back. If the number of support staff is cut without cutting the amount of paperwork, this will give an immediate saving, but in the longer run the sales force will end up doing their own paperwork and this will cut back on time spent selling.

■ Territory management

Forecasts and budgets need to be devolved down to the salespeople who have to deliver the sales. These salespeople need to have a fair chance of working within the budgets set, and thus achieving, or exceeding, the forecasts. The budget will be developed as both a forecast of the revenue each salesperson is expected to bring in, and a forecast of the expenditure each salesperson will be allowed to commit the firm to in order to bring in the sales. In order to make these figures achievable, salespeople will need to be allocated territories in which the revenues are available and the expenditure will remain within the budget; for example, a salesperson covering a remote area of Scotland will undoubtedly incur more expenditure on travelling and will have less time available for selling than would a salesperson based in a heavily populated area such as the English Midlands.

The purpose of establishing fixed territories is to ensure that the salespeople know where and to whom they are supposed to be selling, and to ensure that effort is not duplicated by having several salespeople calling on the same group of prospects. Territories are usually, but not always, geographical in extent, since this minimizes sales-force travelling time. Occasionally territories will be designated according to types of customer (IBM use this system) but the price of this method is that sales-force expenses will rise considerably. The advantage is that the salespeople concerned gain greater understanding of the business sector they are dealing with, and are thus more able to assess customer needs.

Table 9.4 shows the main reasons for establishing territories. Not all firms will establish territories for all of the reasons, but these are the main reasons for doing so.

The main issue with territory planning is to ensure that the territories are as nearly equal as is possible. If territories are not equal, the salespeople concerned will often develop resentment towards their colleagues and the management, and in any case it will prove difficult or impossible to make comparisons between territories. Having said that, creating equal territories presents a number of problems:

- Travelling distances may be greater in a rural territory, even though the number of prospects may be the same.
- Some regions may contain more large customers than others, so order values are greater.
- Some regions may have more competitive activity than others.
- Different products may be more popular in some parts of the country than in others; for example, Scotland consumes more canned food than England, whereas frozen food is more popular in England.

- Different salespeople have different strengths and weaknesses with particular types of customer, with particular geographical areas, or with particular products.

For nine out of ten sales managers, sales territories are either inherited from a previous manager or they develop on an ad hoc basis as the firm expands. Occasionally a sales manager will have the opportunity to allocate sales territories from scratch, and of course virtually all sales managers have the power to revise sales territories and make alterations as necessary.

The task of designing, or redesigning, territories follows distinct stages, as shown in Figure 9.3.

The first stage is to select the basis on which the territories will be allocated. There are three bases for allocation; according to customer type, according to product type, or according to geography. The comparison between them is as shown in Table 9.5.

The second stage in territory design is to determine the size and scope of the territory within the overall base. This is true for all three types; if territories are allocated by product type, each salesperson may be allocated more than one product, or more than one salesperson might be allocated to a single product category. The same is true for customer types, and there will be circumstances in which it is appropriate to combine approaches. For example, a computer software house might allocate one salesperson to sell training systems to banks, and another to sell training systems to insurance companies; a third might be allocated to sell accounting systems to the same banks that the first salesperson is selling to. Given

TABLE 9.4 Reasons for establishing territories

Reason	Explanation
Performance evaluation	Comparison between territories and comparison of results from different time periods within the same territory are easier when the territories are clearly established on a fair basis.
Defining responsibilities	Having a specific territory enables the salesperson to have a clear understanding of what is expected. If the territory is based on customer type rather than on geography, the salesperson is able to determine which prospects are fair game and target effort accordingly; if the territory is geographical, the salesperson is able to establish ownership of prospects within the area.
To ensure that the market is covered thoroughly	The market can be divided up and allocated to salespeople so that the sales manager is confident that each prospect has been allocated a salesperson. If this were not the case, salespeople might converge on the most profitable, or easily sold to, prospects.
To ensure continuity for customers	If territories have been allocated appropriately, the salesperson concerned in each territory will be able to establish long-term relationships with the firm's customers within the area. This is reassuring for customers, and makes life easier for the salespeople also, since they become attuned to customers' needs.
Cost reduction	Geographical territories ensure that salespeople do not waste time and money pursuing deals which are a long distance from their homes or offices.

the complexity of the systems and the customers' needs, plus the high order values of such products, this might be a prudent way to organise the sales force.

Fine-tuning of the territories can be conducted according to sales potential, customer servicing needs, or workload. Table 9.6 shows how this operates.

A second approach to territory design is to build each territory up from individual accounts, areas or products. This has the advantage of ensuring that each territory has equal potential for the salespeople servicing them, and is an improve-

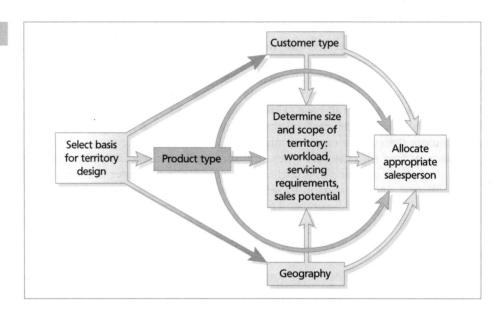

FIGURE 9.3

Designing territories

TABLE 9.5 Bases for allocating territories

Basis	Advantages	Disadvantages
Product	The salesperson becomes expert in the particular product type. Where products are complex, the salesperson is able to deal with fellow experts on an equal basis.	Can lead to product orientation. Also the salespeople can spend inordinate amounts of time travelling, unless the prospects are clustered in a small geographical area; for example, head offices of UK banks are almost all in the City of London.
Customer type	The salesperson becomes expert in the customers' problems and is more able to anticipate needs, and transfer solutions from other customers facing similar problems.	Again, travelling time may become excessive. There may be some difficulty in deciding who the main players are in a particular market, and thus allocating territories fairly may prove difficult.
Geographical	The only real advantage is that the salesperson saves on travelling time. In some industries, for example tourism, local knowledge might also be a factor in selling success.	Salespeople are unlikely to have the detailed product knowledge needed if the range of products being sold is wide; equally, customer knowledge may not be comprehensive if many different types of customer are involved.

ment on another common method, which is to break the territory down from the company's aggregate sales potential. The main drawback of the latter method is that it is conceptually unsound; it assumes that sales forces result from sales, rather than the other way round.

A third approach is the incremental method, where new sales territories are created on the basis that there is sufficient sales potential in the new territory to make it worthwhile employing someone to service the area. This is particularly useful to firms which are expanding into new areas, or new countries.

TALKING POINT

ACORN (a classification of residential neighbourhoods) is a system which breaks down areas of the country according to the type of housing it contains. The theory is that the type of house someone lives in says more about them than their income or occupation.

ACORN is a useful tool for dividing up sales territories. In some cases, the type of product is likely to sell better in some areas than in others, and in other cases the classification can be used to ensure that territories are equally divided.

TABLE 9.6 Fine-tuning territories

Method	Explanation
Sales potential	The sales potential for the whole firm and for its market segments is estimated, then divided according to the salespeople available to do the work. The advantage is that each territory has the potential to produce the same amount of business; the drawback is that the territories might show marked differences in difficulty of coverage, competitive activity and customer density.
Servicing requirements	In markets with a large number of repeat customers, servicing existing accounts is the main issue. Often accounts are classified as A, B or C accounts according to potential: A accounts are those which will generate the most business, but are most susceptible to competitive pressures; these will be called on most frequently; B accounts are steady, loyal customers who might be called on regularly; C accounts are marginal, and would receive less servicing, perhaps by telesales rather than personal visits.
Workload	The workload approach includes more factors in the calculation, including such issues as topography and competitive activity. Territories are divided according to the amount of work it is estimated will be needed to produce a given result. The main problem is that too many factors are involved; this makes the calculation difficult, and often inaccurate because the wrong factors are included.

The final stage in territory design is to assign the right person to service the territory. This can be problematical; a salesperson can succeed in one area, and fail miserably in another owing to differing account mixes (Parasuraman 1975). This may come about due to personality differences between the salesperson and the customers, or it may be due to the demoralizing effect of change.

Future developments affecting territory design

Traditionally, territories have mainly been created on a geographical basis, due to the need to maintain coherent lines of communication. Developments in electronic communications technology have reduced the necessity for such considerations; in the same way as the invention of the motor car reduced salespeople's dependence on railway routes, the advent of video conferencing, fax equipment, and e-mail have reduced their dependence on face-to-face meetings. This has eroded the main advantage of geographical territory design, and opened up possibilities for team selling.

■ Time management

One of the many areas in which IT can help the sales force is in time management. Careful planning of calls will reduce the time spent on the motorway, and also ensure that the sales force allocates time appropriately to customers and prospects. The problem falls into three parts; the amount of time that should be spent with different types of customer, the amount of time which should be spent with different types of prospect, and the division of time between prospecting and servicing existing accounts.

Computerized systems such as CallPlan can help integrate the various factors involved in an interactive way and devise the most efficient route and time allocation system for the salesperson. Parasuraman and Day (1977) have developed a further model called PAIRS (purchase attitudes and interactive response to salesmen) which integrates the following factors:

- Classification of customers into groups based on their responsiveness to selling effort.
- Assessment of the skills of the salesperson, by different customer groups.
- The impact of selling effort based on sales ability and calls made.
- The average purchase cycle to determine a planning horizon.
- Variations in time per sales call required for various groupings.
- Expected volume of sales from each type of customer.

The basic data on which the program works is collected from salespeople and sales managers, so the system is truly interactive. It generates an estimate of sales revenue from each group or customer for each period within the planning horizon. This allows the salespeople to allocate effort to those groups which are likely to show the greatest return.

SUMMARY

Sales-force activity needs to be planned around a clearly forecast future; if the firm does not know where it is going, then any route will do to take it there. Predicting the future and taking action to meet its threats and opportunities is becoming increasingly complex, and increasingly immediate; the past is no longer a reliable guide, and the pace of change is increasing to the point where change is a process rather than a series of events.

The key points from this chapter are as follows;

- Sales forecasting should be a process, not a one-off annual activity.
- The fewer the variables, the simpler the model; the greater the number of variables, the more detailed the model.
- Market research is more accurate than sales-force anecdotes.
- The relationship between sales and time is tenuous, so time-series analysis may not always be accurate.
- Consensus methods are less accurate than objective methods, but are often useful for explaining the root causes of sales fluctuations.
- Spending money on one aspect of the budget means that it cannot be spent on another; budgets are therefore sources of conflict between managers.
- The sales force should be regarded as an investment, and returns on the investment need to be calculated.
- Territories should be as near equal as possible, even though this is difficult to achieve in practice.
- Territories can be based on product categories, on customer categories, or on geographical territories.

REVIEW QUESTIONS

1 Since the sales team is the only department which generates income, why should they not have complete control over the budgets?
2 How might a sales manager avoid the problem of the automation system not living up to expectations?
3 Why can time series analysis not be used to predict the sales of a new product?

4 How might improved time-management techniques be built into forecasting?

5 What prediction methods might be most useful in the computer software industry?

REFERENCES

Battersby, A. (1968) *Sales Forecasting*, London: Cassell.

Blythe, J. (2003) *Essentials of Marketing Communications*, Harlow: Financial Times Prentice Hall.

Box, G. and Jenkins, G. (1976) *Time Series Analysis, Forecasting, and Control*, San Francisco, CA: Holden Day.

Cox, J. E. (1989) 'Approaches for improving salesperson forecasts', *Industrial Marketing Management* 18(1): 51–5.

Donaldson, W. (1998) *Sales Management Theory and Practice*, London: Macmillan.

Fouss, J. H. and Solomon, E. (1980) 'Salespeople as researchers: Help or hazard', *Journal of Marketing* 44 (Summer) 36–9.

Gonek, J. (1978) 'Tie salesmen's bonuses to their forecasts', *Harvard Business Review* 56 (May–June): 116–23.

Mathews, B.P. and Diamantopoulos, A. (1986) 'Factors influencing the nature and effectiveness of subjective revision of objective sales forecasts: An empirical analysis', *Contemporary Research in Marketing*, Proceedings of the XVth Annual Conference of the European Marketing Academy, Helsinki: 913.

Parasuraman, A. (1975) 'Assigning salesmen to sales territories: some practical guidelines', *Industrial Marketing Management* 4(6): 336.

—— and Day, R. L. (1977) 'A management-orientated model for allocating sales effort', *Journal of Marketing Research* XIV (Feb.): 22–3.

Peterson, R.T. (1990) 'Sales force composite forecasting – An exploratory analysis', *Journal of Business Forecasting* 8 (Spring): 23–7.

Robertson, T. S. (1967) 'The process of innovation and the diffusion of innovation', *Journal of Marketing* 31 (Jan.): 14–19.

Rogers, E. M. (2003) *Diffusion of Innovations*, 5th edn, New York: Free Press.

Van Rycke, R. (1986) 'Overconfidence leads to unrealistic sales forecasts', *Sales and Marketing Management in Canada* 27 (May): 16–17.

WIRELESS CUSTOMER-RELATIONSHIP MANAGEMENT

Customer-relationship management systems in most companies are about ensuring rapid communication of customer needs to the sales force. Whether this means passing leads out quickly, or getting messages from existing customers out fast, rapid communications is a key factor in sales success. As a result, many companies are giving their field sales forces access to the Internet via wireless connections. The problem in the past has been that the technology has not been available to co-ordinate corporate networks in a wireless protocol.

Aprisma Management Technologies, a company which produces infrastructure management software, has a particular problem in this respect. Demand for Aprisma products is volatile. Typically they are faced with a flurry of leads for their products when they exhibit, or when they run a telesales campaign, and these leads need to be followed up quickly. Exhibition leads, in particular, degrade quickly because prospects have almost always seen and contacted the firm's competitors. There is therefore a powerful need to get leads out to the salespeople as quickly as possible.

Aprisma has closed the gap with a suite of products from MarketSoft. MarketSoft's eLeads management software helps solve the problem by sending data direct to salespeople's hand-held mobile phones. Information from the firm, and about customers, can now be downloaded remotely by e-mail direct to the user's telephone.

'The quicker we can get those leads into the hands of our sales team or our channel partners, the better opportunity we have to turn it round into real revenue,' says Aprisma's marketing man, Darren Orzechowski. Darren controls a staff of 70 direct salespeople, and also controls channel partnerships with Compaq and Cabletron Systems.

The lead management software resides on Aprisma's server. Their own IT staff wrote a program which prioritizes prospects and sorts the leads into separate types, so that they can be delivered to the appropriate salespeople. The salespeople are allowed to specify how they are to be notified of the new leads or information, so they are not compelled to receive leads via their phones. Other options include e-mail to a PC or fax.

Aprisma does not need to use the WAP system because the MarketSoft software delivers the leads as e-mail. So far, salespeople who use the system have overwhelmingly opted for e-mail delivery. Aprisma has very fast methods for entering leads into the system. For example, at exhibitions and trade fairs where people often wear magnetic-strip or laser name tags, Aprisma can swipe the customer's details into the computer and have the lead out to a salesperson before the prospect has left the stand.

The overall result of introducing the new system is that Aprisma has dramatically increased their response times to customer enquiries, and have more than recouped the £70 000-plus cost of the software. Salespeople love the system – it means they sell more, and have less paperwork. From the sales manager's viewpoint, keeping all that information about customers and leads on a database makes planning much easier.

Case-study questions

1 What effect might the software have on territory design?
2 What are the major problems for Aprisma in forecasting sales?
3 What are the implications for time management of Aprisma's systems?
4 What possible basis might there be for allocating leads to salespeople?
5 What issues does MarketSoft need to consider when forecasting its own sales?

10

MONITORING AND FEEDBACK

Learning objectives

After reading this chapter, you should be able to:

- Understand how to set sales objectives.

- Develop systems for monitoring the achievement of objectives.

- Explain the differences between ordinary company meetings and sales meetings.

- Explain the use of management information systems.

- Describe the sources of information that are available to sales managers.

- Explain the purpose of feedback.

Introduction

No system of management can function unless the outcomes of the workforce effort are evaluated, and corrective measures taken. For this reason monitoring and feedback form a substantial part of the sales manager's responsibility to the company and to the sales force. Employees, in the main, would rather do a good job than do a bad one; provided their activities are monitored, and they are given suitable feedback, most employees will take action to correct their own mistakes and will get back on course without any further intervention by the managers.

Jean-Marc Chaput was born in Montreal, Quebec. A Harvard graduate, Jean-Marc began his working life as a lecturer, teaching office administration and sales courses at University of Montreal. Moving into sales, he sold life insurance and subsequently became a salesman in the tobacco industry. He entered 1969 as a millionaire, but then his luck took a turn for the worse – some bad investments left him virtually bankrupt. His wife, Celine, advised him, 'Start all over again. But this time sell the only thing you have left – yourself.' So Jean-Marc began calling on the companies he used to deal with, offering to inspire their sales teams. His ability to speak from experience, and his sense of humour, led to his becoming one of Canada's leading motivational speakers.

His book, *Vivre c'est vendre* (To live is to sell) helped raise his profile to the point where he spoke to full houses at the Grand Théâtre de Québec and the Place des Arts in Montreal. In 1999 the Canadian Professional Sales Association voted him one of the eight inaugural laureates of the CPSA Hall of Fame. His courage and the ability to pick himself up from defeat have been instrumental in his success, far more so than his degrees and experience, powerful though these are.

Feedback systems

When a discrepancy appears between the expected performance and the actual performance, the sales manager or the salesperson will need to take action. This action will typically take the following sequence:

- Determine the reason for the discrepancy. Was the original plan reasonable? Have competitors seized the initiative in some way so that the situation has changed? Has something else changed in the business environment? Is someone at fault?
- Feed these findings back to the salespeople. This can happen at a meeting to discuss the situation, or in e-mails, memos and reports.
- Develop a plan for correcting the situation. This will probably involve the co-operation of all the staff concerned, not just the salespeople.

Feedback should be both frequent and concise, and any criticisms should be constructive; managers should never, for example, go to a sales meeting and offer only criticisms since this sends the sales force out with negative feelings about themselves and the company.

Sales strategy and planning is much like any other planning exercise. It relies on good information, a clear idea of where the organization is going, and regular examination of both outcomes and methods to ensure that the plan is still on target.

Managers often misjudge the seriousness of problems confronting their staff (Lilly *et al.* 2003). Frequently they will assume that a problem which is outside the control of the staff or the sales manager is actually more serious than a problem which is within their control. In fact, this is not the case, so managers' bias in this direction is, in general, counterproductive.

▌ Control systems

The purpose of any strategic control system is to decide whether the current strategy is correct, and should therefore be retained, or whether circumstances have altered in such a way that the strategy should be scrapped and a new one formulated.

Most control is reactive; it seeks out variances in performance, and applies a correction to redress the variance. Such feedback is called negative feedback, because it acts against the trend of the variance in order to reduce it. Feedback which tends to increase the variance is called positive feedback, and is generally considered to be counterproductive since it creates a situation where the system runs away with itself entirely in one direction. In some cases, a variation which is self-correcting, i.e. a temporary blip in performance, may be over-compensated for, so that variance increases rather than decreases. This comes about because of time delays in the feedback systems. Figure 10.1 illustrates how this works in practice.

In Figure 10.1, the first arrow shows how feedback applied too late will send sales rocketing too high. This may seem like a good outcome, but it is likely that the feedback applied will have been a costly sales-boosting exercise such as a major sales promotion or an advertising campaign, the result of which is a fall in profits, possibly a fall in competitive position, and at worst provokes an insupportable competitive reaction. The second arrow shows a correctly applied negative feedback, which helps the fall in sales to bottom out and return to normal.

Some fluctuation is inevitable. Minor deviations from the plan will always occur sooner or later; the difficulty for managers lies in judging the extent to which such deviations are permissible before action must be taken.

The concept of feedback and control is borrowed from engineering. The controls for a machine are intended to maintain the status quo; some controls are

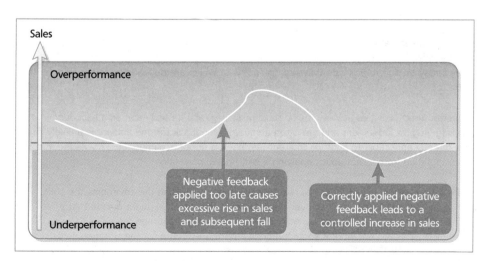

FIGURE 10.1

Positive and negative feedback

automatic (for example, the governor on a steam engine) while others are designed for used by a machine operator (for example, the accelerator on a car). In either case the machine will obey the control systems, because that is what it has been designed to do.

Human beings are not machines. The most difficult management issues concern the control of human beings, and this is the area where feedback systems most often break down. For the purposes of feedback and control, processes can be divided into systematized processes such as repetitive telesales or order-taking tasks, and unstructured processes, which are activities requiring judgement (Dermer 1977). Examples of the second type would include major-account selling, and within the firm they would include senior managerial tasks and one-off projects. For most 21st century firms, unstructured processes are in the majority, simply because repetitive work has been taken over by computers and most routine work has been automated. Since Dermer first formulated this division in 1977, the number of people working in manual jobs has more than halved.

Difficulties with control systems

The type of thinking that applies to engineering problems is not necessarily applicable to human problems. Each has its own set of assumptions which may not hold true for the other; certainly many of the assumptions made by managers prove to be false when attempts are made to put them into practice. Finlay (2000) says that there are four assumptions borrowed from engineering which do not transfer to management. These are shown in Table 10.1.

TABLE 10.1 Assumptions underlying control systems

Assumption	Problems with this view
Objectives can be devised and can be stated precisely.	Most organizations do not have clear objectives, but rather have broad goals. In most cases it is possible to set objectives for the sales force, but whether the objectives are realistic is another matter entirely.
Achievement can be measured and a measure of variance can be calculated.	Without measurable objectives, achievement cannot be measured. Even if there is a measurable objective, the reason for the variance may be difficult to calculate – a fall in sales may be due to a great many factors, some of which are beyond the salesperson's control.
Variance information can be fed back.	Unstructured activities such as major-account selling, and indeed most small-account selling, involve judgement and are often unique, so feedback for one activity is unlikely to be directly applicable to another. Indirect feedback is about accumulating knowledge and extrapolating from it, not about applying a set, known correction.
The feedback is sufficient to maintain control.	The system will only work if the applied feedback is bigger than the environmental shift. For example, a company selling over-the-counter cold medicines might decide that a fall-off in sales should be followed by an incentive scheme to encourage the sales force to sell more. This will not work if someone finds a permanent cure for the common cold.

Because of these problems, firms need to use adaptive controls. While much of the control system can be automatic, managers need to use human judgement to override the system when necessary, otherwise long-term change is unlikely to happen. Hofstede (1978) uses a biological analogy to explain this in terms of a living cell, but it may be more appropriate to think of a more complex organism. Fluctuations in outside temperature can be compensated for by the body's natural homeostatic mechanisms – sweating when the temperature is too high, shivering when it is too cold – but beyond certain limits of comfort a human being will exercise judgement and either go somewhere cooler or wear something warmer, as appropriate. In a similar way, organizations need to exercise judgement when the environment behaves in a way that is beyond the control system's capacity.

Two methods of control exist: firstly, to change the sales force's behaviour in some way to overcome the difficulty and reach the objective, or secondly to change objectives and aim for something that is achievable rather than something that is not. The ancient Greek philosopher Diogenes was perhaps the greatest exponent of the latter course; in order to avoid the problems of earning enough money to live in a house, he chose to live in a barrel instead. This option may not always be the optimum one.

Controls come in hierarchies, and levels of control are exercised at different levels of the organization. Three generic ways of controlling the course of events in the business are available: firstly, changing the inputs to the system; secondly, the process itself can be controlled; thirdly, the objective of the organization can be changed.

Tactics of control

There are three basic types of control, as shown in Table 10.2 (Johnson and Gill 1993).

Administrative control is often exercised through planning systems which control the allocation of resources and monitor the utilization of resources against the plan. Planning systems might be top–down, centralized systems in which the

TABLE 10.2 Types of control

Type of control	Explanation and examples
Administrative control	Based on systems, rules and procedures, administrative control is typical in hierarchical organizations which often have large numbers of rules and regulations.
Social control	The control exercised by workmates and the organizational culture. This is common in organismic organizations and smaller organizations.
Self-control	Control exercised by individuals on themselves, based on their own interpretation of correct behaviour. This is common in organizations composed of professional people, who may be working to a professional code of ethics rather than a set of rules laid down by the employer.

standardization of work procedures is paramount. Within a devolved organizational structure, administrative control is more likely to centre on bottom–up planning, carried out within an overall set of budget constraints. In these circumstances, each division needs to reconcile its activities with other divisions in order to ensure consistency. This can become the main role of senior management within the organization. The risk of bottom–up planning is that key strategic issues are left out of the equation, because each division focuses on its own part of the problem without seeing the overall picture. Again, co-ordination is a function of senior management; the centre needs to establish the boundaries and reconcile the plans of the divisions, which may in turn mean that the centre should benchmark in order to establish best practice.

Control through direct supervision is common in small organizations, where one person is able to control resources effectively. In large organizations it is only really possible in conditions of stability or during times of crisis (for example, if the survival of the organization is threatened). Autocratic direct control by one person might be the only way the necessary changes can be forced through – although, of necessity, this is a route which is likely to lead to considerable resentment among lower-grade staff who are displaced or undermined.

Control through performance targets is common in sales management. Setting the correct performance indicators is far from easy; indicators often give only a partial view of the overall situation, and it is usually the case that the activities which are measured are the ones that get done, regardless of the real-life situations faced by the staff and managers in the organization.

Social and cultural control comes from the standardization of norms of behaviour within the organization. In such organizations, administrative controls have a lower priority: people behave in the way they do because it is the right way to behave, not because they have a boss applying the yardstick at every stage. In the 21st century organization, this type of control is likely to become much more prevalent since people are becoming more individualistic and more idealistic, and less inclined to obey orders blindly. Also, social controls are much more effective in sales organizations, in which it is impossible to lay down fixed procedures for dealing with every possible eventuality.

Social controls can sometimes work the other way, by hindering senior management when changes become necessary. The reason is that cultural norms are difficult to change, and people who regard themselves as professionals are likely to prove difficult if asked to do something which they feel impinges on their professional prerogatives.

In some respects, the 21st century sales force is likely to be less about controls and more about influences. Managers may not be able to impose fixed procedures on salespeople, partly because such procedures will be difficult to formulate, and partly because a well-educated, independent-minded sales force is unlikely to be as prepared to accept management by diktat as people were 50 or a 100 years ago. Influence can come from many sources, but the greatest influences are likely to be social ones, created by and in turn creating obligations between the sales team. This implies that managers will need to be charismatic rather than autocratic, and lead rather than drive the workforce.

▌ Evaluating salespeople's activities

Evaluation of sales-force activities is not always simple. Some sales managers take the view that only results count – either the salesperson made target, or did not make target. This results-focused attitude can cause resentment, or engender a selling orientation – the salesperson aims to bring in sales at any cost, sometimes alienating customers or damaging business in the longer term. In a major account selling situation this would, of course, be disastrous. The other problem with this approach is that it does not give the salesperson any clues as to what to do to correct the situation if the results are not achieved.

Evaluation is necessary so that the salesperson can identify above average or below average performance and make the necessary adjustments. Above average performance in one area of activity might well be linked to below average performance in another area; also, the average performance is obviously below the best possible performance. This means that in each case the salesperson needs to consider what should be the appropriate level of performance, given the other constraints.

A second problem with evaluating sales-force activity is the sheer volume of factors which make for selling success. In one review of the research undertaken into selling success, 1653 possible associations were identified (Churchill *et al.* 1985). Only an average of 4 per cent of variation in salesperson performance can be explained by any one variable, and since selling is a dynamic social process conducted between individuals it is unlikely that any single variable will emerge to explain what makes for selling success. The variables which appear to show some correlation with success are as follows:

- *Aptitude*: This is the individual's basic predisposition towards being successful at learning a given skill. Unfortunately, aptitude has many components, some of which are disputed between researchers and practitioners alike.

- *Skill*: Somewhat difficult to define, skill implies a pre-existing level of aptitude plus a training component. Like aptitude, it has many components, but the level of skill itself can be evaluated and tested fairly easily. In other words, although the components of skill are too numerous to be easily tested, the overall outcomes can be tested.

- *Motivation*: This is difficult to measure, and therefore difficult to evaluate in practice.

- *Role perception*: It is difficult to measure how the salesperson perceives his or her role, but there is a strong link with selling success. This is probably of limited practical value in evaluating performance.

- *Personal variables*: Some of these do exhibit consistent correlation with success, but again the number of variables makes it difficult to use in practice.

- *Organizational and environmental factors*: Correlations here are low and inconsistent, probably due to the complexity of the problem. Very few researchers have tried to assess these factors in terms of evaluating selling success.

The relationship between these factors is shown diagrammatically in Figure 10.2.

Sales-force evaluation programmes need to be realistic and fair, and preferably discussed and agreed with the salespeople themselves. Setting unrealistic targets or expecting more than is possible from the sales force will only lead to demotivation; on the other hand, setting targets too low does not give the salesperson anything to aim for. There are two basic approaches to setting up evaluation systems: outcome-based systems and behaviour-based systems. Outcome-based systems focus on what has been achieved; number of sales made, value of those sales, level of cancellations, profitability of the business won and other similar measures. Behaviour-based systems focus on issues such as the number of sales calls made, customer satisfaction measures, proportion of time spent in calls as opposed to being on the road, and other such measures of activity. Behaviour-based systems tend to work best in major-account selling situations, where outcomes may take months or even years to become apparent. Outcome-based systems are more common in fast-moving consumer goods areas, but should be used with a degree of caution. Outcome-based systems can easily lead to selling orientation, as explained earlier.

Planning the evaluation system involves two stages: deciding the strategic issues, and deciding the tactics to be used. Strategic issues are the objectives which the sales force, and the company, needs to reach; tactical issues are the methods used for reaching those objectives. Strategic objectives are often handed down by senior management, but could also be agreed between the sales manager and the marketing department. Table 10.3 shows the areas which need to be addressed.

Because selling is inherently creative, and because no two selling situations are identical, sales managers should not be too prescriptive in determining which activities are appropriate and which are not. Usually the activities that are being measured are the ones that will be prioritized, since the sales force will naturally concentrate on areas which they feel might be assessed later. For many people, that which is not measured does not exist. This can create distortions in working practices, but salespeople do need to be aware of what measures are being applied to their activities. It would not be seen as fair to measure an activity without telling the sales force that the measurement is being taken, and it would also remove the motivational effects inherent in the assessment process.

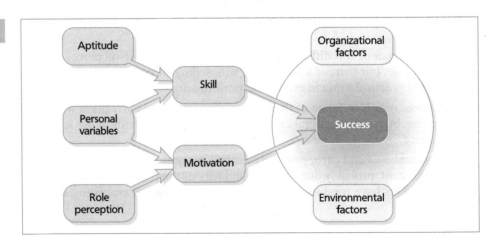

FIGURE 10.2

Factors in sales success

TALKING POINT

Bristol Myers Squibb is one of the leading pharmaceutical companies in the United States. The company is well known for its commitment to staff training and to developing people's skills; as one sales manager put it, 'What's kept me here for 15 years is the BMS culture. It's a culture that's directed towards its people. BMS wants to take care of those who are willing to work hard and do the right things.'

Pharmaceutical selling is dominated by missionary selling. The sales force is rarely in front of a buyer; usually they talk to doctors, hospitals and even State organizations which have influence over the decisions made. Pharmaceutical selling can almost be seen as a public-relations exercise, except that the results, in terms of sales, are much more tangible. The pharmaceutical industry is also characterized by a continuous training need as new, ever more complex products arrive on the market.

During the summer of 2002 BMS revamped its entire hardware and software support systems for its sales force. This included the M-Power office automation system, including the field sales force automation system CallMex. This system enabled BMS to manage sample distribution, capture doctors' signatures electronically, record and analyse data on prescribers, prepare reports, and use pen-tablet systems to communicate with head office. The new software also complied with new legislation (the Prescription Drug Marketing Act). The purpose of the software is to enable the company to track sales success in an industry where salespeople never actually take an order.

TABLE 10.3 Strategic and tactical issues in evaluation

Issue	Explanation
Strategy: Setting objectives	These may be sales objectives, such as a desired level of turnover, or they may be marketing objectives concerned with market penetration, response to competitors, or establishing a particular brand. Objectives are more than mere aims; an objective needs to be measurable if it is to be achievable, whereas an aim can be expressed in more general terms.
Strategy: Deciding on the tasks which need to be carried out in order to meet the objectives	Translating objectives into tasks may also involve deciding who is to carry out each task. For example, there may be a split between the marketing department and the sales department regarding some tasks; within the sales force, there may be division of labour between the field salespeople and a telesales team.
Tactic: Rewriting job descriptions	The salespeople's job descriptions should, ideally, contain a clear statement of their responsibilities, and these should reflect any redesigning of tasks. Rewriting job descriptions can be contentious, so it is advisable to involve the sales force and any other interested parties in the decision-making process.

TABLE 10.3 *(cont.)*

Issue	Explanation
Tactic: Establish the evaluation measures to be used	Sales do not always result directly from sales effort; sometimes a great deal of effort is applied but no sales result, at other times sales come very easily. Evaluation methods should take account of both effort and outcome; salespeople should be encouraged not only to work hard, they should also work smart.
Tactic: Ensure that the measures are used, and that they remain relevant	Measures may not be used if they are cumbersome to operate or if they are perceived as threatening. For example, if salespeople are compelled to fill in a lengthy report after each sales call, the likelihood is that they will leave the reports until the end of the day, or even the end of the week, which will almost certainly lead to inaccuracies. Equally, if reporting measures are used as a stick to beat salespeople with, the information given is likely to be less than accurate. Finally, sales managers need to take care to ensure that the measure being used actually records the activities intended.
Tactic: Apply corrective action	There is little point in identifying a problem if nothing is done to seek a solution. Often salespeople will think of their own answers to the problem of deviation from the objectives, but sales managers need to be prepared to discuss corrective action with the salespeople concerned, and to have answers ready.

Sources of information for evaluation

It is relatively easy to collect information on sales-force activities; the difficulty lies in deciding which information should be collected and which should not. Since the collection of information invariably takes time, either on the part of the sales manager or, more importantly, on the part of the sales force, there is a cost attached to information. Table 10.4 shows some of the more commonly used information sources, with their advantages and disadvantages.

Traditional evaluation systems tend to be geared to the E. K. Strong model of selling (see Chapter 4) rather than the more modern relationship or solutions model of selling. This means that there tends to be an emphasis on call rates, closing rates and order values rather than on relationship-building issues such as customer satisfaction and corporate reputation. In fairness, these are difficult to measure; most attempts to measure the customer's attitudes will inevitably mean contacting the customer, and many buyers would find this irritating or unsettling. Done on a regular basis such evaluations are likely to do more harm than good, and if the salesperson's bonuses or commission rest upon favourable reports from customers, the potential for damage is even greater.

The evidence is that salespeople will pursue organizational objectives more effectively when they are evaluated according to behavioural measures. When evaluated according to outcome measures, they tend to act in their own self-interest (Anderson and Oliver 1987).

Management information systems

Management information systems (MIS) are designed to ensure the regular collection, collation, analysis and presentation of information for management decision making. Such systems provide the management with information on a daily, weekly or monthly basis in the form of summaries, reports and statistics which give constant feedback on what is happening in the firm and in the market. MIS differ from one-off fact-finding exercises in that it is an ongoing process, with more or less permanent systems in place to provide a constant flow of relevant information. Information systems can be seen as holistic, all-encompassing systems which collect and collate all the information available within the company, or as a set of subsystems. In the former case, the quantity of information is likely to be so large that a sophisticated computer-based system will be needed to handle it. In the latter case, each department operates its own systems, which may or may not be computer based.

The advantage of using a subsystems approach is that it enables each department to be flexible in the type of information it collects, and to tailor the system to its own requirements. In a holistic system, the main advantage is that it is more cost effective, but also it ensures that information is available to all departments and thus it becomes easier to co-ordinate planning.

If a subsystems approach is being used, the sales management information system would probably be a subsystem of the marketing information system, which

TABLE 10.4 Advantages and disadvantages of information sources

Source	Advantages	Disadvantages
Company records	Easily available, relatively cheap to access, usually accurate and almost invariably relevant.	Only refers to the past, and therefore has no information on new customers or new market conditions. May not be in a form that is useful to the manager.
Sales reports	Salespeople would normally keep records of each visit; these have the advantage of being available, up to date and highly relevant.	Reports are likely to be incomplete or inaccurate if the salesperson thinks that the manager will be seeing them, particularly if there is a possibility that some material benefit or punishment might result from management scrutiny.
Field visits	Good for comparing different salespeople. Also reinforces the relationship between the salesperson and the supervisor.	Can be subjective. Salespeople may also ensure that the manager is only taken to calls where a favourable impression will be gained.
Customer contact and feedback	Collecting feedback direct from customers provides instant, up-to-date information about the salesperson's activities. It is independent of the company and therefore likely to be more objective.	Sometimes salespeople regard this as spying; it can also undermine the customer–salesperson relationship by making the customer think something must be wrong with the salesperson. If the customer puts the salesperson in a bad light this can also be damaging.

would itself be a subsystem of the general corporate management information system. The different approaches are compared in Figure 10.3.

In the holistic system, the management information system contains all the other systems; those shown are there for illustration only. Each of the subsystems allows information in and out on all sides so that information is shared through the overall management information system. In the subsystems approach, the overall management system sends and receives information to each subsystem, but the subsystems do not communicate with each other except through the filtering process of the overall management system. Instead of swimming in a sea of information, the subsystems own their own information, and exchange some of this with the main system.

The issues involved in developing a management information system are as outlined in Table 10.5.

Because of the rapidly changing nature of sales management, and indeed business life in general, systems need to be as open and flexible as possible. Rapid change is a feature of life in the early 21st century, and has wide-reaching implications, not least of which is that most employees are distrustful of changes in working practices, often with good reason. This applies equally to changes in information gathering systems and in feedback methods.

Management information systems often develop problems, or have problems built into them at the outset. Table 10.6 shows some of the most common problems, with possible solutions.

TABLE 10.5 Issues in MIS design

Issue	Explanation
Nature of the problem	The problem facing salespeople may be structured in the same way every time. For example, home-improvement salespeople tend to maintain fairly consistent closing rates on average, so a fall-off in orders can usually be traced to a fall-off in the number of presentations being conducted. On the other hand, the problem may be unstructured, as is usually the case with major-account sales. For structured problems, standard procedures and remedies can be laid down; for unstructured problems, judgements will have to be made.
Use of the information	If information is to be used for planning (for example if it is general market intelligence), it will be used at a strategic level. If it is to be used for control (for example information on a single salesperson's activities), it will be most useful at the tactical level. Strategic information will go to the sales manager and marketing people, tactical information to the sales manager and the salespeople themselves.
Type of decision	Some decisions can be pre-programmed, in the sense that the information coming in can be predicted, at least at an either-or level. For example, a decision could be made that if the sales figures for a particular area exceed a certain amount, extra salespeople will be hired to cover the area. Other decisions are not programmable because the information is unpredictable, as for instance when a competitor launches a new product.
Source of the information	Internal sources of information may lend themselves to programmed decision making because such information will usually follow a fairly predictable pattern. External information is coming from a less-controlled environment, and is therefore more likely to lead to unprogrammed decision making.

FIGURE 10.3

Management
information
systems

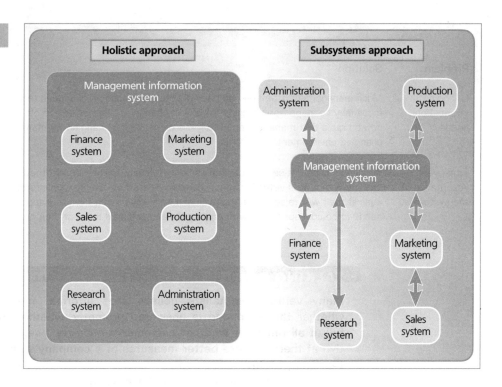

FIGURE 10.3

Management
information
systems

TABLE 10.6 Problems with MIS

Problem	Solution
Information overload	Computer technology has the ability to deliver far more information than the human brain can handle. The system needs to focus on information which is actually going to be used to make decisions, not on information which is collected simply to satisfy curiosity. The bulk of this information will be collected from the sales force, who probably have better things to do. Requests for 'all the available information' are almost certainly counterproductive, so the solution lies in identifying correctly what is the relevant information.
Inaccurate data	The main cause of inaccurate data input is likely to be salespeople who see the information-gathering process as a threat, and therefore only provide information which puts themselves in a favourable light. Overcoming this fear can be difficult, but two tactics will help: firstly, the information should never be used to punish people, and secondly the salespeople should be kept fully informed as to how the information is to be used. If the information gatherers feel that they have a stake in providing accurate information, they are more likely to be honest.
Language barriers	MIS systems are often developed by computer technicians who know how to provide information, but do not know what to provide; the sales managers, on the other hand, often know what they need information on, but do not know what other information could be provided, or how much more easily it could be presented. Sales managers and technicians can overcome this problem to some extent by talking through the problem at great length, and by being prepared to ask questions and seek clarification.

TABLE 10.6 *(cont.)*

Problem	Solution
Changing information needs	Much management attention has been devoted to managing change in recent years; in fact, this focus may be inappropriate since it looks at change as a series of one-off events. Change is now so rapid that managers need to focus on managing changing, or managing in a constantly changing environment.
Employee acceptance of the system	If employees do not see the system as being relevant to their needs, they are unlikely to co-operate with it. It is virtually impossible to force staff to comply with information gathering against their will; false information will almost always result from this approach. The system needs to be concept tested with employees and adjusted to meet their needs.

TALKING POINT

Many venture capitalists believe that informal measures such as whether the telephone is answered promptly, whether the car park is full at all times, or whether customer-service representatives are effective at their jobs are better measures of a company's potential than are the financial figures.

Few venture capitalists would have wanted to invest in WorldCom, the fraudulent firm set up by Bernie Ebbers. WorldCom's vice-president in charge of customer service, Thomas Barton, did not even exist – although his signature appeared at the bottom of response letters.

Integrating sales management information systems with the other information systems within the firm is another area where problems might arise. It is very easy to end up duplicating effort, or demanding far more information than is necessary; the costs and benefits of collecting the information need to be taken into account. Because sales managers are usually managing by remote control, in other words have few opportunities to observe the sales force in action, they often become tempted to ask for too much information. It is often better to trust the salespeople to get on with the job, rather than be constantly asking for information by which to monitor them.

Feedback

Feeding back the information to the sales force is important for two reasons: firstly, they need to be able to see the benefit of collecting the information in the first place, and secondly they need to be able to correct any discrepancies in their behaviour. There are three main ways of feeding back information to the sales force:

1 Written material such as reports, newsletters and e-mails.
2 One-to-one meetings at which problems are discussed.
3 Group meetings where information is exchanged in a positive way.

A factor that complicates the issue of giving feedback to salespeople is the need to put almost everything in a positive light. Salespeople can easily become infected with negative thinking, and this affects their performance seriously. Therefore any feedback given needs to emphasize benefits and solutions rather than drawbacks and problems.

For example, if the government is introducing a new tax on the goods the firm sells, this will give an opportunity for extra sales in the period immediately before the tax is imposed. Expressed this way, the new tax becomes an opportunity rather than a threat. The ability to think of positive outcomes is a useful one for sales managers; more experienced salespeople tend to develop this ability in the course of handling objections, but rookies and less experienced salespeople can become demotivated by negativity.

Written material

E-mails, newsletters and reports are only useful if the recipient reads and understands them. Given the ease with which such materials can be produced (especially e-mails), employees are often overwhelmed with information and therefore do not read all of what is sent them. Salespeople are more likely to read the information if:

- They can see the relevance of it.
- They know that they will be asked about it later.
- It is presented in an interesting and readable manner.
- They need to respond to it in some way, for example if they are asked to send back comments on it.

Newsletters are often used at national level, and usually contain profiles of successful salespeople around the country, articles on how to improve sales, details of forthcoming competitions and the winners of previous ones, and information about forthcoming opportunities for the company. Newsletters should be bright and interesting, and written in an accessible style; larger firms use professional journalists to write them.

E-mails need to be succinct and factual, but should still be positive even if the main information being conveyed has negative implications. Global e-mails should be avoided wherever possible – much of the time wasted on e-mails is spent deleting irrelevant messages.

Reports are often heavy going, which is why most of them contain an executive summary. Managers need to recognize that often it is only the executive summary which will actually be read, so there is a question mark over whether the rest of report needs to be sent out at all.

One-to-one meetings

The only time that negative issues can be discussed without causing demotivation is during one-to-one meetings with the salesperson concerned. In these circumstances the salesperson should feel at liberty to express concerns freely and without the risk of being criticized or belittled for it; on the other hand, it is the responsibility of the sales manager to resolve the issues raised and inject some positive mental attitude into the meeting.

For example, it is not unusual for salespeople to have dry periods where sales are low, or even non-existent. This usually results in feelings of inadequacy and loss of confidence. Rookies in particular can begin to believe that their earlier sales were a matter of luck, and that they do not have what it takes to be a salesperson. These feelings can be very strong, but might be resolved by showing the salesperson statistics on selling, by explaining that everyone has occasional dry periods and by carrying out a field visit. Typically, the feelings of inadequacy recede once the salesperson wins a sale, but may return in the next dry period.

Sales managers need to remember that 'telling isn't selling' in this context, as is also the case in selling situations. Salespeople need to be led to the appropriate conclusion, in the same way as a prospect is led to a sale by asking questions such as 'What do you think you ought to do to raise sales?' or, 'If your closing rate has fallen to one in five, how about just doing more presentations until things improve?'

There is some risk of bias arising from social interaction between the manager and the salesperson. Managers who like a salesperson, either for work-related reasons or for social reasons, are likely to be biased in their appraisal of the employee (DeCarlo and Leigh 1996).

Sales meetings

Sales meetings are much more about creating positive mental attitudes than they are about exchanging information. Sales meetings need to have a structure or agenda, minutes to record what has been agreed, and an action plan for implementing decisions made. In this respect a sales meeting is much like any other meeting. Where the sales meeting differs from other meetings is in its content and environment.

Sales meetings are essentially motivational. They exist for the purpose of congratulating success so as to inspire others and for demonstrating that success brings rewards. They also exist for demonstrating the superiority and innovativeness of the firm's products, the helpfulness of the new promotion campaign from the marketing people, and any other motivational factors. The elements which will be included in a sales meeting are as shown in Table 10.7.

At no time should negative comments be allowed in a group sales meeting. If salespeople have problems or personal difficulties with the firm, its products, its customers, or with their own attitudes and capabilities, these should be raised afterwards in private. Salespeople should also be discouraged from raising negative issues with each other; these should be saved for one-to-one meetings with the sales manager, who presumably has broad enough shoulders to cope with negativity.

Sales meetings should never become boring; although meetings do have a serious purpose, it is important that the sales force does not regard them as a waste of time. The frequency of meetings is a matter of debate – some sales managers hold meetings weekly so as to maintain morale and make best use of the motivational value of the meetings, whereas others prefer to hold meetings monthly, thus reducing the time salespeople spend off the road. If meetings are held less frequently, the sales manager might contact salespeople individually by telephone to maintain the momentum between meetings.

Meetings are frequently held at the company headquarters. This has the advantage of keeping costs low, and also allows the sales force to discuss individual issues with other people within the organization, such as administrators or technical staff. If the sales force is normally widely scattered this can be a useful opportunity. Alternatively, sales meetings can be held at conference centres or hotels; this would be a normal procedure if the sales force is large. Holding meetings away from the office has the advantage that interruptions are less likely, and, if the sales force is large, it is often the case that suitable accommodation at the company offices is not available. Wherever the meeting is held, there should be adequate space, refreshments as necessary, and adequate facilities for presentations (flip charts, overhead projectors, etc.). It is not unusual for sales meetings to conclude with lunch, paid for by the company. This has the advantage of allowing a more informal atmosphere to develop, and to emphasize the sense that meetings are enjoyable social occasions.

TABLE 10.7 Elements of a sales meeting

Element	Explanation
New product demonstrations	Any innovations from the company should be presented in an exciting and positive way; they offer new opportunities for making sales. Apart from the sales of the new product, the innovations provide a talking-point for salespeople even when demonstrating better-established products. New products are almost always motivational.
Congratulating rookies on their first sales	The round of applause the rookie gets from experienced salespeople is often a greater reward than any bonus or ice breaker award that the company provides. It appeals to the rookie's need to belong to the group.
Announcing competitions, or competition winners	Competitions are always occasions for celebrating success and motivating staff to even greater efforts. In national sales competitions, sales managers will often emphasize that they want their team to scoop the national prizes; this can help engender a team spirit and ensure that any competitive practices are directed at teams in other areas, rather than within the local team.
Visits by national or regional management	A pep talk from a senior manager helps to ensure that the local sales team feels part of the larger picture. This can have strong motivational effects, especially if the team is made to feel that they are better than other regional teams.
Talks from experienced salespeople	Sharing experiences, techniques and skills can be motivational both for the listeners and the speaker. Listeners gain useful ideas which they can try in practice, and the speaker gains esteem from colleagues.

■ Sales-force automation

Sales-force automation has been defined as the process of converting manual sales activities to electronic processes through the use of various combinations of hardware and software (Errfmeyer and Johnson 2001). The degree to which the sales force becomes automated may vary greatly from one firm to another, within the definition; at one extreme, a paper-based system might simply be transferred onto computers, while at the other extreme automation might allow for orders to be entered, prices to be calculated, presentations to be produced, and payments to be made.

The history of sales-force automation is somewhat chequered. Salespeople often resist automation, because they feel it erodes their traditional position of organising their own pace and schedule of work. Industry figures suggest that more than half of all sales and marketing systems fail to meet the users' expectations (Goodwin 1998); this may be due to failure of the systems, or it may be due to unreasonable expectations on the part of the users, but results so far have been disappointing. The reason for this failure may be due to a reluctance to change working practices in ways that will make the best use of the systems; often firms see this as the tail wagging the dog, believing that the automation systems should adapt to existing practices. This view is fallacious, because it does not take account of the computer revolution. Because information can be gathered and shared in ever-increasing amounts, selling can become much more of a team effort. Everyone in the company can sell to the customer, to a greater or lesser extent, and this means that information, and customers, become shared.

If salespeople are not committed to the organization's technology, customer alliances and future relationships are likely to be hindered (Jones *et al.* 2002). The benefits to the salesperson may seem obvious: reduced time spent in preparation, reduced number of follow-up visits, and faster access to information (Taylor 1993) as well as reduced number of errors, improved closing rates, and an increase in the average selling price due to more accurate pricing information (Verity 1993).

Jones *et al.* (2002) found that a total of eight factors contributed to the degree to which salespeople adopt automation. These are shown in Table 10.8.

Ultimately, the success of the automation system will depend on infusion, which Jones *et al.* (2002) define as the extent to which the full potential of the innovation has been embedded within the organization's operational or managerial work systems. Schafer (1997) estimates that for every two successful implementations there have been three failures, and since some research seems to indicate that sales-force automation is usually driven by the company rather than the salespeople, this is perhaps unsurprising (Widmier *et al.* 2002). In areas where the thrust of the automation has been concerned with controlling the sales force, salespeople have often simply ignored the technology, but when the automation has been geared towards information gathering, presentation preparation and contact management most salespeople will use it (Widmier *et al.* 2002).

TABLE 10.8 Factors contributing to sales-force automation	
Factor	**Explanation**
Personal innovativeness	The degree to which the individual salesperson likes new technology. The greater the degree to which the individual is open to new ideas, the greater the likelihood of adopting automation technology.
Perceived usefulness	The degree to which the person believes that using the new system will improve his or her job performance. Again, a greater belief in the usefulness of the system will increase the likelihood of adopting it.
Attitude towards the new system	This is the overall view of the system, which is only partly dependent on its usefulness; a system may be difficult to use, but still useful, for example. A positive attitude will obviously encourage adoption.
Compatibility with existing system	The degree to which the proposed system fits in with the adopter's existing values, previous experiences and current needs (Rogers 1995). The greater the compatibility, the more likely the adoption.
Facilitating conditions	This is the degree to which the individual believes that the organization has provided suitable resources and support for the adoption.
Subjective norms	The degree to which the salesperson believes that customers, superiors and colleagues would want them to use a particular system.
Ease of use	The easier the system is to use, the more likely it will be adopted.
Intention to use	This is the degree to which the person believes that he or she will use the system, and is a composite of the other factors.

Database management

Databases can be constructed from the company's existing customer records, from computer returns, from enquiries received during advertising campaigns or exhibition attendance, or from buying in ready-made lists from other firms. In most cases, the databases will be used by the marketing people, who sometimes feel that they own the database and can be reluctant to share it with the sales force (Blythe and Yandle 1999).

The role of the database develops strategically within the firm, as shown in Table 10.9. The process described below is not necessarily a tidy one, and firms may skip stages, but it does illustrate a hierarchy of commitment to the use of the database as the driving force in the company's communications activities.

Integrating all the firm's activities around a single database increases the coherence of the marketing communications and increase the possibilities for establishing relationship marketing. A single database puts the company in the position of the small corner shop; the company knows all its regular customers, and can therefore anticipate and satisfy their needs much more effectively both in terms of product and in terms of communications.

For salespeople, automation often represents a threat; in the past, their status and earnings within the organization were based on the number of sales and quality of customer they brought in. This meant that most salespeople tended to defend their territories jealously, and as a result defend their information sources equally jealously. In an automated system, they are expected to share information, to log all their sales visits onto the system, and to expose their activities for all in the company to see. Many salespeople are used to the idea of doing their planning on the back of an envelope, of changing their route plan to seize a good opportunity, and of only telling the sales manager what they think he or she ought to know. This way of working is clearly unhelpful in an automated system, and salespeople need to be persuaded of the benefits. The ways in which this should be done are shown in Table 10.10.

The database can come to be seen as a threat, since it will take over many of the traditional areas which salespeople have handled: lead generation, aftersales service, and repeat business have all passed into the domain of database marketing in some firms (see Table 1.3 in Chapter 1).

Ultimately, the efficiency gains which can be made from automating the sales force will ensure that such systems will become widespread in use. No sales force in the country can afford not to automate, in the long run, and, like the car and the telephone before it, computer technology will inevitably generate major changes in business practice.

TABLE 10.9 Strategic position of the database

Phase of development	Explanation
Phase 1: Mystery lists	The firm regards the database as an adjunct to its main business, as a stand-alone operation next to its main marketing activities.
Phase 2: Buyer databases	There may be several databases in use, each carrying different information. For example, the sales force may use one database for special customers, the distribution department may have a separate one containing delivery details and scheduling, credit control may have yet another one. The Phase 2 focus is on broadening the databases, defining target markets, improving list quality, segmentation, credit scoring, response handling, testing, and management systems for campaign planning.
Phase 3: Co-ordinated customer communication	Databases are amalgamated so that one database drives all the customer communication, including sales. The database is used to identify prospects within the broader market, review past performance and segment the market.
Phase 4: Integrated marketing	Most functions automate within closed loops, but need each others' information for the plan-execute-monitor-report cycle. Each functional subsystem gets its information from every other subsystem within the context of the main database. Common IT architecture ensures maximum automatic feedback, combining lifetime management of customers with the management of campaigns for particular brands.

TABLE 10.10 Introducing sales-force automation

Action	Explanation
Explain the benefits	As a general management principle, explaining clearly and truthfully why the changes are taking place will often win over 70–80 per cent of the workforce. The same is true of salespeople; seeing the benefits, and accepting the inevitability of change, will always help considerably.
Ensure that adequate support is available	IT hotlines, training, where appropriate, and plenty of opportunity to practise using the new systems are all essentials if the system is to be credible. If the users experience problems in the first few weeks after introduction, it may take a long time to re-establish confidence in the system.
Decide what information should be transferred	Salespeople's diaries are a particularly sensitive area. A clear division needs to be agreed on what is company-specific information and what is individual-specific information. Obviously information about the salesperson's family commitments and social engagements is individual specific; borderline areas might include a golf appointment with a client, or confidential information about a client's family circumstances which might have a bearing on the business relationship.
Ensure that information is available back to the salespeople	Sometimes company managers are reluctant to allow access to all the available information – not without good reason, as it has been known for someone to accept a job, download all the firm's information, and go to work for a competitor. The risks of this happening are relatively small, set against a certainty of inefficiency and disaffection if the management does not allow the sales force access to the information it has, as a group, collected. A large part of the payoff for salespeople is easy access to information; without this, they are unlikely to co-operate fully with the system.
Ensure that the system provides real benefits for the sales force	Many automation systems are designed as management information systems, to make planning simpler for the management. If this is the case, there is no incentive for the sales force to co-operate with the system, and they will tend to do the minimum, or even circumvent the system entirely.
Show the sales force that non-participation is not an option	Control on the sales-force input to the system is essential, with sanctions to be applied to those who do not participate. Equally, bonuses or other incentives can be applied to those who do co-operate with the system (see Chapter 8).
Change the business culture	Acceptance of change must come from the top; management in the 21st century is about handling change, not as a series of discrete events, but as a continuous process.
Revise the system of sales-force incentives and rewards	If selling becomes a shared process, salespeople must not feel that their financial position is threatened. The system of commission and bonuses will need to be revised to allow for the possibility that a salesperson might spend a great deal of time on developing an account, only to have a telesales operator or database marketer close the deal and get the credit. This in itself can be a powerful incentive for salespeople to log all their calls and appointments into the database in order to establish their priority in dealing with the prospect.

SUMMARY

Evaluation is mainly about ensuring that the right things are being done, and that things are being done right. The problem is more complex for sales managers than for managers of other staff because salespeople are out of sight most of the time, and therefore the sales manager needs to rely much more on written material and discussions than most other managers.

The key points from this chapter are as follows:

- The variables which determine sales success are so numerous that it is difficult to know which should be evaluated.
- Evaluation programmes need to be realistic, fair and agreed with the salespeople themselves.
- That which is measured is that which gets done.
- Collecting information almost always incurs a cost.
- Change is rapid, so systems need to be flexible.
- Feedback should always be positive in tone.
- Sales meeting are primarily motivational tools, with feedback running a close second.

REVIEW QUESTIONS

1 How might a sales manager handle a situation in which a group of salespeople raise a problem which has collective significance – for example, a complaint about a change in company policy?

2 How might the sales manager make use of communications technology to give salespeople rapid feedback?

3 What feedback might be given for major account salespeople?

4 What factors might be critical for evaluating salespeople in retail environments such as consumer durables?

5 When managing a sales force which sells fitted kitchens, which is more appropriate: outcome-based control systems, or behaviour-based control systems? Why?

REFERENCES

Anderson, E. and Oliver, R. (1987) 'Perspectives on behaviour-based versus outcome-based salesforce control systems', *Journal of Marketing* 51(4): 76–88.

Blythe, J. and Yandle, J. (1999) 'Role, dominance and conflict between sales and marketing – A grounded theory approach', *New Marketing, New Relevance*, Proceedings of the Academy of Marketing, July, Stirling University.

Churchill, G.A., Ford, N.M., Hartley, S.W. and Walker, O.C. (1985) 'The determinants of salesperson performance: A meta-analysis', *Journal of Marketing Research* XXII (May): 103–18.

DeCarlo, T.E. and Leigh, T.W. (1996) 'Impact of salesperson attraction on sales managers' attributions and feedback', *Journal of Marketing* 60 (Apr.): 47–66.

Dermer, J. (1977) *Management Planning and Control Systems: Advanced Concepts and Cases*, Homewood, IL: Irwin.

Errfmeyer, R.C. and Johnson, D.A. (2001) 'An exploratory study of sales force automation practices: Expectations and realities', *Journal of Personal Selling and Sales Management* 21 (2/Spring): 167–75.

Finlay, P. (2000) *Strategic Management*, Harlow: Financial Times Prentice Hall.

Goodwin, C. (1998) 'Mind the cultural gap', *Marketing Business*, November.

Hofstede, G. (1978) 'The poverty of management control philosophy', *Academy of Management Review* 3 (3/July): 450–61.

Johanson, J. and Vahlne, J. E. (1990) 'The mechanism of internationalization', *International Marketing Review* 7(4): 11–24.

Johnson, P. and Gill, J. (1993) *Management Control and Organisational Behaviour,* London: Paul Chapman Publishing.

Jones, E., Sundaram, S. and Chin, W. (2002) 'Factors leading to sales force automation: A longitudinal analysis', *Journal of Personal Selling and Sales Management* 22 (3/Summer): 135–43.

Lilly, B., Porter, T. W. and Meo, A. W. (2003) 'How good are managers at evaluating sales problems?' *Journal of Personal Selling and Sales Management* 23 (1/Winter): 51–60.

Rogers, E. M. (1995) *Diffusion of Innovation*, New York: Free Press.

Schafer, S. (1997) 'Supercharged sell', *Inc.* 19 (9/July): 42–8.

Taylor, T. C. (1993) 'Computers bring quick return', *Sales and Marketing Management* 145 (Sept.): 22–5.

Verity, J.W. (1993) 'Taking a laptop on a call', *Business Week* (3342/25th October): 124–35.

Widmier, S.M., Jackson, D.W. Jr. and McCabe, D. B. (2002) 'Infusing technology into personal selling', *Journal of Personal Selling and Sales Management* 22 (3/Summer): 189–98.

ALPHA (PTY) SOUTH AFRICA

Alpha (Pty) Ltd's core business is the supply of building materials for civil engineering projects. In the main, the company supplies road-building materials, but of course the same materials are used in major building works, for laying foundations of large structures and so forth. Alpha has three divisions: cement, ready-mixed concrete and stone.

The Alpha Group recognized that it needed a sales-lead tracking system and plant-forecasting tool that could be used to consolidate information across the company's sales forces in the three divisions. The system would also provide management reporting for capacity planning and marketing purposes. Since the three divisions worked entirely independently of each other, each sales manager had developed a mix of paper-based tracking and Excel spreadsheets for tracking information about the sales force. In addition, sales teams in different parts of South Africa had developed their own local systems – in such a large country, such an outcome was almost inevitable.

Oakwell, a South African solutions company, designed a web-based system which is available to salespeople throughout the country and across all three divisions. The system enables the salespeople to keep track of the projects that are assigned to them. They can extract or receive (via e-mail) a weekly project overview with follow-up dates, tasks and reminders. The system tracks each lead right through from initial contact to final order stage, and the system also allows salespeople to record all contact names and details. Importantly, because salespeople from each division often work on the same contracts, the system ensures that they liaise automatically with each other – a feature which the paper-based, independent systems would not allow. This means that salespeople can 'sing from the same song sheet' when dealing with clients, and are less likely to make conflicting statements.

The system includes a management reporting tool which provides facilities for forecasting sales volumes, for monitoring competitor activity, including tenders, and monitoring salesperson performance. The latter is achieved through a string of key performance indicators (KPI) reports. Parameter-driven reporting is delivered through the web browser interface, which allows managers to access the information from any location. The system also allows seamless access to different levels of management, so that reporting happens instantly at all levels. An automatic report is delivered weekly to executives' desktop computers, via e-mail.

Detailed analysis of market, product, plant and competitor trends can be carried out using Excel, which is also built into the system. Analysis of sales data across geographies, divisions, product lines, clients, competitors and, importantly, sales representatives are all easily managed by the system.

The result of all this is that the salespeople are able to track their own behaviour (and obtain instant feedback), management are able to monitor their people, and salespeople can collaborate more effectively across divisions. At the strategic level, senior managers can estimate future capacity needs, plan and review marketing campaigns, and predict competitor responses. Sales forecasting is much more accurate, and problems with individual salespeople become apparent much earlier. Perhaps most importantly, salespeople have a large degree of control over the system, and can use it for their own purposes to improve their own working lives and success rates.

Case-study questions

1 What might be the drawbacks of having a unified, computer-based system throughout the company?

2 What would be the barriers to implementing such a system?

3 Why does it matter that the salespeople are able to monitor themselves through the system?

4 Why would a manager need a computer system to track salesperson activity, rather than simply talking to the salesperson?

5 How might a salesperson circumvent such a system in order to fool a manager?

INTERNATIONALIZATION

Learning objectives

After reading this chapter, you should be able to:

- Explain the cultural difficulties of dealing in overseas markets.

- Describe the main ways of entering overseas markets.

- Compare theories of internationalization.

- Explain the main issues surrounding overseas postings for salespeople.

- Describe the main forms of selling organization used in overseas markets.

- Describe the differences between running a directly employed sales force and indirect selling in overseas markets.

▮ Introduction

As world trade expands, more and more firms are seeking a direct route into overseas markets. Although it is still very common for firms to export, using local agents or distributors in the target countries, the increased control that having a directly employed local sales gives encourages firms to take this route.

Running an international sales force requires knowledge of local culture, laws and employment issues in an international context. Whether the sales force is a permanent fixture in the foreign market, or making a one-off sales visit to secure a greenfield contract, the sales management problem remains: handling an interpersonal process outside the normal cultural contexts that the firm operates in.

SUCCESS STORY – ESTÉE LAUDER

On 1st July 1910, above a hardware store in New York, Esther Mentzer was born. She married Joseph Lauter in 1930 (they later changed their name to Lauder), and settled down to start a family. But this wasn't enough for Esther – changing her name to Estée, because it sounded French and exotic, she persuaded her uncle, a chemist, to start producing cosmetics which she sold to department stores and holiday complexes. When she started, in 1946, she simply outworked everyone else in the cosmetics business. She stalked the bosses of New York department stores, using every possible approach she could think of – she even burst into tears at Saks of Fifth Avenue in order to melt the heart of a particularly tough buyer (she got the sale).

Lauder never stopped selling, never stopped thinking about people's needs. She once gave a young journalist from Vogue three recipes for chicken, in order to help the young woman to woo her boyfriend into marrying her. It worked – and the young journalist went on to become editor-in-chief at *Vogue*, a strong ally to have.

Estée Lauder certainly knew how to think globally and act locally. She would turn up at Saks on a Saturday and explain to the sales staff how to sell the cosmetics by giving personal attention and a free gift – and she was still doing this when her company was turning over millions of dollars. Now, Estée Lauder Cosmetics has 45 per cent of the US market for cosmetics, operates in 118 countries, and has a turnover of $3.6 thousand million, larger than the gross national product of several African countries and most Central American republics. Her son Leonard took over the running of the company in 1982, but his mother continued to act as an adviser until her death in 2004.

Cultural problems

Culture encompasses religion, language, institutions, beliefs and behaviours which are shared by the members of a society. Cultural differences are not always obvious, and it is easy to cause offence (or, of course, be offended) by innocent remarks or behaviour. The most obvious cultural differences stem from language and religion, but more subtle differences of customs and expected behaviour can easily create traps for the unwary. For example, it is obvious that Germany is a German-speaking, largely Protestant country. What is less obvious is that Germans regard lateness as extremely rude, and are unlikely to forgive lateness on the part of foreigners in the same way as they would forgive, say, a mistake in speaking the German language.

Language itself is more complex than it at first appears; apart from the spoken language, there is the language of gestures and body language (there is more on this later in the chapter). Also, the way language is used varies between cultures; Germans tend to be direct when speaking, whereas most English speakers equate indirectness with politeness. To a German, English speakers seem almost impossibly diffident, whereas to an English speaker, Germans seem direct to the point of arrogance. Similar problems exist between other cultures, and when one considers that the German culture and the British one are actually very similar, one can imagine the difficulties which arise when dealing with, say, Japanese or Egyptian businesses.

For communication to work between people from different cultures, there must be at least a common language. In practice, there also needs to be a clear understanding of each others' cultural basics. Figure 11.1 shows a communication model which illustrates the problem (Schramm 1971).

The sender of a message must first encode the message, that is put it into words, pictures, gestures or some other form for transmission. The encoding takes place within the sender's frame of experience; partly this is to do with language, but there will also be assumptions about meanings attributed to the context of the message and to the existing knowledge of the sender, some of which is shared by all the members of the same culture. For example, it is quite common for native speakers to refer to advertising tag-lines, titles of popular songs, famous newspaper headlines, proverbs or film titles to convey meanings (often as jokes). Such half statements and literary allusions may be lost on someone from another culture.

The message will need to be decoded by the receiver in order to grasp its meaning, and again this takes place within the receiver's cultural contexts. Provided the words mean the same to the receiver as they do to the sender, communication will result; unfortunately, this is not always the case even when both parties are speaking the same language. For example, the term 'middle class' has different meanings according to whether the speaker is British or American.

Classic examples of errors arising from language differences abound. The General Motors Nova brand name translates as 'no go' in Spanish. Gerber means 'to throw up' in colloquial French, creating problems for the baby-food manufacturer of the same name, and Irish Mist liqueur had to be re-named for the German market since 'mist' means 'excrement' in German. Many cultural problems are

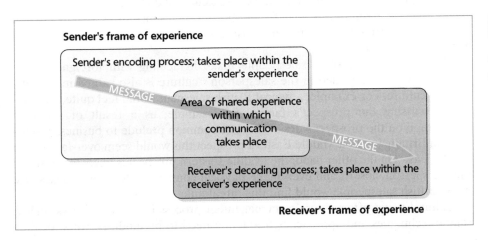

FIGURE 11.1

Culture and communications

more subtle, and have to do with the way things are said rather than the actual words used. In Japanese, 'yes' can mean 'Yes, I understand' but not necessarily 'Yes, I agree.' Portuguese has a total of seven different words for 'you', depending on the status and number of people being addressed.

Gestures are also not universal. The American sign for 'OK', with the thumb and forefinger making a circle, is a rude gesture in Brazil (equivalent to sticking up the index and middle finger in Britain, or the extended middle finger in the US and most of Europe). Showing the soles of the feet is considered insulting in Thailand, and Americans often feel threatened by people standing too close, which is perceived as an invasion of personal space.

Even topics of discussion are subject to cultural norms: while Americans are usually very happy to hear about an individual's personal wealth and success, Australians are less likely to take kindly to somebody acting like a 'tall poppy' in this way.

In general, managers need to be wary of ethnocentrism, which is the tendency to believe that one's own culture is the right one and that everybody else's is at best a poor imitation (Shimp and Sharma 1987). It can be easier to aim for countries where there is some psychological proximity. These are countries with some cultural aspects in common. For example, English-speaking countries have psychological proximity with each other; Spain has psychological proximity with most of Latin America; and the former Communist countries of Eastern European are close. Within countries with large migrant populations there may be sub-cultures which give insights into overseas markets; Australia is well placed to take advantage of Far Eastern and Greek markets as well as other English-speaking markets, and Brazil has good links with Germany as well as with Portugal, Angola and Mozambique. In an interesting reversal, Ireland also has good contacts in many countries due to the Irish diaspora of the last two hundred years.

In most West African countries tribal loyalties cross national borders, so that people from the same tribe might inhabit different countries. In a sense, this is paralleled in the Basque Country of France and Spain, and in the language divide in Belgium.

From a marketer's viewpoint, cultural differences are probably reducing as consumers become more globally minded; foreign travel, the widespread globalization of the entertainment media, and existing availability of foreign products in most economies have all served to erode the world's cultural differences (Ohmae 1989). Increasingly, marketers are able to identify distinct subcultures that transcend national boundaries, for example the world youth culture fuelled by media such as MTV (Steen 1995).

The commonest mistake salespeople make in dealing with foreigners is to assume that what is valued in the salesperson's culture is also valued in the customer's culture. For example, a typical British salesman would feel quite comfortable discussing the prospect's family, for example, as a result of seeing a photograph on the prospect's desk. This is a common prelude to business discussions in Britain, but to a Middle Eastern prospect this would seem over-familiar to say the least. On the other hand, the Middle Eastern prospect is likely to approach the salesperson closely, and even make physical contact, early in the discussions; many British salespeople would find this threatening.

Cultural issues affect the sales management process in two main ways: firstly, selling techniques and approaches frequently need to be modified when dealing internationally, and the process is often considerably slower since it takes longer to be sure that both parties fully understand the situation. The second area where culture makes a big difference is in personnel management issues. This is dealt with more fully in a later section.

Political factors

The political environment of the target country will also affect the entry decision. Table 11.1 shows some of the issues.

Entry strategies

Often it is the marketing department or the board of directors who dictate the entry strategies to be used. From the sales-management viewpoint, it is useful to understand the different entry strategies as these affect the sales-management decisions; marketers might decide to keep the product and the promotion the same, they might decide to keep the product the same but change the promotion, they might decide to change the product but keep the promotion the same (as when selling a major capital investment such as a hydroelectric dam) or they might decide to change both the product and the promotion.

Having decided on an approach to the promotion and product development strategies, the firm needs to choose an entry strategy. The stages of development model (Johanson and Vahlne 1990)suggests that firms seeking to internationalize go through a series of stages. These stages are shown in Table 11.2.

TABLE 11.1 Political factors in international market entry

Political factor	Explanation and implications
Level of protectionism	Some governments need to protect their own industries from foreign competition, either because the country is trying to industrialize and the fledgling companies cannot compete (as in some developing nations), or because lack of investment has resulted in a run-down of industry (as in much of Eastern Europe). Sometimes this can be overcome by offering inward investment (to create jobs) or by agreeing to limit exports to the country until the new industries have caught up.
Degree of instability	Some countries are less politically stable than others, and may be subject to military takeover or civil war. Usually the exporter's government's diplomatic service can advise on the level of risk attached to doing business in a particular country.
Relationship between the marketer's government and the foreign government	Sometimes disputes between governments can result in trade embargoes or other restrictions. Obviously this is particularly prevalent in the arms trade, but trade restrictions can be applied across the board to unfriendly countries. For example, the USA still has a trade ban with Cuba for many items, and Greece has a trade embargo against Northern Cyprus.

Broadly speaking a firm can decide on a globalization strategy, by which the company's products and attitudes are basically standardized throughout the world (examples are Coca-Cola and IBM), or a customization strategy where the company adapts its thinking and its marketing to each fresh market (examples are Sony and Nestlé). As global barriers to trade break down, more and

TABLE 11.2 Stages of development approach to internationalization

Stage	Description	Implications for sales managers
Exporting	Here the manufacturer sells the firm's products to a foreign importer who then handles the marketing of the product. The advantage of this approach is that it involves the least cost; the disadvantage is that the exporting firm has little or no control over the way the product is marketed or used in the foreign market.	Export agents bring together buyers and sellers and are paid on commission; export houses buy goods for export to foreign countries. Sometimes foreign buyers will deal direct with companies, and some major foreign stores (for example Sears in the USA) maintain buying offices in foreign capitals. In all these cases, the sales process is the same as when dealing with any other wholesaler or retailer.
Establishing a sales office in the foreign market	This is an increased financial commitment, but also gives more control.	The sales manager will need to decide whether to hire salespeople in the host country, or to send salespeople over from the parent country. Hiring local salespeople is a tougher recruitment option, since it is much harder to judge the ability of salespeople, due to cultural differences; conversely, they will have local knowledge which is unavailable to imported salespeople trained in the home country.
Overseas distribution	This involves establishing a warehousing and distribution network in the foreign country. This gives more control over the marketing of the product, but still relies on importing from the home country.	The distributors are responsible for the sales operations, but are usually contracted to a set of guidelines which would fall to the sales manager from the parent company to administer.
Overseas manufacture (includes warehousing and distribution)	This allows the firm to shorten the lines of supply and to adapt the product more easily for the overseas market. In some cases the manufacturing costs are lower in the foreign market so there will be further economies to be made.	The company is likely to establish its own sales force in the overseas country, but could conceivably prefer to rely on a network of distributors; this is usually the approach taken by car manufacturers, for example.
Multinational marketer	The true multinational firm manufactures and markets in those countries that offer the best advantages. Although such a company may have originated in a particular country, it may well employ far more foreigners than it does its own nationals, and will think in global terms rather than national terms.	The likelihood is that a firm operating on this scale would have a complete sales, and marketing, operation in each country. Co-ordination and strategy setting would only occur at main board level, although sales managers from the different countries would usually meet periodically to exchange ideas. In some firms such exchanges also take place at sales representative level, but usually only in exceptional circumstances.

more companies will be taking an international view of their marketing opportunities, and will be seeking to do business across national borders and cultural differences.

Recent research into standardization of advertising showed that relatively few firms use an entirely standardized approach (Harris 1996). Of 38 multinational companies surveyed, 26 said that they used standard advertisements, but only four of these were completely standardized; the others varied from limited standardization (perhaps only a corporate logo in common) through limited standardization of the key executional elements, to standard execution with some modifications. Even though the sample of firms is relatively small, it appears likely that the majority of multinationals would adapt their approaches to fit the markets they are targeting. This is particularly true in the case of personal selling; given the one-to-one nature of most personal-selling activities, it is inconceivable that the salesperson's approach would not be adapted to meet local cultural norms.

Dunning's eclectic theory

An alternative view of internationalization strategy is the eclectic theory proposed by Dunning (1993). Broadly, this theory supposes that the firm will look at its specific advantages over other firms both at home and overseas, and will plan its market-entry strategies accordingly, without necessarily going through a series of stages. For example, a firm with a strength in franchising is likely to use franchising as a market entry method into overseas markets, rather than begin by exporting, then setting up a sales force and so forth. The eclectic paradigm also has implications for production, since a true multinational will produce in whichever country offers the best advantages.

If a firm is adopting an eclectic approach to internationalization, the sales manager is likely to be involved in discussions about the sales policy. There are several routes to establishing a sales presence in a foreign country which do not involve directly employing salespeople; Table 11.3 shows the advantages and disadvantages of the main options.

In all the cases listed in Tables 11.3 it is important to maintain a good relationship with the overseas partners. This is very much a case of major-account management; ensuring that the agents, distributors or export houses are well

---

TALKING POINT

Ford produces all the engines for its European cars in Wales, exporting them for assembly into car bodies in Germany, and perhaps re-importing them back into the UK. Since transport costs are relatively low compared with the final price of the car, Ford deem it worthwhile to centralize production of the various components. In addition the company can take advantage of government and European Union incentives to locate in high-unemployment areas, and can also use transfer pricing to minimize its tax liabilities.

cared for is often part of the sales manager's responsibilities. In particular, overseas partners can sometimes become victims of their own success, because success in the market may encourage the firm to set up its own directly employed sales force in the foreign country, thus depriving the agent or distributor of the contract.

This means that agreements with overseas partners will usually need to be long term, and they will require safeguards to prevent the parent company from cutting them out once it is convenient to do so. Some firms offer the overseas partner a

TABLE 11.3 Advantages and disadvantages of international sales force options

Option	Advantages	Disadvantages
Agents: firms or individuals who act on behalf of the firm	The main advantage is that agency agreements are cheap to set up, and minimize the financial risk. Agents are usually paid on a commission-only basis, so if they do not bring in business there is very little cost attached to using them.	Agents usually work for more than one firm, and are likely to divide their time and effort according to their own objectives, usually to maximize their commission. This is likely to mean that new firms (with new products) receive less attention than established firms with known products (and therefore known sales potential).
Distributors: firms or individual which buy and sell the goods themselves	Because the distributor is actually buying the goods, the firm has no stockholding problem in the foreign market, and the distributor has made a financial commitment to the products and the firm, so is more likely to make an effort to sell the goods on to the final customers.	Since the distributor is running an independent business, the firm has little or no control over the final prices the goods are sold at. Also, the distributor might engage in dubious selling or marketing practices which damage the parent firm's reputation in the longer term.
Licensing: the overseas firm negotiates a licence to manufacture and market the product	This works best for products which are difficult or impossible to export; for example, glass. Pilkington make more money internationally from licensing their float-glass method of manufacture than they do from making glass themselves.	The overseas manufacturer has, at least potentially, a great deal of control over the marketing of the product. The key to success is to ensure that the licence agreement covers these issues comprehensively, and that systems are in place to enforce the agreement if necessary.
Export houses: firms which handle the exporting of goods on behalf of manufacturers	In some cases, these firms take title to the goods and can therefore be treated in the same way as ordinary wholesalers. In other cases they may carry out only part of the total function of exporting. The main advantage is that they often have expertise and contacts in a large number of markets overseas, and can therefore get a small firm some very wide distribution at low cost.	The main disadvantage is the almost total lack of control over what happens to the goods when they reach the foreign market. Export houses will usually use overseas agents and distributors, so will have little control themselves; but even at the home country end of the operation, the manufacturing firm can expect to have little control in the transaction. This can prove damaging in the longer term.

long-term role in running any sales force that might be set up; this ensures a degree of continuity, while being fair to both parties. In some cases, the agent's position is protected by law, but ultimately the firm's reputation in the overseas market is likely to be of greater importance than any short-term savings made by divesting itself of its agents.

European agency law

European law regarding the employment of agents has been rationalized by the Commercial Agents Directive 1986, which lays down minimum conditions under which agents can be employed. The main points are as follows:

1 The Directive only applies to agents based in, and operating within, the EU. It does not cover distributors or anyone else who takes title to the goods, nor does it cover agents who are based in the EU but operate outside it.

2 The agent is entitled to whatever remuneration is standard in the place where the activities are carried out. This means that the agent is entitled to the commission rate which is customary in the country where sales are made, not the one prevailing in the country where the goods are produced. This commission rate can be, and usually is, agreed between the parties when the agency agreement is first created.

3 Agents are entitled to commission on transactions which are completed after the agency agreement has run its course, provided they can demonstrate that the sale resulted largely from their efforts during the contract period.

4 Agents are entitled to statements of commission due, and to inspect the company's books to check that the figures are correct.

5 Each party is entitled to terminate the agreement by giving notice, unless the agreement is entered into for a fixed term. The notice period is laid down by law and cannot be varied; the period is one month during the first year of the agreement, two months during the second year, and three months thereafter.

6 Agents are entitled to compensation if the contract is terminated by the principal, unless the agent is in breach of contract. Compensation may also be payable if the agent terminates the contract due to age or illness, or if the principal is in breach of contract or acts in a way that effectively terminates the contract, for example, by refusing to supply goods.

The purpose of the legislation is to ensure fair treatment of agents when dealing with large firms against whom they would otherwise have little power. In order to avoid the legislation, some firms replaced their agency network with distributors, who are not covered by the law; this has the drawback of reducing the exporting firm's control over events, however.

■ Establishing a direct sales force

Establishing a sales force in the overseas country can follow three basic routes:

1 Hiring an entirely local, autonomous sales force.
2 Hiring salespeople in the home country and posting them overseas.
3 A combination strategy of using home-country salespeople alongside the overseas recruits.

Table 11.4 shows the advantages and disadvantages of each approach.

One of the most effective compromises involves sending out a sales manager from the home country, and recruiting locals as sales representatives. This overcomes many of the problems outlined above, although the sales manager concerned needs to strike a balance between being respectful of the local sales force and its customs, and maintaining continuity with the company's own culture. Sales managers should certainly not act as if the home-country methods are invariably superior to those of the host country.

For example, Latin cultures tend to emphasize analysis and reasoning, whereas Germanic cultures such as that of the UK have a stronger emphasis on doing and achieving. This affects the way salespeople think about their roles, and indeed the way they go about selling (Rouzies and Macquin 2003). Latin salespeople tend to be more adaptive, whereas German and British salespeople tend to use one

TABLE 11.4 Recruiting international salespeople

Route	Advantages	Disadvantages
Hire entirely local sales force	They will have intimate local knowledge of businesses and of the cultural background of the country. Some of them will have worked for local competitors, and will therefore already have some contacts.	It may be difficult to instil the appropriate corporate culture in the sales force; an understanding of company policies and attitudes needs to grow over time, and much of it is conveyed by existing employees. Extensive product training will also be needed.
Posting home-country salespeople to the host country	These people will already be familiar with the company, its policies and products.	Considerable training will need to be given if the salespeople are to cope with the local culture. Also, overseas postings often fail because of culture shock, or because the employee's family fail to adapt. Most employees expect to be very well paid to compensate for the disruption to family life caused by an overseas posting.
Hiring a mixture of overseas and home-country salespeople	The local salespeople are able to assist in understanding the culture, while the home-country salespeople understand the company's products and policies.	Culture clashes and resentment often develop, as the home-country salespeople sometimes feel superior to the locally recruited salespeople.

favourite set of techniques. In other words, working smart comes more easily to Latin salespeople than it does to Northern Europeans.

Cultural differences mean that the basics of sales-force management will change. Motivation, recruitment and training will all differ when dealing with foreign staff, but there are also issues relating to home-country staff posted overseas.

Motivation

Motivating an overseas sales force will more often mean a shift in emphasis rather than a complete rethinking of motivators. For example, Americans tend to be more money-oriented than most Europeans; the Japanese tend to be motivated better by feeling part of the team; the French tend to be motivated by being given greater autonomy in their work. The important point to keep in mind, though, is that individuals differ much more between each other than average members of a given culture differ from average members of another culture. In other words, the most money-oriented Japanese person is a great deal more money-oriented than the least money-oriented American. The tendency to treat all members of the same culture as if they were identical twins should be avoided. Having said that, commission is rarely used in Japan, and salary increases are almost always based on seniority (Hill *et al.* 1991).

Motivation of home-country staff posted overseas will depend very largely on the staff member's reasons for seeking an overseas posting. In many cases, the motivation stems from a desire to travel and to experience foreign cultures, and this could be turned to the firm's advantage, for example by offering extra time off to enable the employee to see the country, or by offering side trips to other countries.

Sometimes the differences in remuneration and motivation between home-country staff and the overseas sales force can cause resentment or perceptions of unfairness. In most cases, staff posted overseas are paid considerably more than their local counterparts in order to compensate for the disruption of switching countries, and this may lead to demotivation among locally recruited staff. This problem is obviated if the only people permanently posted overseas are senior management.

TALKING POINT

Motivating a multicultural sales force is far from easy. Americans tend to be motivated by money and top-of-the-range consumer durables. British salespeople tend to be motivated by experiential gifts such as meals out or weekends away. Japanese staff tend to be motivated by wanting to belong in the group. A gift of champagne would please a Brit, puzzle a Frenchman and offend a Muslim.

Often companies will outsource their sales incentive programmes to firms such as Sales Performance Group or Reward Strategies. These companies organize sales compensation programmes on behalf of clients. Companies can use different local agencies in each country in which they have a sales force, thus ensuring compatibility with local cultures.

Within Europe, the introduction of the euro has made comparisons much easier among salespeople. Within Europe, salespeople's reliance on commission is much less than in the United States, where commission counts for an average 40 per cent of total earnings compared with around 10 per cent in most European countries (Rouzies and Macquin 2003).

One study of expatriate salespeople in Saudi Arabia showed that promotion autonomy, task identity and feedback increased job satisfaction, as it would for any salespeople, but that increasing job variety had the opposite effect (Bhuian and Menguc 2002). The same study found significant differences in ethical attitudes – notably that the expatriates were more appreciative of being rewarded for ethical behaviour.

Training

Much of the training of overseas recruits will involve product and company knowledge, since it is usually wise to recruit people who are already familiar with the market and with selling techniques. Training foreigners in home-country sales techniques would be counterproductive, since the point of recruiting an overseas sales force is to take advantage of their local cultural knowledge; sales techniques are always culturally rooted. The training may involve bringing the salespeople to the home country in order for them to gain some understanding of the parent company's corporate culture, and also to gain some first-hand experience with the firm's products.

Sending salespeople overseas for extended periods will mean a considerable period of training in the local culture. This includes language, but language skills are not sufficient; the executive will need to feel comfortable with the way of life of the people in the host country. In most cases, executives will be taking their families with them; research shows that the majority of overseas placements which fail do so because the families of the executives are unable to adjust to life in the new country. Children may have difficulty fitting into the new schools, husbands or wives may have trouble finding suitable work (or may be prevented from working at all) and the unfamiliar food, difficulty of making new friends, and other problems will often result in culture shock. This usually strikes several months into the placement; the initial excitement at being in a new country will carry people through until then.

It is certainly useful to allow the executive and his or her family the opportunity to visit the country extensively before committing to the placement. It is also advisable to give the whole family formal training in settling into the new country; this training can be provided by a number of specialist agencies in the UK, whose trainers have direct experience of living in the host countries they prepare people for.

SUMMARY

Setting up an international sales operation is not merely a matter of extending the company's home country policies into the international arena. Culture, law, economics, and political factors all need to be taken into account. The main pitfalls lie in failing to take account of local culture, both in terms of selling techniques and in terms of managing foreign salespeople.

Ultimately, it would be impossible to provide an in-depth analysis of every cultural nuance in the world; for this reason, sales managers entering a foreign market need to rely heavily on local advice or local staff or both.

The key points from this chapter are as follows:

- Communication requires an area of common ground, culturally speaking, if the messages are to be understood by all the parties concerned.

- Most managers try to solve problems from within their own cultural context; this approach is inadequate in overseas markets.

- Cultural differences affect personnel issues as much as they do selling issues.

- Firms may go through a series of stages to achieve full internationalization, or they may go straight to the position that best suits their circumstances.

- Firms can choose between using a global approach, or using a customizing approach; the customizing approach is probably more expensive, but is easier to achieve.

- If the firm is to use indirect selling approaches (using agents or distributors) good relations with the intermediaries are essential.

- Agents are protected by law within the European Union, but in any case it is better for the firm's reputation to treat agents fairly.

- Recruitment, training and motivation are all different in the international context.

REVIEW QUESTIONS

1 How might a firm manufacturing consumer electronics products go about entering overseas markets?

2 Why do few firms adopt an entirely standardized approach to their international marketing?

3 How should a sales manager prepare for handling a foreign sales force?

4 Why might car manufacturers use distributor networks, whereas a food manufacturer would typically have a directly employed sales force?

5 If most overseas postings fail because the executive's family are unable to adjust, why not send single people to the foreign country?

REFERENCES

Bhuian, S. N. and Menguc, B. (2002) 'An extension and evaluation of job characteristics, organizational commitment and job satisfaction in an expatriate, guest worker, sales setting', *Journal of Personal Selling and Sales Management* 22 (1/Winter): 1–10.

Dunning, J. H. (1993) *The Globalisation of Business*, London: Routledge.

Harris, Greg (1996) 'International advertising: Developmental and implementational issues', *Journal of Marketing Management* 12(6): 551–60.

Hill, J. S., Still, R. R. and Boya, U. O. (1991) 'Managing the multinational salesforce', *International Marketing Review* 8(1): 19–31.

Ohmae, K. (1989) 'Managing in a borderless world,' *Harvard Business Review* 67 (3/May–June): 152–61.

Rouzies, D. and Macquin, A. (2003) 'An exploratory investigation of the impact of culture on sales force management control systems in Europe', *The Journal of Personal Selling and Sales Management* 23 (1/Winter): 61–72.

Schramm, W. A. (1971) 'The nature of communication between humans', in W. A. Schramm and D. F. Roberts (eds) *The Process and Effect of Mass Communication* Urbana, IL: Illinois University Press.

Shimp, T. and Sharma, S. (1987) 'Consumer ethnocentrism: Construction and validation of CETSCALE', *Journal of Marketing Research*, 24 (Aug.): 280–9.

Steen, J. (1995) 'Now they're using suicide to sell jeans', *Sunday Express*, 26 March.

TJAEREBORG HOLIDAYS

During the late 1970s, Tjaereborg, the Danish holiday-tour operators, set up a marketing organization in the UK. From a Danish perspective, the UK market appeared very tempting; with almost ten times the population of Denmark, and a high propensity to travel, the UK seemed to offer almost unlimited growth potential for the firm. Tjaereborg made a strong commitment to the market; at one time, meetings of the Danish board of directors were held entirely in English, even though all those present were Danish, to ensure that board members were oriented towards the UK.

Tjaereborg's unique selling proposition was that it sold holidays direct to the consumer, without using travel agents, unlike the existing UK tour operators. This gave the firm a 10 per cent price advantage through cutting out one layer of the distribution chain, but much of this was eroded by the extra marketing costs incurred in re-educating British people to buy holidays directly from the tour operators rather than through travel agents. However, because the company was used to dealing directly, their natural inclination was towards continuing to do so when they needed a sales force.

In the early 1980s the company acquired Club LaSanta, a sports and apartments complex in Lanzarote. LaSanta was popular with Olympic athletes as a winter training base, but not so popular as a holiday destination; Tjaereborg decided to sell off the apartments as timeshare properties, but quickly saturated the small Danish market. This led them to set up a sales force in the UK, to operate alongside the holiday operation.

At first, they used the UK office to hire salespeople who had an interest in sport. Some were national-class athletes in their own right, others were salespeople known to the British manager of the UK office. At first, sales appeared to go well, but it soon became apparent that the people who had been hired had little selling experience, and the company had not appointed a sales manager to guide them. The company therefore arranged for a recruitment consultancy to draw up a detailed person specification, and hire some top-flight salespeople. The salary was based on Danish pay scales, so it appeared very generous by UK standards; this encouraged over 400 people to apply for the posts. Of these 400, only two survived the selection procedure and were given a job.

Sales management was handled by the manager of the London office, who had considerable experience of office management but no knowledge of managing a sales force. Morale among the salespeople fell, and eventually a top Danish salesman was recruited as sales manager in London. He handled the job by commuting regularly between Copenhagen and London, but eventually this arrangement proved impossible to maintain, and the lack of contact with the sales force resulted in poor sales performances and lack of direction.

Eventually Tjaereborg was forced to abandon the UK market almost entirely, and the sales force was disbanded.

Case-study questions

1 How might Tjaereborg have avoided the loss of morale among the sales force?
2 What other ways could the firm have used to recruit a sales force?
3 What role did ethnocentrism play in the story?
4 Why might there have been such a high fallout rate from the recruitment consultancy's testing procedures?

12

EXHIBITIONS AND TRADE FAIRS

Learning objectives

After reading this chapter, you should be able to:

- Describe the key benefits and drawbacks of using exhibitions.

- Explain how exhibitions can be used in key-account management.

- Explain ways of making exhibitions more effective.

- Explain the role of exhibitions and trade fairs in the sales cycle.

- Describe ways of assessing the effectiveness of exhibition activity.

- Identify the main issues in planning an exhibition.

- Describe some of the pitfalls in manning exhibition stands and managing the staff on the stand.

Introduction

Exhibitions and trade shows provide a temporary marketplace where producers and marketers of a product category can show their products to prospective buyers, often with the opportunity to demonstrate the products as well. Agricultural shows fulfil a similar function, but are usually biased more towards competitions among livestock breeders and other types of farmer rather than being purely about promoting products.

Exhibitions can be categorized as selling or non-selling: selling exhibitions exist as marketplaces where buyers can place orders for products, whereas non-selling exhibitions exist purely as promotional vehicles, with no actual buying and selling taking place at the exhibition. Some exhibitions are open to the public, while others are business-to-business vehicles.

Considerable controversy exists as to whether exhibitions are effective, and which promotional objectives they best address; the area is not well researched, and much of the existing research has been conducted by parties with vested interests who may or may not be entirely unbiased in their findings. Nonetheless, exhibitions are used by most firms at one time or another, and are often considered as part of the sales manager's responsibilities.

SUCCESS STORY – SCOTT JACOBS

Scott Jacobs was born in Newfoundland, and at the age of 14 months he contracted polio. This crippling disease left him partially paralysed, but this did not stop him from attending Memorial University of Newfoundland and graduating with a BA in political science.

Scott became a life-insurance salesman. For four years he sold insurance, building up his knowledge and experience of marketing and of understanding customer needs, until eventually he decided to go into business for himself. He now has an organic gardening company, Organic Green, which specializes in organic lawn care, organic fertilizers and landscaping. He has a 400-client customer base, and a rapidly growing turnover.

The most rewarding aspect of owning his own business is, for Scott, 'The ability to make a difference, having satisfied customers, and the respect from my peers.' Scott believes in being recognized for his ability, not his disability.

■ Exhibitions and trade fairs as communication

Exhibitions and trade fairs represent a substantial commitment on the part of marketers. Total expenditure on exhibitions and trade fairs in the UK is consistently higher than the spend on advertising in the trade press, and is also higher than the combined expenditure on outdoor, cinema and radio advertising. Yet few exhibitors assess the effectiveness of this activity in any realistic way, and there is continuing academic debate about whether exhibitions are actually effective in communicating with target markets. Attitudes are polarized among exhibitors: some believe strongly that exhibitions are excellent promotional tools, whereas others believe exhibitions are marginal at best (Blythe and Rayner 1996).

One of the areas of dispute is the split between activities relating directly to making sales (generating leads, identifying prospects, even making sales pitches on the stand) and the non-sales benefits of exhibitions (public relations, enhancing corporate reputation, carrying out market research, etc.). Most exhibitors are concerned mainly with immediate sales (Shipley *et al.* 1993, Kijewski *et al.* 1992, Blythe 1997). Having said that, some exhibitors are more concerned with non-selling activities.

Exhibitions occupy a key role in business-to-business marketing, since they allow contact with buyers whom the vendor otherwise might never meet due to geographical or time constraints. This is particularly the case with international exhibitions such as those held in Germany, where exhibitions occupy a more important role than in most other countries. Exhibitions such as these can bring together people who might otherwise not have known of each others' existence. Since contact at an exhibition takes place on neutral territory, both parties can feel more relaxed, so exhibitions offer an opportunity for the relationship between the buying company and the selling company to develop more fully, and perhaps develop in unexpected directions. Since many visitors to exhibitions are technical people or administrators rather than buyers, there are many opportunities for establishing contacts at all levels of the organization.

As a public relations exercise, exhibitions have much to offer. Since buyers are only a tiny minority of visitors to exhibitions (less than 10 per cent) (Blythe 2000, Gramman 1994), selling objectives are probably not the most important activities to be undertaken. Having said that, almost everybody who visits has some interest in the industry for which the exhibition is organized. This means that many of them will be influential in the buying decision, or at the very least might talk to people who are influential.

In terms of semiotics, trade fairs provide signs about the company and its products. For some firms, the sign is the main reason for exhibiting – being at the trade fair at all gives a signal that the company is at the forefront of the industry, or at least is not one of the laggards. In most cases, though, trade fairs are the vehicle by which signs are delivered. Sign systems of trade fairs are well known – the stand, the suited personnel, the product samples, the free gifts, the product demonstrations and set-piece displays are typical of trade fairs. Each system has an accepted etiquette so that visitors and exhibitors know what their role is when attending the show.

Syntactically, trade shows tend to be stylized. The meaning of a brochure offered at a trade show is not the same as the meaning of a brochure offered by a salesperson at a customer's office. Because trade shows have a cultural context of their own, the resulting meanings differ from those encountered outside the exhibition hall.

■ Research into exhibitions

Most research into managers' perceptions of exhibitions confirms that most managers see them in terms of making sales. This is true of both US and UK shows; even when managers do not expect to take orders at the exhibition, they do see the exhibition as an opportunity to generate leads, qualify prospects and open sales. This is particularly apparent in the staffing of stands; managers predominantly staff them with salespeople, even though there is evidence to suggest that visitors do not like this (Tanner and Chonko 1995, Skerlos and Blythe 2000).

Shipley *et al.* (1993) identified 13 reasons for exhibiting, of which seven were directly related to selling with six representing non-selling activities. Research conducted by Blythe (1997) showed that the selling aims were ranked highest in importance by the majority of exhibitors (see Table 12.1); note that the first five aims on the list are all directly concerned with selling.

Attempts to determine whether exhibitions are effective or not are also coloured by the assumption that they are primarily selling devices. Sharland and Balogh (1996) defined effectiveness as the number of sales leads generated, followed up and successfully closed, and efficiency as the comparison between the cost of trade show participation versus other sales and promotion activities. US research by the Trade Show Bureau in 1988 put the cost of a trade show lead at $132 compared with $251 per call in the field (Trade Show Bureau 1988). UK research showed the comparable figures to be £30 per useful contact at a trade show, compared to £150 for a field call (Centre for Leisure and Tourism Studies 1994). Although a useful contact may not be the same as a sales lead, the general conclusion of researchers is that trade shows and exhibitions generate leads more cheaply than other methods.

The problem lies in determining the strength of these leads. A useful contact may not be a buyer at all – which is not a problem if the individual can act as a gatekeeper or influencer in reaching the decision makers. Even a qualified lead

TABLE 12.1 Ranking of exhibition aims

Reason for exhibiting	Ranking
Meeting new customers (selling)	1
Launching new products (selling)	2
Taking sales orders (selling)	3
Interacting with existing customers (selling)	4
Promoting existing products (selling)	5
Enhancing the company image (non-selling)	6
General market research (non-selling)	7
Meeting new distributors (selling)	8
Keeping up with the competition (non-selling)	9
Getting information about the competition (non-selling)	10
Interacting with existing distributors (selling)	11
Getting an edge on non-exhibitors (non-selling)	12
Enhancing the morale of the staff (non-selling)	13

from a buyer may not be strong, since such a buyer will almost certainly be visiting the firm's competitors, who will undoubtedly be at the same venue.

Some early research by Kerin and Cron (1987) showed that some exhibitors do pay attention to the possibilities of non-selling activities. Although the emphasis was still on selling, other aims were present (see Table 12.2).

For this particular group of respondents, corporate image came out highest, although the next two highest-scoring aims were selling aims. The dissidents may well be right, since there is a discrepancy between the exhibitors' view of exhibitions and the visitors' view. If exhibitions are about communicating, it would seem reasonable to suppose that the visitors and the exhibitors should have compatible aims in attending, that is to say, their aims will not be the same, but they should be complementary. In the case of exhibitions, visitors are quite clearly seeking out at least some of the communication. Figure 12.1 shows the comparison between visitors' tactics and strategies, and exhibitors' tactics and strategies.

Personal selling clearly happens on exhibition stands, although probably not to the extent that exhibitors believe it does. The main reason for the interaction not to happen is the absence of a buyer – fewer than 10 per cent of visitors to exhibitions are buyers.

▍ Visitor expectations

Research conducted among visitors to trade fairs shows that most of them are not directly involved in purchase decisions, and many of them have no role whatsoever in purchasing. (Skerlos and Blythe 2000, Gramman 1993, Bello and Lohtia 1993, Munuera and Ruiz 1999). The Skerlos and Blythe (2000) research showed the breakdown of job titles illustrated in Table 12.3.

TABLE 12.2 Importance of trade show aims

Aim	Mean score (out of 10, with 10 as highest)
Enhancing corporate image	5.32
Introduce new products	5.14
Identify new prospects	5.08
Getting competitive information	4.94
Servicing current customers	4.69
Enhancing corporate morale	3.75
Selling at the show	2.79
New-product testing	2.17

When asked about their role in purchasing, 40 per cent of the respondents said they had no role whatsoever. The respondents' reasons for visiting the exhibition were as shown in Table 12.4. Respondents were allowed to state more than one reason.

Those who stated that they had no role in purchasing were substantially more likely to be there to see new products and developments; this is not surprising, since they are likely to be technical people.

Visitors were invited to rate their overall satisfaction with the exhibition in terms of the extent to which their aims were met. Research and development people were significantly less satisfied with the outcomes than were the sales and marketing people, and engineers showed a similar pattern. Visitors' experience of the

TABLE 12.3 Visitor job profiles at a business-to-business exhibition for the food-technology industry

Job	Percentage of respondents
Sales and marketing	24%
General administration	26%
Design	14%
Engineering	22%
Research and development	14%

TABLE 12.4 Reasons for attending

Reason for visiting	Percentage citing
To see new products and developments	54%
To try new products and go to demonstrations	23%
To obtain technical or product information	21%
To see new companies	12%
To discuss specific problems and talk with the experts	10%
To compare products and services	7%
To make business contacts	6%
To see a specific company or product	5%

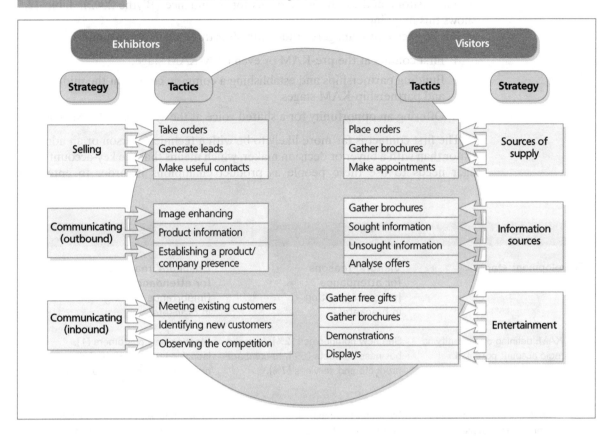

FIGURE 12.1   Exhibitor and visitor strategies and techniques

trade show is therefore clearly related to their jobs, which is unsurprising since the job will tend to dictate the visitor's needs and requirements from the show. Failure to meet these needs will result in visitor dissatisfaction with the show.

■ Exhibitions in key-account management

Key-account management is about creating long-term relationships with other firms (see Chapter 5). As we saw in that chapter, relationships go through stages, at each stage of which the focus is on a different type of problem.

In the context of key-account management, exhibitions offer few opportunities to make immediate sales. What they do offer is an opportunity to initiate relationships by approaching influencers and users, for example technical people and administrators; these opportunities are much greater than the opportunity to meet buyers, simply because of the numerical preponderance of these people. Opportunities to deepen existing relationships by meeting key-account firms' technical or administrative people are obviously present, and may represent the real strength of exhibitions. In some cases these people may not have been involved directly with the supplying company as the relationship is being established, but are able to become part of the process by meeting people on the exhibition stand.

Using the KAM/PPF model outlined in Chapter 5 (Wilson 1999), it is possible to map visitors' and exhibitors' reasons for attendance (Blythe 2002). Table 12.5 shows this mapping.

For key-account managers, trade fairs offer three main opportunities:

1 First contact at the pre-KAM or even early-KAM stage.
2 Building partnerships and establishing a common culture at the mid-KAM and partnership-KAM stages.
3 Offering an opportunity for a shared voice at the synergistic-KAM stage.

The first contact is far more likely to be with a technical person or an administrator than with a buyer or decision maker, which means that the key-account manager needs to use these people as product champions in order to enter the

TABLE 12.5 Exhibitions and the KAM/PPF model

Development stage	Visitors' reasons for attendance [percentage citing in brackets]	Exhibitors' reasons for attendance [importance ranking in brackets]
Pre-KAM: defining and identifying strategic account potential.	See new companies [12%], to make business contacts [6%], to compare products and services [7%].	Meeting new customers [1], launching new products [2], meeting new distributors [8], promoting existing products [5].
Early-KAM: account penetration, seeking preferred supplier status.	To obtain technical or product information [21%].	Interacting with existing customers [4], interacting with existing distributors [12], enhancing the company image [6], taking sales orders [3].
Mid-KAM: building partnership, consolidate preferred-supplier status.	To discuss specific problems/talk with the experts [10%].	Interact with existing customers [4], interact with existing distributors [12].
Partnership-KAM: develop spirit of partnership, build common culture, lock in customer.	To discuss specific problems/talk with the experts [10%].	Interact with existing customers and distributors (possibly by sharing exhibition space).
Synergistic-KAM: continuous improvement, shared rewards, quasi-integration.	No real role. At this stage the companies are very close together, and may even be sharing their promotional activities, including exhibiting at trade fairs.	No real role.
Uncoupling-KAM: disengagement.	To see new customers, products, developments and companies.	To meet new customers and distributors and to take sales orders.

prospective customer's firm. Given that these technical people are at the trade fair for the purpose of finding out what is new in the field, exhibitors might be well advised to put some of their own technical people on the stand in order to explore possible synergies. In the pre-KAM stage, when the parties are feeling each other out, it appears that exhibitors place a high importance on finding new customers and launching new products. Unfortunately, only 12 per cent of visitors cite seeing new companies as a reason for attending, only 6 per cent cite making business contacts, and 7 per cent cite comparing products and services.

At the early-KAM stage, when the parties are aiming to increase the volume of business and build a social network, the exhibitor's aim of interacting with existing customers will be most appropriate. The 21 per cent of visitors who cited obtaining technical information as a reason for attending will also probably be catered for. Where the prevailing strategy is concerned with building networks, the trade fair offers a neutral territory on which people who would not normally have the chance to meet are able to network with the exhibiting firm. For the exhibitor, the key strategy here is to ensure that the partner firm's technical, administrative and marketing people are specifically invited to the stand, possibly with the objective of meeting their opposite numbers. Interaction between these individuals is likely to encourage the identification of problems, the finding of creative solutions and a closer relationship between the organizations. However, the research indicates that many technical people's needs are not being met – the opportunity to discuss specific problems, which is a common reason for visiting the exhibition, is unavailable because the exhibiting firms tend to concentrate mainly on selling activities.

In the mid-KAM stage, visitors may wish to discuss specific problems (and 10 per cent gave this reason for attending). Exhibitors will wish to interact with existing distributors and customers, the latter of which aims is rated fourth in importance by exhibitors.

At the partnership-KAM stage the two parties are probably too closely intertwined to need to meet in an exhibition hall, and may even be sharing stand space.

At the synergistic-KAM stage, firms develop strategic congruence. At this point, trade fairs provide the opportunity to share a voice. This is, of course, true of other communications media, but trade fairs allow congruence across a broader spectrum of activities than most because of the interactive nature of the medium. For example, trade fairs can be used for concept testing of new products, allowing the partners to obtain quick feedback on the market viability of the product.

At the uncoupling-KAM stage, when the partnership is dissolving, the parties are likely to use the trade fair to seek new partners. Obviously there is likely to be considerable overlap between the separate stages and activities, but as the relationship deepens the role of trade fairs is likely to become less.

Using trade fairs effectively as a tool in key-account management means understanding how trade fairs work and who the visitors are. As in any other area of marketing, the key issue is to meet the needs of those visitors effectively in order to facilitate exchange. Using the courtship analogy, the exhibition hall is the business equivalent of the dance hall. It is a place for chance encounters that may lead to romance, or it is a place to go to on a date. Whether chance or pre-arranged, the key-account manager can only make the best of the event by setting objectives and being clear about achieving them.

An important issue here is to ensure that the right people are on the stand in order to discuss issues with the visitors. If the exhibitor intends to relate to technical people, it would seem sensible to ensure that some of the exhibitor's technical people are on the stand to answer questions. If the intention is to establish links with key accounts at other levels in the organization, it may be sensible to arrange for senior managers to be on the stand, at least for part of the time; these people frequently have few opportunities to meet customers.

Why exhibitions fail

Exhibitions frequently do not work for firms. In most cases, this is because exhibitors have not thought through their strategies clearly enough, have not set objectives and have not evaluated their activities sufficiently rigorously, or at all (Blythe 2000). As in any other area of marketing, failure to meet the needs of the customer (in this case the visitor) will result in a failure to communicate effectively and hence a failure of the exhibition.

Referring back to the dance-hall analogy, a key-account manager should be seeking a long-term relationship, and should set objectives accordingly. Whether the encounters are chance or pre-arranged, the key-account manager can only make the best of the event by setting objectives and being clear about achieving them.

In other cases, exhibitions fail because the exhibitors have inappropriate objectives. Going to an exhibition with the objective of making sales, either at the exhibition or through follow-ups, is almost certainly unrealistic in most cases because so few buyers are present as a proportion of visitors. Even when buyers are present, they are likely to be in the information-gathering stage of the buying process and are unlikely to be in a position to place an order anyway.

As in other areas of business, much of the risk of failure can be reduced by planning ahead. Unfortunately, many exhibitors leave the planning of the exhibition to the last minute and do not prepare sufficiently in advance.

Planning for exhibitions

Failure to plan an exhibition may be caused by the view that exhibitions are merely flag-waving exercises aimed at showing the corporate face and nothing more. In other cases, companies do not plan because they regard the exhibition as a one-off event, and so do not wish to impose extra burdens on the marketing team. In other cases, however, failure to plan is simply a result of lack of knowledge or lack of the will to take trouble over ensuring that the exhibition is successful.

Planning an exhibition properly can easily take up six months or more, if pre-preparation and post-exhibition activities are taken into account. The stages of planning an exhibition are as follows:

1 *Decide on the objectives*: This goes beyond merely deciding what the reasons are for exhibiting; the objectives need to be measurable (and systems need to be in place to do this), achievable (within the context of the firm's resources), and realistic (considering the visitor profile and competitive pressures at the exhibition).

2 *Select which exhibition to attend*: This relies on the range of choice, the visitor profiles (obtainable from the organizers, though the figures may have been massaged), the cost of exhibiting, the availability of suitable space in a good location, the timing of the exhibition relative to the firm's business cycle, the competitive level and the prestige value of the exhibition.

3 *Plan the staffing of the stand*: Most managers tend to use the sales force to man the stand, but often this is inappropriate; much depends on what the objectives of exhibiting are. Using salespeople also has the disadvantage of taking salespeople off the road at a time when enquiries are likely to be at their highest. Since visitors are likely to be in the information search stage of the buying process, it is probably too early to involve salespeople anyway.

4 *Plan the support promotions*: These may include direct mailshots to visitors, advertising campaigns in advance of the exhibition, press releases in the trade press, and sales-force activity before the exhibition (inviting existing customers to visit the stand) and afterwards (following up on enquiries).

5 *Decide on the layout of the stand and its contents*: Since visitors are usually information gathering, the layout needs to be attractive and eye catching, but should also convey solid information. It is often a good idea to have a private area so that customers can discuss business in private; this area can double as a rest area for stand personnel. Refreshments can be made available within this area; opinions are mixed as to whether alcoholic drink should be available.

6 *Arrange the follow-up activities after the exhibition*: A surprising number of exhibitors fail to do this, with the result that the sales force is not able to follow up on leads generated, the company is not prepared to send information out to those who requested it, and the PR momentum obtained from the exhibition is wasted (Blythe and Rayner 1996). The biggest problem with delaying follow-ups is that prospective customers will almost certainly have contacted the firm's competitors at the same exhibition, so a delay is likely to mean that the competitors will get the business.

7 *Plan the logistics of the exercise*: Ensure that sufficient promotional material has been produced, that the staff are transported to the exhibition, that the hotels are booked and are of a suitable standard, that stand personnel are briefed and prepared, that equipment, furnishing, samples and so forth all arrive at the right time and in the right condition.

Once the exhibition is over, evaluation needs to take place. Many firms do not evaluate their activities effectively, or at all, which seems perverse considering the amount of money and effort which is expended on exhibition attendance. The reasons for not evaluating might be as follows (Blythe 1997):

1 The firm lacks the resources to carry out the evaluation.
2 The activity is not important enough to warrant evaluation.
3 The evaluation would be too difficult or expensive.
4 The firm is owner-managed and therefore the owner feels able to estimate the effectiveness of the exhibition without formal evaluation.

▍ Managing the exhibition stand

Stand management is straightforward provided the planning has been carried out effectively, and the necessary equipment and staff have arrived. Designing the layout of the stand is an important part of the process; most exhibitors tend to make the company name the most prominent feature of the stand, with brand names and product specifications lower on the list of priorities. This is a reasonable policy if the purpose of the stand is to raise the corporate profile, but in most circumstances the visitors' need for solid information will dictate the design and layout of the stand.

In many cases, firms assume that the visitors will recognize the company's name and will know what products are available. This is something of a leap of faith; overseas visitors to exhibitions may not be familiar with the firm and its products, and even domestic visitors may be more familiar with brand names than with company names, since that is what is usually given the heaviest promotion.

Exhibitions are tiring for the visitors as well as for the exhibitors, so visitors usually only spend significant time at a few stands. This may be as few as 10 or 12 stands, and this figure does not rise if the exhibition is larger since most visitors only spend one day there. This means that large exhibitions with many stands do not increase the number of visitors who will see the stand; statistically, large exhibitions actually reduce the chances of particular visitors seeing a particular stand since there are more stands to choose from. The problem of clutter is probably greater at exhibitions than in any other environment, as exhibitors all compete for the visitors' limited attention. For this reason the stand must be designed with the visitors' needs in mind, as well as with the exhibitor's objectives in mind.

For example, if the exhibition objective is to raise corporate awareness the company name needs to be prominent, and a plentiful supply of brochures and leaflets needs to be available. Temporary promotion staff could be employed to hand out leaflets in other parts of the exhibition so that exhibitors who have not visited the stand might be encouraged to do so, or at least go away with some information about the firm. The stand might have some kind of stunt or gimmick to raise awareness; a product demonstration or some spectacular event will attract attention.

On the other hand, if the aim is to make sales or generate leads the stand should show the brand names prominently, with plenty of information on product benefits. The stand should be staffed with some technical people and some salespeople, and brochures should only be given to visitors who are prepared to

TALKING POINT

Arthur Guinness, the world-famous beer company now owned by Diageo, has a reputation for its innovative exhibition displays. Recently the company has commissioned the design of a table-top display, supplied by Exhibit Solutions Inc. The display allows Guinness to exhibit easily at small exhibitions, conferences and other events where a major presence is not needed, but a smart and eye-catching stand is. The whole stand folds small enough to fit into the boot of a salesperson's car, and can be erected in minutes.

leave their names and addresses; some exhibitors will only mail out brochures rather than give them out on the stand. This ensures that follow-up calls can be carried out. Promotions and stunts should be used to collect names and addresses; for example, a free draw for a prize. Special exhibition-only discounts or promotions can be used, and pre-publicity can reflect this in order to get buyers onto the stand. In these circumstances, casual non-buying visitors are less important and might even be actively discouraged – although (for the reasons outlined earlier in the chapter) this may be a short-sighted policy since most exhibitions are probably not good selling venues, and the casual visitors may be the exhibitor's best future customers.

The following is a checklist for organizing the stand itself:

- Ensure that displays are easily accessible and informative.
- Check that stand members have a clear brief.
- Have clear objectives in place and, where possible, set targets for stand members.
- Have an area where prospects can be taken for a private conversation if necessary.
- Ensure an adequate supply of drinking water and other refreshments.
- Establish a rota for stand staff to ensure regular breaks.
- Have a record-keeping system for leads and useful contacts.
- Have a feedback system for visitors' comments.
- Set up some fun activities for stand staff.

It is useful for stand staff to have the opportunity to tour the rest of the exhibition (this also gives them a break) and it is worthwhile to give them objectives for doing this, for example, making it the time for gathering information about competitors. Staff will need a break at least every hour; long periods of standing, smiling and relating to large numbers of people is both physically and psychologically exhausting. This requires careful planning to ensure that there are enough suitably qualified people left to man the stand during breaks.

The main problem concerning stand staff is maintaining their motivation over the period of the show. After a few hours on the stand, the visitors seem to meld into a single mass, most of the enquiries seem like a waste of time, and the smile begins to wear a little thin. For this reason it is a good idea to have some activities running which keep the stand personnel interested. For example, a competition for collecting business cards, with an appropriate small prize, can keep staff interested. Demonstrations throughout the day can help to break the monotony for staff as well as visitors, particularly if the demonstrations are given by stand members in rotation. Again, a small prize could be offered for the best demonstration.

Exhibitions are often held away from the firm's home base, and therefore away from the staff's homes and families. Sometimes it might be appropriate to allow staff to bring their partners with them, but in most cases this is problematical, so every opportunity should be given for staff to telephone home, and it almost goes without saying that their accommodation and meals should be of a high standard – this compensates to a small extent for being away from home, but in any case it reflects better on the firm.

Overall, exhibitions need to be planned in fine detail, with everything leading towards the planned objectives. Choice of exhibition, pre-publicity and post-follow-ups, stand design, staffing and what to exhibit should all be chosen with clear objectives in mind.

◼ Alternatives to exhibitions

Because of the cost and commitment attached to exhibiting, not least the disruption to the exhibitors' normal routine, firms are beginning to look for alternative routes for meeting buyers and promoting their products. Since one of the major advantages of exhibitions is the neutral-territory aspect, allowing buyers and sellers to discuss matters in a more relaxed way, many exhibitors are moving towards private exhibitions or road shows to exhibit their products.

Exhibitors who look for alternatives to exhibiting are usually seeking out ways of contacting customers on neutral territory, but without the presence of competitors. From a sales manager's viewpoint, any prospect who asks for a presentation as a result of an exhibition is likely to have asked for presentations from some or all of the firm's competitors. This means that exhibition leads go stale very quickly, and must be followed up immediately even if this disrupts other activities.

Private exhibitions

Private exhibitions are sometimes run at venues near to the public exhibition, and coinciding with the main event. Typically such events are held in hotels or small halls where the buyers are invited.

The main advantages are:

- The atmosphere is usually more relaxed and less frenetic than in the main exhibition.
- No competitors are present to distract the visitors.
- The exhibitor has much more control over the environment than would be the case at the public exhibition, where the organizers may impose irksome regulations.
- Superior refreshment and reception facilities are available.

- If the event is held in a hotel the staff will have access to their rooms and can easily take breaks.
- Sometimes the overall cost is less.

The main drawback of the private event is that visitors will only come to it if they are given advance warning, and even then may decide only to visit the main exhibition. The invitations need to be sent out early enough so that visitors can make allowance for the event, but not so early that they forget about it, and some incentive to make the necessary detour may also need to be in place. It is extremely unlikely that the list of desirable visitors will be complete – one of the main advantages of the public exhibition is that some of the visitors will be unknown to the exhibiting company, and a first contact can be made.

Private exhibitions work best in situations where the company has a limited market, where the costs of the main exhibition are high, and where a suitable venue is available close to the main site.

Road shows

A road show is a travelling exhibition which takes the product to the buyer rather than the other way round. In some cases these are run in hotels, in other cases trailers or caravans are used. Road shows are useful in cases where large numbers of buyers are concentrated in particular geographical areas, and where many of them would not make the journey to visit a national exhibition. In some countries (for example the United States) industries may be geographically concentrated (e.g. the film industry in California or the steel industry in Pennsylvania), which makes a road show more economical.

Like private exhibitions, road shows allow the exhibitor to control the environment to a large extent. Road shows can be run in conjunction with other firms, which reduces the cost and increases the interest level for the visitors; this can be particularly effective if the firms concerned are complementary rather than competing.

In common with private exhibitions, the roadshow's organizer is entirely responsible for all the publicity. In the case of a major public exhibition the exhibition organizers and even the firm's competitors will ensure that a certain minimum level of visitors will attend; in the case of a road show the exhibitor will need to produce considerable advance publicity, and even send out specific invitations to individual buyers and prospects. This adds to the risk as well as the cost.

SUMMARY

Although exhibitions and trade fairs are often considered as a form of sales promotion, they do in fact have totally separate features and advantages. Exhibitions offer a wide range of communications possibilities between all levels of the organizations which exhibit, and those which attend. Like an old-fashioned marketplace, exhibitions allow all interested parties to meet if they so wish, but this opportunity is often squandered by an overemphasis on making immediate sales.

The key points from this chapter are as follows:

- Buyers are very much in the minority at most, if not all, exhibitions.

- Most visitors are on an information search, not on a shopping trip.

- Most exhibitors are focused strongly on selling, whereas they should be focused on making useful contacts.

- The dissonance between exhibitors' aims and visitors' aims often results in disappointment for both parties.

- Exhibitors should establish objectives for their activities, but rarely do so.

REVIEW QUESTIONS

1 How might an exhibitor evaluate the aim of enhancing the company image?

2 What objectives might be appropriate for a first-time exhibitor?

3 What would be the most appropriate staffing approach for an exhibitor seeking to relate to existing customers?

4 What are the main advantages of allowing staff time off from the stand to tour the exhibition?

5 How might salespeople use exhibitions to generate leads? What might be the dangers of doing this?

REFERENCES

Bello, D. C. and Lohtia, R. (1993) 'Improving trade show effectiveness by analyzing attendees', *Industrial Marketing Management*, 22(4): 311–18.

Blythe, J. (1997) 'Does size matter? Objectives and measures at UK trade exhibitions', *Journal of Marketing Communications*, 3 (1/March): 51–9.

—— (2000) 'Objectives and measures at UK trade exhibitions', *Journal of Marketing Management* 16(1): 203–22.

—— (2002) 'Using trade fairs in key account management', *Industrial Marketing Management* 31: 627–35.

—— and Rayner, T. (1996) 'The evaluation of non-selling activities at British trade exhibitions – An exploratory study', *Marketing Intelligence and Planning*, 14(5): 20–4.

Centre for Leisure and Tourism Studies (1989), *EIF Exhibition Effectiveness Survey*, London: Exhibition Industry Federation.

Graman, J. (1994) *Independent Market Research*, Birmingham: Centre Exhibitions with National Exhibition Centre.

Kerin, R. A. and Cron, W. L. (1987) 'Assessing trade show functions and performance: An exploratory study', *Journal of Marketing* 51 (July): 87–94.

Kijewski, V., Yoon, E. and Young, G. (1992) *Trade Shows: How Managers Pick their Winners*, Institute for the Study of Business Markets.

Munuera, J. L. and Ruiz, S. (1999) 'Trade fairs as services: A look at visitors' objectives in Spain', *Journal of Business Research* 44(1): 17–24.

Sharland, A. and Balogh, P. (1996) 'The value of non-selling activities at international trade shows', *Industrial Marketing Management* 25(1): 59–66.

Shipley, D., Egan, C. and Wong, K. S. (1993) 'Dimensions of trade show exhibiting management', *Journal of Marketing Management*, 9 (1/Jan.): 55–63.

Skerlos, K. and Blythe, J. (2000) 'Ignoring the audience: Exhibitors and visitors at a Greek trade fair', *Proceedings of the Fifth International Conference on Corporate and Marketing Communication*, Erasmus University, Rotterdam 22nd and 23rd May.

Tanner, J. F. and Chonko, L. B. (1995) 'Trade show objectives, management and staffing practices', *Industrial Marketing Management*, 24(4): 257–64.

Trade Show Bureau (1988) *Attitudes and Opinions of Computer Executives Regarding Attendance at Information Technology Events*, Study no. 1080, East Orleans, MA: Trade Show Bureau.

EARL'S COURT TOY FAIR

Each year in January, Earl's Court hosts the Toy Fair. This exhibition is attended by toy buyers from all over the UK and the world – and is one of the premier showcases for British toy manufacturers.

Because 80 per cent of toys are sold at Christmas, the toy industry needs to operate on long lead times and needs to have orders booked well in advance in order to schedule production. For some firms, the difference between a successful exhibition and an unsuccessful one is the difference between surviving the year and not surviving. The Earl's Court exhibition, and another one in Harrogate, are widely believed to be the most important in the industry.

Apart from the buyers there are a number of other types of visitor. Some are there to sell things to the exhibitors: marketing consultants, machine tool manufacturers and financial services salespeople are all likely to be among those present. Also, many students attend the exhibition. Some are design students, looking to pick up ideas and make contacts, and some are business students observing the process of exhibiting. Another large category of visitor is the technical people: the engineers and programmers who build mechanical and electronic toys for rival firms and are simply on a spying mission to see what is happening with the competition. There are even some visitors who are having a day out of the office or are retired from the industry altogether – in other words, have no power to buy anything at all, and are simply there for the entertainment value of spending all day in a giant toy shop.

In fact, only a relatively small number of the visitors is engaged in buying anything at all. This presents a problem for the exhibitors, many of whom are small firms who are staking their year's profits on doing business at the show.

For AM Games Ltd the show is particularly crucial. As a small company starting out in the board games business, AM Games needs the showcase that the exhibition provides, but can barely afford to attend. The company produces a grand total of three board games, and is hoping that, eventually, it will be bought out by one of the bigger games manufacturers. The directors of AM Games realize that they are unlikely to strike it rich with only three games – but establishing them in the market is a way of attracting the attention of the larger manufacturers.

The games themselves are all of the traditional board variety. There are no electronic gadgets involved, just dice and counters: each game has an educational aspect as well as the excitement of a game of chance, and each game was invented and tested by the managing director's son-in-law, a mathematics professor at a university in England's Midlands. AM Games Ltd's managing director, Colin Rogers, is a retired army officer who has funded the company out of his army savings. He wouldn't be destitute if the company failed – but equally he is anxious not to lose his investment.

To this end he hired a firm of exhibition consultants to help him plan and run the stand. The consultants advised him on the design of the stand, and on what he might reasonably expect from an exhibition – and in fact the advice proved to be very useful, because he obtained more than 20 good sales leads from interested buyers in the course of the first day.

Afterwards, Colin considered whether the exhibition had been worthwhile. Of the total of 70 sales leads obtained, he managed to follow up on 50 in the first week after the exhibition, making telephone calls and appointments to see the firms' buyers. The 50 leads actually resulted in 14 firm appointments, which seemed to be a reasonable result. Colin thought it would probably be worthwhile booking a stand at the exhibition for the following year – the sales figures should be enough to carry the company through until then at least. Overall, his gut feeling was that exhibitions are a good way forward for his fledgling company.

Case-study questions

1 What else might Colin have achieved from the exhibition, apart from sales leads?

2 How might Colin have ensured that the right kind of people visited the stand?

3 How might Colin have evaluated the success or otherwise of the stand?

4 What other activities might have been advisable to ensure that the exhibition went well?

5 Should Colin consider going to other toy exhibitions?

13

ETHICS, CONSUMER PROTECTION AND THE LAW

Learning objectives

After reading this chapter, you should be able to:

- Explain the main features of UK law relating to sales.
- Explain the difference between civil law and criminal law.
- Describe the functions of a code of ethics.
- Describe the procedure for drawing up a code of ethics.

◼ Introduction

As with all other interpersonal processes, personal selling contains within it the possibility of deception. Although the widespread mistrust of salespeople by consumers is largely misplaced, there is no doubt that some salespeople will shade the truth, or tell outright lies, in order to win a sale. In some types of selling, particularly where salespeople are paid on a commission-only basis, the temptation to deceive customers can be very high.

In the long run, such behaviour is counterproductive, since it leads to the firm, and the salesperson, developing a bad reputation, which will itself damage further business. Unfortunately many people only think short term, so for this reason most governments have developed a body of law which seeks to protect consumers and others from unscrupulous practices.

Tom Cowie was born in Sunderland and left school at 15 to work in his father's motorbike repair shop. It was here that he established his sales skills, taking over the motorbike-sales side of the business. Unfortunately, his career was cut short by the Second World War, in which he served in the RAF.

After the war, the business was in tatters. Tom had £1000 in capital, and used it to restart the business, selling used motorbikes in Sunderland. His negotiating skills, and understanding of customers, stood him in good stead and the business grew rapidly. He branched out into buying motor dealerships, then into operating bus companies, then into vehicle rental. The Cowie Group's best-known brand is Arriva, introduced in 1997; it operates buses and trains throughout the UK. Corporate turnover is in the hundreds of millions, and Sir Tom Cowie is now (at over 80) lifetime president of the company – not bad for a motorbike salesman from Tyneside.

Ethics

Ethics are the principles that define right and wrong. Ethical thinking divides into the *teleological* (basically that acts should be defined as ethical or otherwise according to the outcome of the acts) and *deontological* (that acts can be defined as ethical or unethical regardless of outcome). The teleological approach implies that the end justifies the means, but is concerned with the greatest good of the greatest number; the deontological approach is best illustrated by Kant's categorical imperative, which states that each act should be based on reasons that everyone could act on, and that actions must be based on reasons that the decision maker would accept for others to use.

In most cases salespeople and managers do not become enmeshed in the deeper recesses of philosophy, but instead rely on the moral rules which are part of the corporate culture. Research shows that most business people have separate sets of morals for work and for home (Fraedrich 1988). For example, much of the jargon of marketing is warfare-based (counterattacks, offensive product launches, etc.) and of course all's fair in love and war; soldiers may kill or maim the enemy, but would not do so in civilian life. Having said that, while the moral code of a company may not be the same as the personal moral code of its employees and managers, there will be less dissonance amongst the staff if the firm conforms reasonably closely to a code of ethics.

Salespeople often face ethical conflicts. Perhaps a salesperson is faced with the dilemma of either correcting a customer's mistaken belief about a product, and thus losing the business, or allowing the customer to continue with the false belief right up to the point of taking delivery of the goods. Once a salesperson has deceived a customer it becomes increasingly difficult to tell the truth later, and eventually the customer will discover the truth anyway. At that point the business will be lost, probably forever. Table 13.1 shows some examples of ethical problems faced by salespeople, with suggestions for solving the difficulty.

Pricing raises ethical issues in the areas of price fixing, predatory pricing (pricing below the cost of production in order to bankrupt competitors) and not revealing the full cost of purchase.

Price fixing involves collusion between salespeople from different companies who agree not to compete on price. Such collusion can be overt, where the salespeople meet and agree prices, or it can be tacit, where there is an unspoken agreement not to compete on price. The latter is extremely common, and is often the subject of investigations by the Monopolies and Mergers Commission in the UK.

Predatory pricing is more commonly decided upon at director level rather than at sales-force level. It is at its most prevalent in international markets, where it is

TABLE 13.1 Examples of ethical problems for salespeople

Problem	Possible solution
A customer has a false belief about the product, for example believing it to be made of superior materials.	The salesperson should apologize for not explaining properly, should correct the misunderstanding, and should try to put the new information in a positive light, perhaps by explaining that the use of cheaper materials helps to keep the cost down.
A misunderstanding means that the customer is offering to pay more than the list price for the goods.	Again, the correction is easily made by telling the customer there has been an error. Keeping quiet about it is not an option, because the customer will almost certainly find out later anyway (quite apart from the dishonesty involved).
The customer agrees to sign the contract providing delivery will be within seven days – but the salesperson knows that delivery will take at least two weeks.	The salesperson must tell the customer about the delivery problem, but could first offer to call the delivery people to find out whether anything might be done to speed things up. If not, it may be worth pointing out that, by the time the customer has spoken to competing suppliers, the actual delivery date might be later.
The customer suggests an unethical action – for example, the customer agrees to buy, provided the selling company gives information about the customer's competitors.	This warrants a straight refusal. Apart from the ethical issue, the customer is demonstrating his or her own lack of ethics, which might make him or her problematical to do business with. Secondly, agreeing to such an arrangement jeopardizes the position of other existing customers. Thirdly, agreeing to the proposal demonstrates to the customer that the salesperson is lacking in ethics, which opens up possibilities of blackmail.
A buyer suggests that an order will be placed provided a suitable cash payment is made to the buyer.	This is not an unusual scenario, particularly in very large firms and some government organizations. Such bribery is illegal in most countries, and could result in jail sentences for both parties. As with the previous problem, it demonstrates that the buyer is not to be trusted – if he or she is willing to betray his or her employer, there is an even greater likelihood of being prepared to betray the supplying firm. Bribery differs from a business gift because a gift is not conditional on business being done. It is usually a token of thanks, given outside the contractual process.

called predatory dumping; the goods are sold at such a low price that local manufacturers cannot compete, while the importing company can make up its losses in other international markets. Predatory dumping is illegal under international trade law, but is notoriously difficult to police – usually the damage is done long before sanctions can be applied.

Distribution ethics involve abuse of power in the buyer–seller relationship. Some major retail stores operate no-quibble sale-or-return contracts which mean that manufacturers have to accept damaged goods back, even when there is no fault in the manufacture; this has been seen as unethical by some smaller manufacturers who have little negotiating power and few choices of outlet for their products. A second area of distribution ethics is the failure of some firms to keep within the agreed terms of payment – large firms frequently delay payment to smaller firms in order to improve their own cash-flow position. The sales force can sometimes be caught in the middle when this happens, particularly if commission is only paid out when payment is received from the customer.

There is evidence that the sales manager's own ethical stance affects the hiring of salespeople. This is partly because the manager will judge reported acts of the salesperson according to the manager's ethical beliefs, but also the manager will have an ethical stance regarding the hiring process itself – in other words, a regard for the fairness or otherwise of the hiring process (Sivadas *et al.* 2003).

■ Stakeholders

The concept of stakeholders is a relatively recent way of looking at businesses and their activities. The theory is that everyone on whom the business impacts should be considered as a stakeholder, and should be considered in terms of their needs and wants. Senior management should try to balance the needs of different stakeholder groups when running the business. From the viewpoint of marketers, stakeholder theory has an important impact on thinking, because marketers have traditionally focused on the customer, whereas stakeholder theory requires managers to consider employees, shareholders, the general public, government agencies, suppliers, neighbours and so forth in a long list. The importance given to each group of stakeholders will vary from one firm to another, depending on the views of the management, but customers are not necessarily given top priority.

This raises some important ethical considerations, because there will be trade-offs between the interests of the different groups. For a salesperson, the customer is likely to come first because salespeople spend more time with customers than with colleagues. This could mean that a salesperson is faced with a choice between keeping a promise to a customer and acting in the company's best interests. Most of the accusations of unethical dealing which are hurled at companies arise from the impossibility of meeting the needs of all the stakeholders. Should a company be environmentally friendly, or should it make money for the shareholders?

There are six basic duties of sellers in respect of consumer rights (Kuhlman 1994). These are as follows:

1 Manufactured and offered products must provide a minimum level of security.
2 Supplier communication must not contain any deceiving or misleading information but rather educate the consumer with regard to important product qualities.
3 Contracts must not be drawn up at the consumer's disadvantage but must enable both parties equally to attain their interests. Furthermore, they should provide the consumer with the right to demand redress for damages.
4 Suppliers should be open to consumers' complaints and attend to their problems as well as to the reasons for satisfaction and dissatisfaction concerning products and services.
5 The environmental pollution caused by the production, distribution use and waste disposal of goods should be minimized.
6 Suppliers of goods can help to educate the consumer. Companies offering high-quality products and services at reasonable prices have nothing to fear from a well-informed customer.

All of these duties result in ethical problems in their observance, since they conflict with the needs of other stakeholders. Table 13.2 shows some of these conflicts. Obviously in some cases the loss to one stakeholder is tiny compared to the potential loss to another – which is why managers need to consider all aspects of the problem.

In practice, most firms find that acting ethically pays off, however, because a good reputation helps sales. Ethical behaviour can be viewed as a hierarchy, as follows (Donaldson 1998).

Level 1 – *the firm is law abiding*: At this level the firm acts within the law, but does no more than this – anything which is not actually illegal is regarded as fair practice.

Level 2 – *the company establishes a set of company regulations*: These are often embodied in the employment contract so that employees are compelled to abide by the rules or risk disciplinary action.

Level 3 – *the company establishes a code of conduct*: This establishes an overall set of aims and aspirations for corporate ethics, going beyond a simple set of dos and don'ts. A code of conduct applies throughout the organization, from senior management down to the lowliest employee.

Level 4 – *social awareness*: At this level the corporation has regard to the wider world, beyond its immediate associates. A responsibility to the wider community is acknowledged.

Level 5 – *proactive level*: The company seeks to pioneer advances in ethical standards, setting the pace for other firms to follow.

Few sales managers are in a position to set the level at which the company's ethical principles will lie, but many are in a position to make recommendations. It is certainly the case that a sales manager is able to set a code of conduct for the sales force.

TABLE 13.2 Conflicts in basic ethics

Duty	Conflict
Manufactured products must offer minimum security.	This will increase prices and create a problem for suppliers and for many employees. There is also a problem for marketers, who may need to get a product to market quickly in order to beat the competition, and may not have time for the type of rigorous testing needed.
Supplier communication must not mislead.	Almost all advertising is intended to put the product in the best possible light. Failing to do this, when competitors certainly will, runs the risk of damaging the business and reducing the job security of employees.
Contracts must not be drawn up to the consumer's disadvantage.	Most personal selling involves negotiation. This means that each party gains from the deal, but the degree to which one gains more or less than the other is a matter for negotiation. Salespeople would be failing in their duty to their colleagues and shareholders if they did not negotiate as strongly as possible.
Suppliers should be open to customers' complaints and attend to their problems.	If a customer complains about an employee there is an implication that the employee is at fault and should be punished. Quite clearly an unconditional acceptance of complaints will damage employee interests: the customer is not always right (although the customer is always the customer).
Environmental pollution should be minimized.	Frequently the minimization of pollution places the company in an uncompetitive position with respect to other, less environmentally friendly, companies. This is why companies prefer the government to intervene, to keep the playing-field level.
Suppliers of goods should educate the consumer.	This again adds to costs, which damages the firm's competitive position. In the long run, the firm may benefit, but in the short term there are costs for shareholders and employees.

Chonko and Hunt (1985) listed the most important ethical concerns of marketing practitioners. These are listed here, in order of frequency of mention:

1 *Bribery*: This includes gifts in advance of making the deal, under-the-table personal payments to decision makers, commissions for agreeing to a deal and cash rebates. A bribe is a payment made in exchange for agreeing to a purchase.

2 *Fairness*: Manipulation of other people, creating conflicts between company and family, and inducing customers to use services which they do not need.

3 *Honesty*: Misrepresentation of capabilities, and outright lying to customers.

4 *Price*: Differential pricing (where different customers are offered the same product at very different prices), charging higher prices than competitors while falsely claiming product superiority.

5 *Product*: Selling products which do not have the claimed attributes or which do not genuinely meet a consumer need. Copyright infringements, poor product safety and exaggerated performance claims also come under this heading.

6 *Personnel*: Unfair hiring, firing and employee evaluation.

7 *Confidentiality*: The use or publication of private, secret or classified information about customers or competitors.

8 *Advertising*: Misleading or false claims, crossing the line between acceptable puff and outright lying.

9 *Manipulation of data*: Distortion, falsifying figures or using misleading statistics, using misleading information.

10 *Purchasing*: Reciprocity in supplier selection (choosing suppliers on the basis that they are also customers).

TALKING POINT

During the 1980s, Thermastor Double Glazing sold its windows, doors and conservatories door-to-door. At that time, double glazing was a relatively new phenomenon; few householders really knew what it was, it was relatively expensive, and it needed to be sold vigorously. Also, there were no repeat sales – once a house was double-glazed, it would never need to be done again.

Thermastor used some high-pressure techniques, and salespeople were renowned for never taking **no** for an answer. However, by the early 1990s the market had matured: many other companies had entered the market, and prices had dropped dramatically. Also, double-glazing salesmen in general had acquired a reputation for being pushy and unpleasant, so suppliers were actually able to generate business by promising that no salesman would call. Unfortunately, Thermastor continued with what was an expensive and outmoded method of selling, and despite having a superior, patented product the company went spectacularly bankrupt. The selling concept clearly was not working for them any more.

These concerns are obviously mirrored in the sales force, who need to consider the extent to which they are prepared to bend the rules in order to win a sale.

Interestingly, a survey of managers in direct-selling industries showed that most of them believe that they act more ethically than others in their industry (Chonko *et al.* 2002). This may say more about perceptions of ethics than about the behaviour itself.

Legal restrictions

The following section is only intended as a guide to the law, and refers to the laws of England and Wales; Scottish and Irish law contain some variations from this. The section is not intended as a definitive statement of law, and of course the law frequently changes as a result of new legislation and new decisions handed down by the courts.

The law falls into two categories: civil law and criminal law. Civil law covers contractual disputes between individuals and firms, and is concerned with redressing balances where one individual or firm has infringed the interests of another. The remedies available under civil law range from damages to be paid by the infringer to the victim, through to injunctions preventing the infringer from continuing to damage the other's interests.

Criminal law is concerned with protecting the interests of society at large, in particular with punishing those who act in ways which damage others' interests. Criminal law is concerned with offences against Acts of Parliament, or against case law as developed by judges and magistrates. Criminal law generally does not concern itself with compensating the victims of wrongdoing, but rather with regulating trade and punishing transgressors. In most cases, business issues are dealt with through the civil courts, because those who feel that they have been dealt with unfairly are more interested in seeking compensation than in seeking revenge.

The basis of most civil cases, at least in the business world, is the contract that exists between the parties. A contract is an agreement which is intended to have a legal status; it can be verbal or written, and it comes into existence as soon as a deal is agreed. Once an offer by one party has been accepted by the other, a contract exists and is legally binding whether or not it is in writing. Written contracts are only intended as proof of what was agreed (except in the case of sales of real estate, in which case a written contract is required), and can even be overturned if one or other party can prove that a verbal agreement nullifies it (for example, if one party can prove that the contract was entered into on the basis of verbal assurances which did not subsequently materialize). In most business transactions it is accepted that the written terms of business are the basis of the contract, but since few buyers, or sellers, read the detail of the contracts misunderstandings will arise. The contract may be drawn up by the purchaser (a contract for supply) or by the seller (an order form).

Typical clauses inserted into purchase contracts are as follows:

● Only orders issued on the company's printed order form and signed on behalf of the company will be accepted.

● The supplier shall be responsible for insuring goods in transit.

- Time is of the essence in this contract. The purchaser reserves the right to cancel in the event of late delivery.
- Faulty goods will be returned at the supplier's expense.

Typical clauses inserted in a contract for the sale of goods (an order form) include the following:

- Title to the goods will only pass to the purchaser once payment has been received in full. This is known as a Romalpa clause, after a famous case in which a supply of aluminium was deemed to belong to the, unpaid, supplier even though the aluminium had been used to make something else. This is an important consideration if the purchasing firm goes bankrupt, because it means that the supplier can seize goods from the liquidator rather than wait for a share from the proceeds of an auction. Since unsecured creditors rarely receive anything in a liquidation, this is an important clause to include in any contract.
- Payment in full is to be made within 30 days of delivery of the goods. This is often difficult to enforce, but under UK law firms are allowed to make interest charges for late payments, which, to an extent, reduces the impact of late payment. The problem for most firms lies in deciding whether to apply the interest charges, and possibly alienate a customer, or whether to write them off to goodwill.
- The supplier accepts no liability for goods damaged as a result of the purchaser's negligence. The difficulty with this clause lies in proving that the purchaser was negligent. For example, if a delivery is made during a lunch break and the purchaser's staff are not available to move the goods inside, a subsequent rainstorm might cause damage. Whether this is the purchaser's fault for not moving the goods, or the supplier's fault for leaving them unattended, is difficult to assess.
- In case of damage caused in transit, the purchaser should refuse delivery of the goods and notify the supplier immediately. No liability will be accepted for goods found to be damaged after delivery has been accepted by the purchaser. Here the difficulty is that few purchasers check the goods thoroughly on delivery. When faced with a delivery driver who wants a signature so he can leave for his next drop, most warehouse staff will sign first and examine the goods later. This can make for acrimonious disputes later.

Contracts such as these become complicated when dealing internationally, since further clauses need to be inserted to cover the specific problems encountered in international dealings. The main problems arise because of the difficulty of suing in a foreign country; attendance at court is usually difficult or impossible, and unfamiliarity with foreign law can also cause problems. For this reason most contracts in international trading contain a clause stating which country's laws should be used in interpreting the contract. In recent years, many contracts in the former Communist countries of Eastern Europe have been drawn up under the laws of England and Wales; the reason for this is that Communist countries lack a system of commercial law, since all enterprises of any size were state owned. Following the collapse of communism in Eastern Europe, companies were privatized but the law is still catching up. For companies dealing in those countries, it has proved much simpler to use the well-established English law rather than wait for the new parliaments of the countries to pass their own legislation.

In the event of a dispute over a contract, or the failure of one party to adhere to the terms, the victim will arrange for a summons to be issued. In most cases, summonses are issued for non-payment for goods. The petitioner will be able to state exactly how much is claimed, and the defendant will be allowed the chance to submit a written defence to the court. This is passed on to the petitioner, who then decides whether it is worth pursuing the matter further. If so, each side's solicitors will prepare a case; frequently, in the course of doing so, a compromise is worked out which will satisfy both parties. The reason this happens is because taking a case to court is costly and inconvenient, with no guarantee of winning.

Salespeople are often caught in the middle of such disputes. Because contracts exist whether written or not, it is a good defence in English law to say that the contract was entered into as a result of verbal assurances by a salesperson. There may, of course, be a problem in proving this, but courts frequently come down on the side of the defendant in such circumstances. Exactly what was or was not said in the course of a sales meeting is difficult to establish, especially several months after the event. At a lesser level, salespeople may be expected to act as go-betweens to resolve a disputed payment between a company and a buyer.

■ Criminal law

Firms and individuals can be prosecuted for making false statements about products. The precise offence varies. Applying a false description to a product would fall under the Trade Descriptions Act 1968, which requires firms to describe products in a fair and reasonably accurate way. Firms, and salespeople, are allowed to use a certain amount of puff in describing goods, but false descriptions are outlawed. For example, to say that a car is 'A lovely little runner' is acceptable if the car performs reasonably well; it is not acceptable if the car is dangerously unroadworthy. To describe a restaurant as 'The best in town' is also acceptable, because to at least some of its patrons it is the best; to describe it as a vegetarian restaurant when in fact all the food is cooked in lard is not acceptable. Most successful prosecutions under the Act result in a fine against the perpetrator, but it is open to the victim to sue in the civil courts for compensation.

At a more serious level, a material deception on the part of a salesperson can result in fraud charges. Fraud is committed when an individual deliberately deceives another individual with the intention of gaining a financial advantage. For example, if a car salesperson sells a car knowing it to be still subject to a hire purchase agreement, a fraud has resulted. In the most serious cases, jail terms can result. However, if the salesperson's boss had not informed him or her that there was a hire purchase agreement in place, the salesperson would be innocent. This is the *mens rea* or guilty-mind defence, under which someone cannot be convicted if they did not know that they were committing a crime. Not knowing the law is not a defence, on the other hand a salesperson would be expected to know that selling a car which is still on hire purchase is illegal, but genuinely not knowing that the car is encumbered is a defence.

The Consumer Protection Act 1987 covers misleading prices. The Act applies if prices are stated to be less than they actually are, if charges are included which are not apparent at the time the price is stated, if it suggested by the salesperson that prices are about to rise when this is not the case, or if the salesperson states that the price depends on circumstances which do not exist. For example, if a sales-person offers a discount contingent on the customer signing a contract immedi-ately, this will only be acceptable if the discount really cannot be offered later. This legislation covers a common situation during the early 1980s in which home-improvement salespeople would offer a '10 per cent tonight-only discount' in order to persuade people to sign up for expensive installations immediately.

The Sale of Goods Act 1979 requires that products must be 'of merchantable quality'. This means that the goods must be fit for the purpose for which they are intended. This lays the onus on the salesperson to ensure that the goods being sold are suitable for the customer's needs; another reason, if one were needed, for checking the customer's need situation in the course of the presentation. From an ethical viewpoint, a salesperson should not knowingly sell a customer something unsuitable, even if the customer is eager to buy. Even so, the law requires that the salesperson should make it clear to the customer that the goods are not appropri-ate for the purpose. The Supply of Goods (Implied Terms) Act 1973 also prevents firms from inserting clauses in their guarantees that exclude them from liability for the quality of the goods.

The Consumer Protection Act 1987 provides for compensation to be paid to vic-tims of defective goods. The onus is on the manufacturer to ensure that products are safe, but manufacturers can defend against this if they can demonstrate that the state of scientific knowledge at the time the product was made would have pre-vented them from knowing about the defect. This Act does not go as far as American law, which provides for strict liability on the part of manufacturers; in other words, any injury caused by the product is the manufacturer's liability. This law almost terminated the manufacture of single-engine aircraft in the US, and is seen as being an unnecessarily strict measure by European legislators.

Law relating to sales management

Sales managers need to be aware of some of the provisions of personnel law. For example, the Employment Protection Act prevents employers from dismissing employees capriciously or without giving the employee a fair chance to improve his or her performance. The law only applies to full-time employees with more than one year's service. Some employers have tried to circumvent this law in two ways: firstly, by employing staff on one-year contracts, renewed annually. This loophole was closed by the European Union, who regard such contracts as representing con-tinuous service if there is not a substantial break between the periods of employ-ment. Another common way to circumvent the law is by classifying the staff as self-employed. This is commonly the case with commission-only sales forces, but in fact the decision as to whether an individual is self-employed or not rests with the tax authorities, not with the employer. Issues such as exclusivity of service and degree of control over activities are taken into account by the authorities when deciding whether an individual is self-employed or not.

Some types of sales-force organization are outlawed, for example pyramid-selling operations. Under a pyramid-selling scheme, the salespeople are required to buy the goods themselves, and either sell to final consumers, or recruit other people to sell. These new recruits are then required to buy from the original salesperson, at a mark-up. The result of most pyramid schemes was that the goods were passed on at ever-increasing mark-ups, without being sold to final consumers in any great quantities. This meant that, eventually, someone would have a garage full of rather elderly washing-powder priced so high that no-one would buy. So many people lost money in these schemes that they were outlawed in the UK in the late 1970s.

Pyramid selling should be distinguished from multilevel marketing (MLM), however. Also called multilevel selling, this a system of direct marketing which relies on the personal contacts of the sales force. Well-known examples are Herbalife, the vitamin and health food distributors, and Amway, the household cleansing products firm.

In a multilevel-marketing organization each salesperson has two areas of responsibility. Firstly, salespeople are responsible for selling the product to family, friends and work colleagues, and secondly they are responsible for recruiting more salespeople. Each salesperson is paid on a commission-only basis, with no basic salary or fringe benefits, and is regarded as self-employed. Most of them sell on a part-time basis, and have other jobs. Each salesperson is also paid an override commission of one or two per cent on the sales of each person he or she recruits; ultimately, recruitment of other people is what makes the exercise worthwhile for most multilevel marketing recruits. Figure 13.1 shows a typical structure for MLM.

What distinguishes multilevel marketing from pyramid selling is that the sales force do not take title to the goods. Their only financial commitment is usually a small deposit on their sales kit and samples, and sometimes even this does not apply. In this way, the multilevel salesperson can only gain.

In practice, most of those who go into multilevel schemes fail to sell any substantial amounts of goods. This is because the training and support levels are generally low, and the motivation to sell is low. As with any commission-only sales force, motivation will tend to be poor at best, and it tends to be an expensive way to distribute goods.

FIGURE 13.1   Multilevel marketing scheme

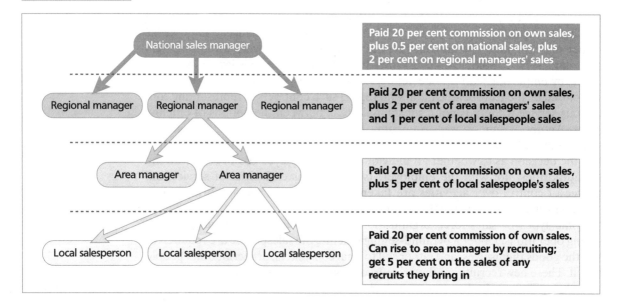

Ethical issues surrounding a manager's dealings with the staff are not always enshrined in law. In general, managers should not abuse their power, or use their position to bully salespeople or apply undue pressure to them. Such behaviour is likely to be outlawed in the near future, and recent cases have indicated that civil courts are prepared to award damages when an employee has been bullied or placed in an unduly stressful situation by the employer.

Government regulation of business also comes about through the actions of semi-autonomous regulatory bodies such as the Monopolies and Mergers Commission. This commission is empowered to investigate cases of price fixing between firms as well as mergers; the remit of the commission is to prevent the abuse of a dominant market position, whether this occurs because one large firm controls the market, or because a group of firms have colluded to control the market. Other Government bodies include the Department of Trade and Industry, which has powers to regulate firms' behaviour, and various bodies which ensure ethical conduct in employment issues such as the Race Relations Board.

To give a comprehensive discourse on business law and the legislation regulating business transactions would be well beyond the scope of this book. Regulations vary from one industry to another, from the highly regulated financial services sector through to the almost entirely unregulated Internet. In most industries the regulations are well known, and it would be advisable for any sales manager to seek advice on what the regulations are for the industry in which he or she is employed.

■ Establishing a code of ethics

Establishing a code of ethics within an organization should not be left to chance. It is better to have a code of practice, and monitor the code in practice, so that employees and others know exactly what the firm is doing about its ethical responsibilities. As with any other question of marketing, the decision as to what the code should contain can be made by reference to the firm's customers and consumers: what would these people regard as ethical behaviour?

Codes of ethics need to be agreed with the people who will have to implement them. This offers them the opportunity to contribute their own ideas on what is ethical and what is not, and also to develop a feeling of ownership of the code, which will help them relate better to its provisions. The code should contain the following:

- Guidelines for what information customers should be given before signing the contract.
- Guidelines on how follow-up visits and aftersales service are to be handled.
- Cooling-off periods, where appropriate.
- Instructions regarding written material, including ensuring that the customer understands what the provisions of the contract actually mean.
- The scope of the code; who and what is covered by the code.

People working within the firm have to be able to live with their consciences, and establishing a code of ethical conduct will help them do so. Most people prefer to feel that they are working for an honest and ethical firm; staff have friends and family at home who might be quick to criticize if the firm is perceived as unethical.

The code of conduct should be published to customers as well as staff, and in some cases it can be publicized further afield. This has the advantage of reassuring customers and potential customers that the firm will deal honestly and ethically, and also provides a degree of policing to ensure that the code is followed by staff. A further spin-off, particularly for industry leaders, is that it may forestall Government legislation controlling the industry. It is almost certainly less irksome for the industry to develop its own controls and regulations rather than have them imposed by Government.

Many industries have trade associations which lay down codes of practice, and where applicable these should be adopted. The reason for doing so is to ensure a level playing field for all firms within the industry concerned. If all firms are following, or exceeding, the provisions of the same code of conduct it becomes difficult for rogues to operate. Ultimately it is not in anybody's long-term interests for an industry to acquire a reputation for unethical practices; industries such as time-share, double glazing and life insurance have spent many years and much effort to shed their former shady images.

SUMMARY

Moral and ethical issues are at the heart of legislation, but in many cases legislation only applies a minimum standard, and is quickly outdated by business practice. Businesses need to establish their own rules of conduct, and frequently do so in order to forestall legislation, or simply from a desire to behave as good citizens.

The key points from this chapter are as follows:

- Most people have different ethical standards when in work from those they apply in their private lives.

- Once a salesperson deceives a customer, the customer is almost certainly lost forever.

- Civil law is mainly concerned with compensation, criminal law with retribution.

- Contracts do not have to be written in order to be binding. The purpose of having a written contract is to be able to prove what the agreement was.

- It is better to self-regulate than to wait for regulation to be imposed.

- Codes of ethics should be agreed with those who will abide by them, and should be based on customers' perceptions of what is ethical.

- Codes of ethics should be publicized to staff, customers, and the firm's other publics in order to increase the credibility of the firm.

- Trade associations normally provide ready-made codes of ethics.

REVIEW QUESTIONS

1　If the most ethical outcome is the greatest good of the greatest number, presumably the salesperson should act for the good of the employees and shareholders of the firm rather than for the good of a single customer. Discuss.

2　Why might pyramid selling be regarded as unethical, whereas multilevel marketing is not?

3　Why is it better for industries to establish codes of practice?

4　If a salesperson were to tell an outright lie about a product, thus obtaining payment under false pretences, why might the aggrieved customer sue through the civil courts rather than bring fraud charges?

5　What steps might you take to draw up an industry code of conduct for selling over the Internet?

REFERENCES

Chonko, L. B. and Hunt, S. D. (1985) 'Ethics and marketing management: An empirical investigation', *Journal of Business Research* 13(4): 339–59.

—— Wotruba, T. R. and Loe, T. W. (2002) 'Direct selling ethics at the top: An industry audit and status report', *Journal of Personal Selling and Sales Management* 22 (2/Spring): 87–95.

Donaldson, W. (1998) *Sales Management: Theory and Practice*, London: Macmillan.

Fraedrich, J. (1988) 'Philosophy type interaction in the ethical decision making process of retailers', PhD Dissertation, Texas A&M University.

Kuhlmann, E. (1994) 'Customer', in B. Harvey (ed.) *Business Ethics: A European Approach*, Trowbridge: Prentice-Hall.

Sivadas, E., Kleiser, S. B., Kellaris, J. and Dahlstrom, R. (2003) 'Moral philosophy, ethical evaluations, and sales manager hiring intentions', *Journal of Personal Selling and Sales Management* 23 (1/Winter): 7–21.

LOCKHEED

Lockheed is a major aircraft manufacturer, based in the United States. In common with other aircraft manufacturers, the company deals worldwide, and therefore operates in a multicultural way. Due to the extremely high order values, the company is also involved in long-term key-account selling, where relationships with buyers are paramount.

Like most companies in their position, Lockheed employs local agents in countries in which they hope to do business. This ensures having someone who understands the local culture, is well connected with the right people in the target country, and who can act to smooth the path of any deals. In Japan, Lockheed's local representative was one Yoshio Kodama, a former war criminal with strong connections to the ruling Liberal Democrat party.

During 1970 Lockheed almost went bankrupt. Aircraft sales worldwide had fallen dramatically, and strong competition from Boeing and McDonnell Douglas left the company on the verge of bankruptcy. Only a US Government loan of $250 million saved the company, and even that loan was controversial. Lockheed's survival was on the line, and A. Carl Kotchian, the president of the company, knew that the Japanese market was a major opportunity. Kodama was hired in 1972 to broker a deal with All Nippon Airlines to buy Lockheed's Tri-Star airliners.

The deal, if it went through, would generate revenues of over $400 million, which would restore Lockheed to solvency and save thousands of jobs. In fact, Kodama was more than successful. He actually negotiated a total of $1.3 thousand million in aircraft contracts, but these deals were eventually cancelled following disclosures of how the deals were made.

Komada had, in fact, simply bribed the appropriate people to place the orders. He had paid a total of $12 million to representatives of the Japanese prime minister, Kukeo Tanaka, through a private company called Marubeni. Toshiharu Okubo was the executive of Marubeni handling the Lockheed account, and he had specifically asked Lockheed for 500 million yen (about $4.5 million) to smooth the path for the sales. Kotchian later stated that he knew the money was heading straight for the Prime Minister's office, but he felt obliged to pay because this was normal practice in the Japanese market and he knew that the alternative was to lose the business to a competitor. What he had done was not against American law, and in any case he had not offered a bribe, it had been requested by his Japanese intermediaries, who then, of course, offered it to the Prime Minister.

When the facts became known, Kotchian was forced to resign. So was the Prime Minister Tanaka, and his successor, Takeo Miki, who was shown to have been involved in a cover-up operation. In 1977, the US Government introduced legislation to prevent such a situation arising again. The Foreign Corrupt Practices Act forbade any American company from making payments to foreign governments or individuals to further their business interests.

From Lockheed's viewpoint, paying a commission to a public official was a normal cost of doing business. From the Government viewpoint, these payments were not normal business costs, and in 1979 Lockheed pleaded guilty to four counts of fraud and four counts of making false statements to the Government, specifically in that the company concealed secret commissions (bribes) under the heading of marketing costs. Their case was not helped by a second scandal in which Lockheed bribed Prince Bernhard of Holland in 1976 to facilitate the sale of 138 Lockheed Starfighters and ex-President of Italy Giovanni Leone in connection with defence sales. Lockheed admitted paying out $202 million in 'commissions'.

Obviously Lockheed felt justified in making these payments, because otherwise the company would almost certainly have gone bankrupt, costing thousands of jobs. From a Government viewpoint, Lockheed had had to be baled out already, and was clearly not operating efficiently enough to be able to play by the rules – on the other hand, no government wants to have thousands of voters thrown out of work. Even management guru Peter Drucker became involved in the debate, arguing that Lockheed had no more choice in the matter than does the victim of a mugging – failure to hand over the money will lead to injury or death, which was of course exactly the situation Lockheed found itself in.

No doubt other companies will find themselves in similar situations in future, and no doubt they will be compelled to make difficult choices. Lockheed paid a high price for their choice, and so did the recipients of the 'commissions', but such arrangements are so common in some countries that this might be regarded as simple bad luck rather than a just outcome.

Case-study questions

1 Since Lockheed had not broken the law, why was there a scandal?
2 Should Lockheed have refused to pay up, or not?
3 How were stakeholders' interests balanced?
4 Why should the US Government be interested in what is, after all, corruption in a foreign country?
5 To what extent is Drucker's view correct?

INDEX